Terrorism and International Justice

Terrorism and International Justice

Edited by
JAMES P. STERBA

Contributors

Shannon E. French • Tomis Kapitan • Noam Chomsky
David B. Burrell • Robert L. Phillips • Zayn Kassam
Louis P. Pojman • Daniele Archibugi • Iris Marion Young
Claudia Card • Richard W. Miller • James P. Sterba
Martha C. Nussbaum

New York   Oxford
Oxford University Press
2003

Oxford University Press

Oxford   New York
Auckland   Bangkok   Buenos Aires   Cape Town   Chennai
Dar es Salaam   Delhi   Hong Kong   Istanbul   Karachi   Kolkata
Kuala Lumpur   Madrid   Melbourne   Mexico City   Mumbai
Nairobi   São Paulo   Shanghai   Taipei   Tokyo   Toronto

Published by Oxford University Press, Inc.
198 Madison Avenue, New York, New York, 10016
http://www.oup-usa.org

Oxford is a registered trademark of Oxford University Press

Library of Congress Cataloging-in-Publication Data

Terrorism and international justice / edited by James P. Sterba.
     p.   cm.
  Includes bibliographical references.
  ISBN 0-19-515887-3—ISBN 0-19-515888-1 (pbk.)
     1. Terrorism.   2. International law.   3. Justice.   4. Rules of law.
  I. Sterba, James P.

  HV6431 .T46144 2003
  303.6'25—dc21   2002192570

Printing number: 9 8 7 6 5 4 3 2 1

Printed in the United States of America
on acid-free paper

CONTENTS

PREFACE

Following 9/11, the U.S. government has made war on terrorism its number one priority. But how should we understand the terrorism that the governments of the United States and other countries oppose? Is it something only our enemies have engaged in, or have we ourselves and our allies also engaged in terrorist acts? More important, is terrorism always wrong, or are there morally justified acts of terrorism? When we actually confront wrongful acts of terrorism, what are the morally defensible responses? Is war a morally defensible response to the terrorism of 9/11? If war is a morally defensible response to terrorism, how is terrorism related to issues of international justice? Do failures of international justice motivate acts of terrorism? Did they do so in the case of 9/11? Are morally defensible responses to terrorism required to correct related failures of international justice? If so, what implications, if any, does this have for the United States achieving a morally defensible response to 9/11?

This volume focuses on evaluating competing answers to these and other central questions relating to 9/11. The volume begins with an introductory essay that provides a brief history of terrorism and a summary discussion of the other essays.

As one would expect, the volume is the result of many helping hands. Special thanks are due to the contributors to the volume whose interest and resolve to work together to complete this project matched my own. I also wish to thank Robert Miller, executive editor at Oxford University Press, who endorsed the project from the very beginning, and the Institute for Scholarship in the Liberal Arts at the University of Notre Dame and the National Humanities Center in North Carolina for their financial support. Finally, I would like to thank the reviewers for their helpful suggestions, including Jeff McMahan, University of Illinois at Urbana-Champaign; Andy Wible, Muskegon Community College; Christopher W. Morris, University of Maryland; and Joshua Cohen, Massachusetts Institute of Technology.

CONTRIBUTORS

DANIELE ARCHIBUGI is a director at the Italian National Research Council. He has worked at the universities of Sussex, Cambridge, Naples, and Rome. Archibugi has been active in the reform of the United Nations and on the history of peace ideas, and he is one of the promoters of cosmopolitan democracy. *Cosmopolitan Democracy: An Agenda for a New Worder* (Polity Press, 1995), *Global Democracy* (special issue of *Peace Review*), *Re-imagining Political Community* (Polity Press, 1998), *Innovation Policy in a Global Economy* (Cambridge University Press, 1999), and the *Globalising Learning Economy* (Oxford University Press, 2001). *Debating Cosmopolitics* will be publshed in 2003 by Verso.

DAVID B. BURRELL, C.S.C., is currently Theodore Hesburgh Professor in Philosophy and Theology at the University of Notre Dame. He has been working since 1982 in comparative issues in philosophical theology in Judaism, Christianity, and Islam, as evidenced in *Knowing the Unknowable God: Ibn-Sina, Maimonides, Aquinas* (Notre Dame University Press, 1986) and *Freedom and Creation in Three Traditions* (Notre Dame University Press, 1993), *Friendship and Ways to Truth* (Notre Dame University Press, 2000), and two translations of al-Ghazali: *Al-Ghazali on the Ninety-Nine Beautiful Names of God* (Islamic Texts Society, 1993) and *Al-Ghazali on Faith in Divine Unity and Trust in Divine Providence* [Book 35 of his *Ihya Ulum ad-Din*] (Fons Vitae, 2001). With Elena Malits he coauthored *Original Peace* (Paulist, 1998). He served as Luce Professor of Abrahamic Faiths at Hartford Seminary and University of Hartford in the fall of 1998 and has been asked to direct the university's Jerusalem program, housed at the Tantur Ecumenical Institute, each spring until 2004.

CLAUDIA CARD is Emma Goldman Professor of Philosophy at the University of Wisconsin, where she also has teaching affiliations with women's studies, environmental studies, and Jewish studies. She is the author of *The Atrocity Paradigm: A Theory of Evil* (Oxford University Press, 2002), *The Unnatural Lottery: Character and Moral Luck* (Temple University Press, 1996), and *Lesbian Choices* (Columbia University Press, 1995) and the editor of *The Cambridge Companion to Simone de Beauvoir* (Cambridge University Press, 2003), *On Feminist Ethics and Politics* (University Press of Kansas, 1999), *Adventures in Lesbian Philosophy* (Indiana University Press, 1994), and *Feminist Ethics* (University Press of Kansas, 1991). She is currently a senior member of the Institute for Research in the Humanities at the University of Wisconsin and is at work on a book on responding to atrocities such as genocide and large-scale terrorism.

NOAM CHOMSKY joined the staff of the Massachusetts Institute of Technology in 1955 and in 1961 was appointed full professor in the Department of Modern Languages and Linguistics (now the Department of Linguistics and Philosophy. In 1976 he was appointed Institute Professor. In the spring of 1969 he delivered the John Locke Lectures at Oxford; in January 1970 he delivered the Bertrand Russell Memorial Lecture at Cambridge University; in 1972, the Nehru Memorial Lecture in New Delhi, and in 1977, the Huizinga Lecture in Leiden, among many others. Chomsky has written and lectured widely on linguistics, philosophy, intellectual history, contemporary issues, international affairs, and U.S. foreign policy. His works include *Aspects of the Theory of Syntax* (MIT Press, 1965), *Fateful Triangle* (South End Press, 1983) *Pirates and Emperors* (Claremont Research & Publications, 1986), *On Power and Ideology* (Black Rose Books, 1987); *The Culture of Terrorism* (South End Press, 1988); *Necessary Illusions* (South End Press, 1989); *Rethinking Camelot: JFK, the Vietnam War and US Political Culture* (Black Rose Books, 1993); *World Orders, Old and New* (Columbia University Press, 1994); *New Horizons in the Study of Language and Mind* (Cambridge University Press, 2000); *A New Generation Draws the Line* (Verso, 2000); and *9–11* (Seven Stories Press, 2001).

SHANNON E. FRENCH teaches in the Department of Leadership, Ethics, and Law at the United States Naval Academy, Annapolis, Maryland. Dr. French received her B.A. from Trinity University in 1990 and earned her Ph.D. in Philosophy from Brown University in 1997. Before joining the USNA faculty in June 1997, she taught as a part-time instructor at Incarnate Word College and Trinity University in Texas and at Salve Regina University, the University of Rhode Island, and Brown University in Rhode Island and was a full-time assistant professor at Belmont University (in Tennessee) for three years while completing her dissertation, entitled "The Problem of Motivating Ethical Behavior." Her primary research area is military ethics. She has written several articles, book discussions, and edited texts in this field; her first book, *The Code of the Warrior: Exploring Warrior Values, Past and Present* (Rowman and Littlefield, 2000), features a foreword by Senator John McCain. In the spring of 2000 she was awarded USNA's campuswide Apgar Award for Excellence in Teaching. The courses she teaches at USNA include "Moral Reasoning for Naval Leaders," "The Code of the Warrior," "Philosophy of Religion," and "Knowing Your Enemy."

TOMIS KAPITAN is professor of philosophy at Northern Illinois University. He received his doctorate from Indiana University in 1978 and has also taught at Indiana University, Indiana State University, and East Carolina University. From 1981 to 1986 he taught philosophy and cultural studies at Birzeit University in the occupied West Bank, and during the spring and fall semesters of 2000 he was a visiting professor of philosophy at the American University of Beirut in Lebanon. His research is primarily focused on issues in metaphysics, philosophy of language, and international ethics. He has edited three books, including *Philosophical Perspectives on the Israeli-Palestinian Conflict* (M.E. Sharpe, 1997), and has published over fifty articles on such topics as the free will problem, practical thinking, propositional attitudes, indexical reference, logical form, enthymematic reasoning, the semantics of variables, abduction, terrorism, self-determination, and the Israeli-Palestinian conflict. He has lectured frequently about the Arab world, Islam, and current Middle East tensions.

ZAYN KASSAM is associate professor of religious studies at Pomona College, Claremont, California. She earned her doctorate from McGill University, Montreal, Canada. Her areas of specialization are Islamic and Indian philosophy, and she teaches courses on Islam, Islamic thought and mysticism, Muslim literature, gender in Islamic societies, and comparative studies in religion. Kassam has published several papers on Islamic and Indian philosophy, gender issues in the Islamic world, and teaching Islam. In addition, she has lectured widely to both academic and nonspecialist audiences on topics as diverse as the role of ritual in society, building community, gender issues, and medieval

Islamic philosophy. She is currently working on two books, the first on gender issues in the Islamic world and the second on an eleventh-century Muslim philosopher. She recently won Pomona College's Wig Award for Distinguished Teaching. She is currently cochair of the Study of Islam Section at the American Academy of Religion and has also served as a consultant to the National Endowment for the Humanities.

RICHARD W. MILLER is professor of philosophy at Cornell University. His many writings in social and political philosophy, ethics, epistemology, the philosophy of science and aesthetics include three books, *Analyzing Marx* (Princeton University Press, 1984), *Fact and Method* (Princeton University Press, 1987), and *Moral Difference* (Princeton University Press, 1992), and recent articles on foreign aid, humanitarian military intervention, and economic inequality. His current work in progress includes a book grounding political goals of equality on the proper valuing of relationships of loyalty, cooperation, and trust.

MARTHA C. NUSSBAUM is Ernst Freund Distinguished Service Professor of Law and Ethics at the University of Chicago, appointed in the Philosophy Department, Law School, and Divinity School. She is an Associate in the Classics Department, an Affiliate of the Committee on Southern Asian Studies, and a member of the Board of the Human Rights Program, and the Coordinator of the new Center for Comparative Constitutionalism, which studies the implementation of constitutional rights for women, minorities, and other disadvantaged groups. Her most recent books are *Women and Human Development: The Capabilities Approach* (Cambridge University Press, 2000) and *Upheavals of Thought: The Intelligence of Emotions* (Cambridge University Press, 2001).

ROBERT L. PHILLIPS holds a D.Phil. in philosophy from Oxford University and is currently professor of philosophy and director of the War and Ethics Program at the University of Connecticut. He has previously taught philosophy at Oxford University, Queens University, and Wesleyan University. Dr. Phillips is the author of *War and Justice* (University of Oklahoma Press, 1984) and coauthor of *Humanitarian Intervention: Pacifism vs. Just War* (Rowman and Littlefield, 1996). He has lectured widely on topics in ethics and international affairs and has published many chapters in books as well as articles in such journals as *Global Affairs, Ethics and International Affairs,* and *Latin Mass.* Dr. Phillips serves as a frequent consultant on ethics and international affairs for the national and international media. He is president of the Hartford Chapter of Una Voce International, an organization dedicated to the restoration of traditional Catholic liturgy, doctrine, and morality.

LOUIS P. POJMAN received his D. Phil. from Oxford University. He was a Fulbright Fellow at the University of Copenhagen and a Rockefeller Fellow at Hamburg University. He also has a M.A. in religious studies and Ph.D. in ethics from Union Theological Seminary at Columbia University in New York. He is the author or editor of twenty-six books and eighty-seven articles, including *The Logic of Subjectivity* (University of Alabama Press, 1984), *Religious Belief and the Will* (Routledge and Kegan Paul, 1986), *Ethics: Discovering Right and Wrong* (3rd ed., Wadsworth, 1998), and *Global Environmental Ethics* (Mayfield Publishing Co., 1999). He has taught at Oxford University, the University of Notre Dame, the University of Texas, the University of Mississippi, and, currently, the U.S. Military Academy at West Point. He has read over 100 papers at 50 universities and scores of conferences.

JAMES P. STERBA is professor of philosophy at the University of Notre Dame and a founding faculty fellow of the Kroc Institute for International Peace Studies. He has published twenty-three books, most recently the award-winning *Justice for Here and Now* (Cambridge University Press, 1998) and *Three Challenges to Ethics: Environmentalism, Feminism, and Multiculturalism* (Oxford University Press, 2001). He is past president of Concerned Philosophers for Peace; past president of the International Society for Social and Legal Philosophy, the American Section; and past president of the North American Society for Social Philosophy. He has held visiting appointments at the University of Rochester; the University of Latvia in Riga, Latvia, when that country was part of the Soviet Union; the University of San Francisco; and the University of California at Irvine. He recently completed a point/counterpoint book on affirmative action with Carl Cohen (Oxford University Press) and another entitled *The Triumph of Practice over Theory in Ethics* (Oxford University Press, both forthcoming).

IRIS MARION YOUNG is professor of political science at the University of Chicago, where she is also affiliated with the Human Rights

Program. Her most recent book, *Inclusion and Democracy* (Oxford University Press, 2000), devotes its last chapter to issues of global justice and democracy. She is also author of *Justice and the Politics of Difference* (Princeton University Press, 1990), and *Intersecting Voices: Dilemmas of Gender, Political Philosophy, and Policy* (Princeton University Press, 1997).

Terrorism and International Justice

Introduction

9/11

For Americans, no act of terrorism compares with 9/11. The terrorist attack began on a clear, early autumn morning in New York City. At 8:45 A.M., a hijacked American Airlines passenger plane piloted by Muhamed Atta slammed into the north tower of the World Trade Center. Within twenty minutes, a second hijacked United Airlines plane piloted by Marwan al-Shehhi struck the south tower. At 9:45 A.M., another hijacked plane crashed into the western façade of the Pentagon, and less than a half hour later, a fourth hijacked plane plummeted to the earth in a wooded field outside of Somerset, Pennsylvania. At 9:50 A.M. the south tower of the World Trade Center began to collapse, each floor pancaking onto the one below. Forty minutes later, the north tower seemed to implode. The collapse of the Twin Towers sent dust and smoke billowing through the streets of lower Manhattan as thousands of terrified New Yorkers ran for cover. Initial estimates put the number of dead from this terrorist attack at over five thousand, but later the death toll was reduced to approximately three thousand.

Immediately comparisons were made to the Japanese attack on Pearl Harbor in 1941, when 2,403 sailors, soldiers, and civilians died. But the attack on a military outpost far removed from the American heartland is hardly comparable to an attack against targets in our largest city and in our capital. Nor was 9/11 carried out with the weapons of our old adversaries, but by commandeering commercial aircraft with knives and boxcutters and using them in murderous suicidal missions. So this terrorism we now face is something new, something different, and, as a consequence, many Americans, and many people around the world, now feel vulnerable in a way they would have never thought possible before.

Accordingly, we need to better understand the terrorism we now face and reflect upon how we should best respond to it. That is what

1

this volume aims to assist the reader in doing. To that end, the articles in the volume focus on three central questions:

1. What is the nature and rhetoric of terrorism?
2. Who are the terrorists, and why do they hate?
3. What is a morally justified response to terrorism?

Given that 9/11 has changed the world we live in, answering these and other questions about terrorism is now more important to us than at any time in the past. While the articles in this volume may not provide all the best answers, hopefully they will provide some of the answers we need, and thereby enable us to go on to find additional answers for ourselves. To introduce these articles, a brief history of terrorism follows, as well as a brief summary discussion of the articles as they appear in the volume.

A Brief History of Terrorism

The terrorism of 9/11 is something new, but it is also very old. This is because terrorism, whether practiced by states or by substate groups or individuals, is found throughout human history. Most historical accounts, however, focus on what they take to be forms of terrorism that are practiced by substate groups and individuals.

During biblical times, Jewish Sicarii known for their use of a short sword (*sica*) struck down rich Jewish collaborators who were opposed to violent resistance against their Roman conquerors. Later, in the eleventh and twelfth centuries, a group of Shiite Muslims called the Assassins opposed efforts to suppress their religious beliefs in Sunni-dominated Persia. Using daggers, the Assassins killed prefects, governors, and caliphs in front of many witnesses, thus ensuring their capture and execution because they believed that by their actions they would gain entry into paradise. Eventually, the group was suppressed by the Mongols in the thirteenth century.[1]

In India, from the eleventh century on a group called the Thugs were active until they were destroyed by the British in the nineteenth century. The Thugs ritually strangled their victims with a silk tie. They claimed allegiance to the goddess Kali, who it is said required them to kill in order to supply her with blood for nourishment.[2]

Following the French Revolution, the Jacobins under Robespierre gave us the very term "terror," unleashing a "Reign of Terror" between 1793 and 1794 upon all levels of French society. During this period, more than seventeen thousand people—peasants, workers, aristocrats, moderate revolutionaries, and others—were killed, sometimes without any trial, by means of the guillotine, which was designed by Dr. Joseph Guillontin to be a more "humane" form of execution. When Guillontin first proposed his invention, he told the National Assembly, "Gentlemen, with my machine, I'll take off your head in a flash, and you won't even feel the slightest pain."[3] For the most part, however, the guillotine served simply to facilitate executions, as more than twenty-five thousand people were executed by other methods during the Reign of Terror. Those executed included not only those accused of some offense or disloyalty, but sometimes their children, parents, or even grandparents as well.[4]

In the nineteenth century, the most important revolutionary movement was the Russian Narodnaya Volya (People's Will), whose operations lasted from January 1878 to March 1881. Their armed struggle began with the shooting of the governor general of St. Petersburg; gained momentum with the assassination of General Mezentsev, the head of the czarist political police; and ended with the assassination of Alexander II on March 1, 1881, ironically after most of the members of the group had already been apprehended by the police. Moreover, the assassination of the czar turned out to be counterproductive, at least in the short run, because it replaced the reformer Alexander II with the more repressive Alexander III.[5]

In 1900, the Social Revolutionary Party was founded in Russia at a time when there was greater popular support for the assassination of high government officials than was the case twenty-five years earlier, when Narodnaya Volya had been founded. As a result, between 1903 and 1910, the Social Revolutionary Party managed to kill over two hundred provincial governors and high officials before it was effectively suppressed with thousands of trials and executions.[6]

A third wave of political violence in Russia came after the Bolshevik coup of 1917, but it was directed against both communist leaders and German diplomats in an effort to sabotage the peace negotiations then going on between Russia and Germany.[7]

Yet it is not clear that *all* of these historical examples should be regarded, as they usually are, as acts of terrorism. Without a doubt, they are all cases in which terror (intense fear, fright, or intimidation) is induced in large groups of people, but terrorism, as many have come to understand it, involves more than just this. First of all, many think that terrorism must have a political purpose, that it must aim to achieve some change in a government or government institution or policy. This is true of most of the historical examples just cited, but it is not true of the Thugs of India, whose goals were personal and religious rather than political. Second, many also think that terrorism must directly target innocents, a requirement that does not really hold true for any of these historical examples, except that of the French Jacobins. The Jewish Sicarii targeted Jewish collaborators who, in virtue of their operation with the Romans, were clearly not innocent. The Assassins attacked people in positions of political leadership who were responsible for the religious persecution against Shiite Muslims, and so were not innocent. In the three examples of political violence in Russia, innocents were not targeted, only those whom the revolutionaries reasonably believed were primarily responsible for very unjust institutions and policies. So the only really clear example we have here of terrorism is that of Robespierre's Reign of Terror, directed as it was at innocents as well as at those who were accused of being guilty of some offense. However, in the case of Robespierre's Reign of Terror, what we have is an example of state terrorism, not terrorism as practiced by substate groups or individuals.

In the late nineteenth century, it was thought that the invention of dynamite would provide "a decisive advantage to revolutionary forces," giving them a powerful but easily concealed weapon.[8] Narodnaya Volya was the first revolutionary group to use dynamite in its attacks. They used it in their assassination of Czar Alexander II in 1881. In 1906, the International Association of Bridge and Structural Iron Workers Union also used dynamite to try to prevent U.S. Steel and other companies from imposing open shops at their plants. Between 1906 and 1911, members of the union were responsible for one hundred explosions at bridges, factories, and plants across the United States. This resulted mostly in minor property damage until the dynamiting of the Times Building in Los Angeles in 1910, which killed twenty-one nonunion workers and resulted in $500,000 in damages. When two members of the union were arrested for the bombing and brought to trial, Clarence Darrow agreed to defend them, even though, as the evidence against them mounted, both pleaded guilty to avoid the death penalty.[9] At a subsequent congressional inquiry, Darrow claimed that James B. McNamara, who had placed the bomb in the Times Building, had acted with no selfish criminal motive. According to Darrow, McNamara "was a union man in a great industrial struggle running over the years. He believed in it and believed it was necessary for the welfare of his class; . . . in his mind he thought he was serving his class, and taking his life in his hands without reward. Now, if anyone can condemn him for it, they reason differently from myself. . . . I can not."[10]

Here again, however, it is not clear that the bombing of the Times Building should count as a terrorist act. On the one hand, it could be argued that the workers who were killed in the bombing were, in fact, supporting the owners in their dispute with the union, and so, for that reason, were not reasonably regarded as innocent from the perspective of the union. On the other hand, it could be argued that these workers were so far removed from the owners and elite managers who were the real agents in this dispute with the union that they should have been regarded as sufficiently innocent to be immune from lethal attack even from the perspective of the union.

Of course, some would argue that the workers do not have to be innocent before we regard the bombing as terrorism. According to one definition, terrorism is simply "the use or attempted use of terror as a means of coercion."[11] But defined this way, there will clearly be many justified acts of terrorism, as when, for example, judges impose severe penalties in order to strike fear into the hearts of would-be criminals. Thus, only when terrorism is defined to involve directly targeting innocents will it turn out to be rarely morally justified.

Prior to World War I, there were various anarchist-inspired attacks on high government officials and leaders in France, Germany, Austria, and elsewhere, but since the victims of these attacks were not reasonably regarded as innocents from the perspective of their attackers, the attacks themselves, whether justified or not, cannot rightly be regarded as acts of terrorism. Of course, after the war, Benito Mussolini and his Black Shirt supporters in Italy and Adolf Hitler and his Brown Shirt supporters in Germany clearly did engage in many terrorist acts in their rise to power, eventually succeeding in establishing states through which they practiced an even more widespread terrorism.[12]

Following World War II, the use of political violence by substate groups and individuals shifted from Europe to the Middle East, India, and the Far East. Throughout these areas, colonies and other dependencies launched violent campaigns for independence.[13]

In Palestine, Jews hoping to drive out the British, who maintained a mandate over the region, formed militant groups, most prominently the Irgun under the command of Menachem Begin and the Stern Gang led by Abraham Stern until he was killed by British police in

1942. In the summer of 1946, Irgun detonated a bomb in the King David Hotel in Jerusalem that served as headquarters for the British mandate in Palestine, killing eighty-six—twenty-eight Britons, forty-one Arabs, and seventeen Jews—and wounding forty-six other people. David Ben-Gurion, who in 1948 would become Israel's first prime minister, called Irgun "the enemy of the Jewish people." The Haganah, the main Jewish paramilitary organization, denounced the attack, even though it had been in on the planning. But Irgun survived to continue its terrorist campaign.[14]

During the War of Independence of 1948–1949, Irgun and the Stern Gang cooperated in an attack on Deir Yassin, a village eighteen miles outside of what were then the boundaries of the Jewish state, as part of an overall plan to cleanse the area of Arab inhabitants and establish a corridor between Tel Aviv and Jerusalem. Until attacked, Deir Yassin had avoided being involved in the fighting and had even signed a "nonaggression" pack with its Jewish neighbors as early as 1942. Nevertheless, on April 7, 1948, Irgun and Stern Gang forces attacked the village, going house to house, throwing grenades into the houses and then spraying the insides with gunfire. Later, they began dynamiting houses and then firing on anyone who moved in the rubble. The next day the Red Cross arrived in Deir Yassin and buried 254 Arabs, mostly women and children. The attackers lost five men. According to a report issued by a Haganah regional commander after the attack, "For a full day, [Irgun and Stern Gang] soldiers stood and slaughtered men, women, and children, not in the course of the operation, but in a premeditated act which had as its intention slaughter and murder only."[15] Although Ben-Gurion and the Haganah high command condemned the attack, the leaders of Irgun and the Stern Gang were never punished for it. In fact, in later years, Menachem Begin, the leader of Irgun, and Yitzhak Shamir, one of the leaders of the Stern Gang, both became prime ministers of Israel.[16]

As one might expect, the Arabs retaliated for Deir Yassin with an act of terrorism of their own. On April 13, they besieged a convoy of mainly Jewish doctors and nurses just outside of Jerusalem and killed seventy-seven of them.[17]

In Latin America in the 1960s and 1970s, the use of political violence by the Tupermaros in Uruguay and the Montoneros in Argentina gave rise to repressive dictatorships in each country that eventually destroyed these groups. Moreover, while the groups themselves were fairly discriminate in their use of force, the dictatorships that came to power to suppress them were far less discriminate. In Argentina, thousands were arrested, many were tortured, and many disappeared without a trace. Similarly, revolutionary groups arose in other Latin American countries, but only in Nicaragua were they successful. There the Sandinistas overthrew the U.S.-backed dictator Anastasio Somoza in 1979. The Sandinistas were then attacked and their authority undermined by the U.S.-sponsored Contras, and they eventually accepted defeat to the U.S.-backed candidate, Violetta Chamorro, in a 1990 election. In Chile, the democratically elected Salvador Allende was overthrown in 1973 with U.S. support by the Chilean military headed by Augusto Pinochet. The Pinochet government then employed "death squads" to eliminate and suppress its opponents. More recently, Patricio Aylwin Azocar was democratically elected president of Chile in 1994, and Pinochet stepped down as head of the Chilean army in 1998. A subsequent attempt to extradite Pinochet from the United Kingdom, where he was seeking medical treatment, to Spain to face charges of brutality against Spanish citizens in Chile during his regime was denied on grounds of ill health.[18]

In the wake of the student revolt of 1968, a new wave of revolutionary violence erupted in Europe. In Germany, there appeared the Red Army, or the Baader-Meinhof gang. We can trace the group's origins to a fairly ineffectual fire-bombing of two huge department stores in Berlin as a protest against capitalism and the Vietnam War. Ulrike Meinhof wrote of the motivation for this fire-bombing, "Those who have understood what the war in Vietnam is all about start to walk about with gritted teeth and a very bad conscience; start to realize that the inability to stop this war leads to complicity with those waging it."[19] For the next several years, the Red Army robbed several banks; bombed police stations, government office buildings, and American bases in Germany; and killed a number of bankers, industrialists, government officials, and judges. They followed many of their attacks with explanation papers that attempted to justify their attacks. Meinhof was the acknowledged leader of the group until her capture and imprisonment in 1972 and subsequent suicide in 1976. At a huge funeral for her in West Berlin, more than four-thousand radical students followed the funeral procession, wearing masks so that the police could not identify them. The group continued its acts of political violence after the death of Meinhof, and even after the later suicides in jail of two other prominent gang members. In 1998, however, the group released a document declaring an unconditional end to its violent struggle against "the system."[20]

In Italy, the Red Brigades conducted a similar, but much broader, program of political violence. In the early 1970s the Red Brigade began kidnapping midlevel corporate officials, some of whom were released after they publicly confessed to their crimes, while others were held for ransom. After fourteen of their top members were placed on trial, the Red Brigades responded by kidnapping Aldo Moro, who had five times served as Italy's prime minister, to bargain for the release of their gang members. When the Italian government, under pressure from the United States, refused to bargain, Moro was killed brutally in 1978. The group continued with political violence into the 1980s, but internal conflicts and successful police work eventually decimated their numbers.[21]

Following the 1967 War and the Israeli occupation of the West Bank and the Gaza Strip, Palestinians engaged in a major campaign of political violence within Israel and the occupied territories as well as overseas. In 1968, the Popular Front for the Liberation of Palestine (PFLP), which then belonged to the Palestine Liberation Organization (PLO), began hijacking El Al planes. In 1969, the group hijacked a TWA flight to Damascus. The PFLP released all the passengers except the Israelis, who were released later when the Israeli government freed two Syrians. They then destroyed the plane. In 1970, the group hijacked several passenger jets at the same time, eventually blowing up all of them on the ground, three of them at Dawson Field in Jordan. Ten days after these hijackings, King Hussein of Jordan, sensing that he might be losing control of his country, ordered his army to attack the PLO. After a bloody fight in which around three thousand Palestinian *fedayeen* (sacrificers) were killed, the PLO was driven out of Jordan and took refuge in Lebanon. Following this defeat, Fatah, the largest component of the PLO (led by Yasir Arafat), began to attack targets outside of Israel through a group called Black September (named in memory of their expulsion from Jordan). Abu Iyad, the Fatah leader who secretly headed Black September, said the organization's purpose was "to make the world feel that the Palestinian people exist." The group's most well-known attack was on Israeli athletes at the Munich Olympics in 1972. Eight members of the group broke into the athletes' quarters at the Olympic Village; they killed two of them and took nine hostages. All of the athletes, five members of

Black September, and one police officer were killed at the airport in a police operation that went terribly wrong. While such actions brought the PLO little sympathy, it was thought that it "nevertheless succeeded in establishing the image of its cause as the quest of a victimized people for national self-determination, rather than a neglected refugee problem as it had hitherto been widely regarded."[22] In retaliation two days later, Israel bombed Palestinian refugee camps in Lebanon, killing three hundred to five hundred people.[23]

After its expulsion from Jordan, the PLO continued its operations against Israel from its new bases in Lebanon, as well as participated in a civil war in Lebanon in which Syria intervened. Subsequently, Arafat began to restrain the political violence of the PLO, and the Arab League announced that he was the "sole legitimate representative of Palestinian people." But in June 1982 with little provocation, having just concluded a treaty with Egypt and withdrawn from the Sinai, Israel invaded Lebanon to drive the PLO out. The Israeli invasion left much of West Beirut in rubble and caused thousands of civilian casualties. When the Israeli forces entered Beirut, the PLO left. Subsequently, an international peacekeeping force (representing the United States, France, and Italy) entered the city. In September 1982, while the international peacekeepers were withdrawing, the newly elected Christian Lebanese leader Bashir Gemayel was assassinated. Israeli forces then re-entered the city, allowed the Lebanese Christian Phalangist forces into the refugee camps of Sabra and Shatila, and provided them with assistance so that they could avenge Gemayel's assassination, resulting in the massacre of hundreds of Palestinians. Later, the Israel government accepted "indirect" responsibility for this massacre and Ariel Sharon was forced to resign as defense minister.[24]

With much of the PLO relocated to Tunis, in the late 1980s Arafat tried a new strategy implicitly recognizing Israel's right to exist and rejecting political violence. Militant members of the PLO rejected Arafat's new strategy and formed an organization called Hamas. In 1987, Palestinian youths began a movement that became known as the Intifada, or "shaking off." These youth demonstrated throughout the Occupied Territories, demanding self-government. Despite frequent clashes between these rock-throwing youths and Israeli troops shooting rubber bullets, Israel could not suppress the uprising. After a year, more than 150 Palestinians had been killed, and more than 11,500 were wounded (almost two-thirds of which were under fifteen years of age).[25]

Because of the harsh Israeli response, world opinion began to swing in favor of the Intifada. By 1993, the Israeli government seemed to be willing to take the first steps toward accepting Palestinian autonomy, and an interim peace agreement sometimes referred to as the Oslo Peace Accords established a quasi-national Palestinian Authority empowered to handle domestic affairs in the Palestinian territories. In July 2000, President Clinton convened a summit meeting at Camp David between Israeli Prime Minister Ehud Barak and Chairman Arafat to try to achieve a final peace accord. While Israel had reneged on the interim steps it had agreed to take in the Olso Peace Accords, Barak seemed willing to make a substantial offer to achieve a final peace agreement on an all-or-nothing basis. No partial, trust-building steps were proposed. But from a Palestinian perspective what the Israelis offered was not nearly enough. It certainly was not what the Palestinians were legally entitled to under UN resolutions. But after the Camp David talks broke down, negotiations still continued between the two sides in Egypt, even as a new and more violent Intifada erupted in Israel and the Occupied Territories. In December 2000, both sides issued a joint communiqué saying, "The two sides declare that they have never been closer to reaching an agreement and it is thus our shared belief that the remaining gaps could be bridged with the resumption of negotiations following the Israeli elections."[26] But when Ariel Sharon became prime minister in Israel, he immediately terminated the peace negotiations. Adopting the same strategy of forceful military presence that he had employed in Lebanon as defense minister in the 1980s, Sharon has moved from a policy of temporary occupation of Palestinian territories to now what appears to be a virtual permanent occupation in an effort to further Israel's interests. The idea of withdrawing to the borders that the UN recognized in 1967 has yet to be tried as a way to achieve a lasting peace.[27]

In the 1990s, the use of political violence in Northern Ireland by substate groups, particularly the provisional Irish Republican Army (IRA) appeared to have come to an end through a series of political agreements and institutional changes. While political violence in Ireland goes back centuries, the most recent wave began in 1968–1969, when the British Army in Northern Ireland was perceived to unfairly side with the Protestants against the Catholics. At the time, the IRA responded with a compaign of political violence of its own. Lord Mountbatten, the retired viceroy of India, and Airey Neave, a minister of the Crown, were killed; bombs were placed in commercial centers in London and Manchester, causing much material damage; and an attempt was made to kill then Prime Minister Thatcher and the Conservative leadership at their party conference. But in recent years support for political violence among both Protestants and Catholics has diminished, setting the stage for the negotiated peace and institutional changes that have resulted.[28]

Throughout this brief history of terrorism, I have tried to follow historical practice and focus on forms of terrorism that are practiced by substate groups and individuals, but that is not always easy to do. This is because most of the clear cases of terrorism directed at innocents are cases of terrorism as practiced by states, such as France under the Jacobins, Italy under Mussolini, Germany under Hitler, and Chile under Pinochet, rather than cases of terrorism as practiced by substate groups or individuals. Partly this is because it is states, not substate groups and individuals, that have killed large numbers of innocent people, but it is also because, despite what governments say, many of those targeted by substate groups and individuals are reasonably regarded by them as legitimate targets, and hence not innocents, especially when the targets are government officials. As a consequence, much of the political violence as practiced by substate groups and individuals cannot properly be regarded as terrorism, irrespective of whether or not we regard it as justified, unless one adopts a broader definition of terrorism that allows that there are many cases of justified terrorism. Unfortunately, the fact that the clearest and most striking cases of terrorism are those of state terrorism is ignored in most historical accounts of terrorism and, not too surprisingly, by governments as well. For example, the U.S. State Department defines terrorism so as to exclude state terrorism, at the same time that it recognizes that there is "state-sponsored terrorism." Accordingly, if we want to have an accurate picture of terrorism throughout history, and in our present circumstances, we must continually remind ourselves that the most significant terrorist problem is that of state terrorism or state-sponsored terrorism.

It is also important to bear in mind that the focus of this volume (but not always the focus of this brief historical introduction) is the interface between terrorism and international justice. There are many examples of terrorism that do not raise questions of international justice, although they may raise a challenge to the justice of the domestic institutions of a particular society, as, for example, the Oklahoma City bombing attempted to do. As you would expect from its title, the focus of this volume, however, is on just those forms of terrorism that do raise questions of international justice, such 9/11 and the terrorist practices of the Israel–Palestinian conflict. With that in mind, let us now turn to a brief discussion of the articles in this volume.

WHAT IS THE NATURE AND RHETORIC OF TERRORISM?

In "Murderers, Not Warriors," Shannon E. French is concerned with what moral rules, if any, govern asymmetric conflicts where the two sides are dramatically mismatched. She is particularly concerned with whether the weaker side in such conflicts is required to fight by the same rules as the stronger side. She argues that the same rules should apply to all, but that in asymmetrical conflicts, the rules can be different from those that apply in symmetrical conflicts. For example, it may be permissible for both sides in an asymmetrical conflict to "fight dirty" or for either side to give up its right to prisoner of war status if captured when not fighting according to the traditional rules of war.

French also denies that either side in an asymmetrical conflict could claim that no moral constraints apply to them. In particular, one moral constraint that must apply, according to French, is a prohibition on intentionally killing innocent persons. Innocent persons are then identified with noncombatants—those who are not a threat to one's life. In my contribution to this volume, I challenge whether a prohibition on intentionally killing innocent persons is an absolute moral prohibition. Moreover, according to French, even unintentional killing of innocent persons can be wrong when that killing shows "a *willingness* to strike an inappropriate target." This would be the case, for example, if one side in a conflict used advanced technology and weapons to fight from such a distance that the risk to its own combatants is minimized while the risk to noncombatants on the enemy side is increased.

French thinks that when morally assessing combatants, it is enough to focus on *jus in bello* (that is, whether just means are being used); there is no need to assess combatants in terms of *jus ad bellum* (that is, whether their cause is just). At the same time, French thinks that fighters for Al Qaeda, at least when they target combatants, as in the case of the attack on the *U.S.S. Cole*, should have combatant status because they are pursuing what they believe is a just cause. For French, then, at least in cases of this sort, the question of just cause is still relevant to determining whether such fighters should have combatant status.

Yet it would seem that if the question of just cause is relevant to establishing the combatant status of irregular forces, such as members of Al Qaeda, it should also be relevant to establishing the combatant status of regular forces, such as standing armies. For example, if a country started a proclaimed war of conquest on its weaker neighbor, surely its soldiers, lacking a just cause for fighting, would also lack combatant status, and thus lack any justification for fighting in such a war, even if the soldiers were to limit themselves to using just means (*jus in bello*).

In Chapter 2, Tomis Kapitan focuses on the rhetoric of terrorism, that is, the way that the language of terrorism is used in our contemporary discussion. What Kapitan observes is that whatever definition of terrorism is endorsed, particularly by government representatives, the term "terrorism" is rarely used to apply to the actions of one's own country, or its allies, even when those actions actually fit their own definition. Kapitan claims that this was true with respect to the destruction of Grozny by Russian forces during the Chechnya war of 1999; the U.S. bombing of Tripoli, Libya, in April 1986; the U.S. naval bombardment of Lebanese villages in the Chouf mountains in October 1983; and the Israeli aerial and land bombardment of Beirut in the summer of 1982 that resulted in the deaths of five thousand to six thousand civilians. At the same time, Kapitan notes, speakers routinely label actions of their political adversaries as "terrorist" that do not qualify as such under the definition the speakers themselves are endorsing. This is because their political adversaries are targeting combatants and, hence, not targeting innocents. By so using the language of terrorism, Kapitan surmises, speakers attempt to discredit their political adversaries before the risky business of inquiry into their complaints can even begin.

While Kapitan's point here concerns consistency of usage and calculated distortion, as we noted before in this introduction, some people define terrorism more broadly so that targeting noncombatants or innocents is not an essential feature of terrorism.[29] Yet as we also noted, when the term "terrorism" is so defined, it turns out that many terrorist actions will turn out to be morally justified.

Kapitan goes on to examine in detail how the rhetoric of terrorism is employed in the Israeli-Palestinian conflict. He argues that Israel uses the rhetoric of terrorism to draw attention away from its own land confiscations, settlement building, and human rights violations, directing it at the more sensational reactions by Palestinians. Kapitan further notes that the U.S. State Department's four principles for deal-ing with terrorism (endorsed by Louis Pojman in his contribution to this volume) unfortunately do not require any investigation into the *causes* of persistent terrorist violence. According to Kapitan, not only do we need to give up our reliance on the rhetoric of terrorism, but we also need to investigate the actual causes of terrorism and seek to remove them.

WHO ARE THE TERRORISTS, AND WHY DO THEY HATE?

In "Terror and Just Response," Noam Chomsky accepts as a definition of terrorism "the calculated use of violence or threat of violence to attain goals that are political, religious, or ideological in nature . . . through intimidation, coercion, or instilling fear." This definition of terrorism does not require that innocents be directly targeted for an act to be terrorist. In this selection, however, Chomsky is not so much concerned with the adequacy of any proposed definition of terrorism as with the failure to draw out the appropriate implications whatever definition terrorism happens to be endorsed.

Using the definition he has adopted here, Chomsky argues that we in the United States cannot consistently think that widespread bomb-ing is the appropriate response to terrorist crimes like 9/11 because then, by parity of reasoning, we would have to be committed to the legitimacy of the widespread bombing of our own nation. For exam-ple, we would be committed to the legitimacy of Nicaragua's bomb-ing of the United States for failure to terminate what the World Court found to be its "unlawful use of force" against that country in the 1980s. By this same reasoning, Haiti would be justified in bombing the United States for failing to extradite Emmanuel Constant, who was responsible for thousands of deaths in Haiti, and Sudan would be jus-tified in similarly retaliating for the U.S. bombing of its pharmaceuti-cal plant in 1998, which led to "several tens of thousands" of deaths.

Chomsky goes on to point out that the United States has a long history of engaging in and supporting terrorist acts in Central and South America and in the Middle East, particularly through its virtu-ally unlimited military support of Israel and Turkey. Again, by parity of reasoning with the U.S. military response to 9/11, those oppressed by Israel and Turkey, that is, the Palestinians and the Kurds, would pre-sumably be justified in engaging in retaliatory military responses against the United States.

Chomsky further notes that there was not much support among most countries around the world for our responding to 9/11 with a military attack against Afghanistan. As to the reason for the 9/11 attack, Chomsky points to Osama bin Ladin's opposition to the U.S. military bases in Saudi Arabia. More importantly, Chomsky maintains that unless the social, political, and economic conditions that gave rise to bin Ladin and his Al Qaeda network are addressed, the United States and its allies can only expect that they will continue to be targeted by Islamic terrorists in the future.

In Chapter 4, David B. Burrell sets out two competing narratives with regard to the Israeli-Palestinian conflict. In the first narrative, the Bedouin Arabs ally themselves with the British against the Turks during World War I, for which their leaders receive vague promises of self-determination after the war. In the second narrative, the Balfour Declaration of 1917 endorses "the establishment in Palestine of a national home for the Jewish people," and the immigration of Jews into Palestine is glorified, particularly after the Holocaust, ignoring the adverse effects it has on "the indigenous people." Yet since 1967, Burrell contends, Israel has had to face a stark choice: either cease being a Jewish state demographically by assimilating the people in the land they have occupied into their body politic or cease being a Jewish state ethically by attempting to rule over people whom they have not admitted to full citizenship. In the current setting, this choice is being played out in terms of whether Israel really intends to end its longstanding occupation. In this regard, Burrell suggests that the Camp David offer made to the Palestinians was not that attractive. It certainly was not what the Palestinians are still entitled to under existing UN resolutions.

Burrell also seeks to counter the view that the survival (which may also include the flourishing) of the Jewish people after Auschwitz justified any means. Invoking Socrates, he argues that survival counts for nothing if one betrays his or her humanity in the process. By showing both the contradiction and moral loss involved in favoring the second competing narrative pertaining to the Israeli-Palestinian conflict, Burrell hopes to thereby "remove it from the competition." He compares the transformation required here to the painful process of self-education demanded of Americans by the Vietnam War. But this transformation, Burrell suggests, may be even more difficult to bring about given the Holocaust, the three wars fought in Palestine, and the legacy of marginalization (and worse) of eighteen centuries of Christendom.

Still, Burrell hopes that the transformation can be accomplished, aided by more dialogue and personal contact among Jews, Christians, and Muslims and less pro-Israel bias in the media coverage of the conflict.

In "The War Against Pluralism," Robert L. Phillips seeks to put 9/11 within a larger explanatory framework. Starting with Plato, Phillips notes two fundamental facts. The first is that human beings cannot fully flourish without truth. The second is that human flourishing requires a complete, public conception of the good. In the Middle Ages, these two fundamental facts were recognized, although there was radical disagreement over what was the appropriate complete, public conception of the good according to which society was to be organized. Early on, this disagreement over a complete, public conception of the good existed between Christians and Muslims; later, it arose between Catholics and Protestants as well. Still later developments in the West, especially the Peace of Westphalia set aside the question of religious truth, at least between nations, and subsequent developments took religious truth out of public life altogether (e.g., in the United States with the doctrine of the separation of church and state), thus achieving the triumph of pluralism. According to Phillips, while pluralism does allow for common values, these values are not always admirable because they represent "the lowest possible common denominator" and are "necessarily consumerist," thus endorsing "a culture of infantilism wherein entertainment and sexual gratification become all-consuming."

Not surprisingly, Phillips finds in pluralism, so understood, an inadequate conception of the good for us to use to face the challenge of 9/11. This is because this admittedly partial conception of the good puts us in sharp opposition to traditional Islamic society, which still endorses a complete, public conception of the good, as we once did in the West. Yet Phillips goes further and sees the terrorism of 9/11 as also part of a critique of Western pluralism, a critique that we would do well to respond to by actually ridding ourselves of that pluralism and reestablishing a complete, public conception of the good in which religion is no longer privatized. In so doing, Phillips thinks, we will be able to find more common ground with traditional Islamic societies, and thus there will be less reason for conflicts to arise between ourselves and Islamic societies in the future.

One might wonder, however, whether the shared values that Western pluralism endorses are simply those of consumerism, as Phillips claims. First, many would argue that the core liberal values of the civil rights movement, the women's movement, and the environmental movement represent a much more substantive conception of the good than Phillips recognizes. Second, there is the worry that instituting a complete public conception of the good in the West would lead, as in the past, to another Crusade against the Muslim world. (Some might even argue that the incomplete Judeo-Christian consensus we already have has led to a partial Crusade against the Muslim world.) Third, there is the worry that our real conflict with the Muslim world derives not so much from religion, or the lack of it, or from our different lifestyles, but rather from the military dominance we exercise over the region—our $4 billion yearly support of Israel, our support for undemocratic governments in the region, and the economic sanctions we still impose on Iraq after all these years.

Of course, Phillips shares with Burrell the need to create more of a consensus among "people of religion" in order to adequately deal with the problems of terrorism that we face. But on Burrell's view, but not Phillips's, it may be possible to do this by getting people of religion to recognize the common moral ground they share with each other, and hopefully even with people who stand outside any religious framework.

In her contribution to this volume, Zayn Kassam raises the difficult question of whether Islam actually teaches, promotes, or requires its adherents to engage in terrorism as their religious duty. She argues that historically "jihad" had been understood as a defensive response to aggression and that there was also a "greater jihad" that required no military action at all but rather an inner struggle directed at personal transformation. However, these distinctions, Kassam claims, have been lost in the contemporary postcolonial world. In that world, subject people have looked to Islam to rescue them from subordination, and Muslim conservatives have argued that this rescue requires the re-Islamization of public institutions, while more moderate Muslims have disagreed. Yet seemingly unconditional Western support of Israel and self-serving interventions by Western powers have made it difficult for more moderate Muslims to get a hearing in the Muslim world.

According to Kassam, while Muslim conservatives or Islamists hold that every aspect of a Muslim's life must be governed by Islam, most do not believe in utilizing physically violent means in achieving their aims, although some Islamist groups do have an organizational arm devoted to that purpose. Yet, unlike bin Laden's Al Qaeda network, most Islamist groups also restrict themselves to local causes as far as their militancy goes.

Kassam claims that these groups foster a desire in their recruits to return to a retrospective golden age utopia, supposedly articulated and implemented by the community of the Prophet, in which a total Islamic polity existed, pervading all areas of life. In so doing, they seek to overturn, infiltrate, or take over the government in order to provide such a society, and along the way create civic conditions that are punitive toward Muslim minorities, members of other faiths, and women. Disappointed with the failure of their governments to provide the conditions necessary for healthy, vibrant societies, these groups also provide social services unmet by government, in response to the poverty and material needs of the population.

Kassam argues that the militant Muslim groups pose a significant threat to Muslims and non-Muslims alike. While their interpretation of Islam runs contrary to the largely peaceful and ethical stances taken by the majority of the world's diverse Muslims, nonetheless, their access to arms and networks makes their small number a sizeable source of risk. To prevent such ideologies from gaining ground, Kassam argues that a concerted effort must be made by liberal Muslims and non-Muslims alike to address the issues from which these groups draw support. Otherwise, as witnessed by the world on 9/11, a Muslim, most likely an Islamist, can become a terrorist, even though the Quran forbids it.

Thus, while Phillips hopes for a day when Western societies, particularly the United States, are less pluralistic, Kassam hopes for a day when Western societies embrace a standard of international justice and thereby encourage Muslim societies to be more pluralistic and tolerant.

WHAT IS A MORALLY JUSTIFIED RESPONSE TO TERRORISM?

In "The Moral Response to Terrorism and Cosmopolitanism," Louis P. Pojman argues for short-term and long-term strategies for dealing with 9/11. Terrorism is a problem for us, claims Pojman, because both Israelis and Muslims in the Middle East seem to be committed to a religious fundamentalism that permits massive retaliation for perceived injustices with virtually no protection for noncombatants or innocents. Pojman sees terrorism as a type of political violence that intentionally targets civilians (noncombatants or innocents) in a ruthlessly destructive, often unpredictable manner. Poverty and oppression are, for Pojman, contributing causes of terrorism; the primary cause is a culture that endorses unlimited violent responses to perceived injustices. At bottom, Pojman sees our struggle with terrorism to be one of moral secularity against intolerant religious theocracy.

Obviously, Pojman is far less confident than Phillips and Burrell are that a solution to the problems of terrorism we face can be found by focusing on people's religious commitments, but surely Pojman would not object to getting people of religion to recognize the common moral ground they should share with each other and with people who stand outside any religious framework.

The short-term strategy that Pojman favors justifies a measured military response to punish and deter those responsible for 9/11. This strategy also incorporates the following principles of current U.S. policy.

1. Make no concessions to terrorists and strike no deals.
2. Bring terrorists to justice.
3. Isolate and apply pressure on states that sponsor terrorism, forcing them to change their behavior.
4. Bolster the counterterrorist capabilities of those countries that work with the United States and require assistance.

Furthermore, the strategy also seeks to cut off the financial resources of terrorists and to impose a more restrictive immigration policy.

As a long-term strategy for dealing with terrorism, Pojman argues for

1. National service.
2. Spreading the message of universal morality with universal human rights.
3. A cosmopolitanism based on a secular morality that would utilize some form of world government.

The cosmopolitanism that Pojman endorses is said to be compatible with a "soft" nationalism that recognizes special obligations to one's own country but also recognizes that "our nationalistic obligations may be overridden at times by obligations to mankind at large or to people not citizens of our nation."

In their contribution to this volume, Daniele Archibugi and Iris Marion Young offer two different frameworks for interpreting 9/11. The first sees it as an attack on the United States as a state and its people.

The second views it as a crime against humanity requiring a cosmopolitan vision of political responsibility. Archibugi and Young argue in favor of the second framework over the first. Viewing 9/11 from the first framework has led the United States to overthrow the government of Afghanistan and, in the process, to destroy some Al Qaeda bases, but, according to Archibugi and Young, there is no reason to think that these actions have deterred other would-be terrorists around the world. Employing the second framework, Archibugi and Young suggest that we should view 9/11 as a crime rather than an act of war, to which the proper response is a criminal investigation and a prosecution within a rule of law. They go on to propose five principles to guide international policy to respond to threats and problems of violence. They are

1. Legitimize and strengthen international institutions, especially the United Nations.
2. Coordinate law enforcement and intelligence-gathering institutions around the world, building on such organizations as INTERPOL, the international police organization, with its 179 member nations.
3. Increase financial regulation of the transfer of money around the world.
4. Use international courts—which will be more difficult for the United States to do now that it has withdrawn its signature from the International Criminal Court.
5. Narrow global inequalities that, as long as they remain, demonstrate an indifference to how poor people fare around the world.

Archibugi and Young maintain that their alternative framework for approaching 9/11 would have had less "collateral damage" than the one that has been pursued so far and that it would have had the additional benefit of showing the peoples of the world that the world's powerful leaders are able to support the rule of law and the instruments of justice beyond their own borders.

Yet even those who tend to favor Archibugi and Young's alternative framework, as far as it goes, may think that it requires yet another dimension—the need to rectify the past and continuing injustices imposed and supported particularly by the United States and other Western powers, such as the Israeli occupation of Palestine, the economic sanctions against Iraq, and the support for dictatorial and authoritarian governments around the world.

In "Making War on Terrorism in Response to 9/11," Claudia Card seeks to determine how we might respond effectively to 9/11 without doing further evil. For her, the 9/11 attacks are paradigms of evil deeds, but she is less sure that they are acts of terrorism. To determine whether they are, Card applies Carl Wellman's definition of terrorism. According to Wellman, terrorism is coercive political violence characterized by two targets. It has a direct (but secondary) target at which harm is aimed, and, by way of that harm, a message is sent to an indirect (but primary) target about what the perpetrator wants the indirect target to do in order that more direct harm be avoided. Card claims that the evidence we have does not unambiguously reveal what was the purpose of the attacks. It is possible that their purpose was simply punitive, in which case the deeds would not be terrorist in Wellman's sense.

This definition of terrorism, which we took note of before, is much broader than those usually found in the literature, and it is also broader than those adopted by most of the other contributors to this collection. For example, an armed robber trying to threaten her victim to hand over his wallet is a terrorist by this definition. So is a judge sentencing a condemned criminal to death if she is attempting to deter would-be criminals by using the death penalty. Other definitions of terrorism require the purpose of the act to be political, and still other definitions also require that terrorist acts be directly targeted at innocents. The first of these additional constraints limits the range of what we can call terrorism. The second limits the possibility of there being justifiable acts of terrorism. Yet whichever of these definitions we use, the ambiguity of the purpose of the attackers of 9/11 does make it a bit difficult to classify their actions, although the bin Laden tapes and recent statements by Al Qaeda spokespersons do seem to rule out a purely punitive purpose.

Yet Card is most concerned not with a definition of terrorism but with determining whether the U.S. war on terrorism is justified. Here she considers two cases in which women dealt with the serious harms that were being inflicted upon them. In one case, known as "the burning bed," Francine Hughes poured gasoline over her former husband as he slept in bed and ignited it after years of having endured his battering and many times having appealed unsuccessfully to the law for protection for herself and her children. In another case, after receiving a phone call threatening her with murder, Inez García pursued and shot at two men, one of whom had raped her minutes before while the other, who weighed three hundred pounds, stood guard to prevent her escape. Her shots killed one man (the second), and she only regretted not having succeeded in killing the other as well (he was never charged with any crime). Card argues that when a nation makes war on terrorism, it takes matters into its own hands in a manner that is analogous to what Hughes and García did. In so acting, a nation steps somewhat outside the bounds and processes of international law. She further claims that if it was justifiable to try Hughes and García, as was done, or if it would have been justifiable at least to hold an inquest or hearing regarding the killings, then perhaps it would also be justifiable, for similar reasons, for international tribunals to do the same with respect to the leaders of nations who make war on terrorists, especially when the wars kill large numbers of civilians. Such inquiries would also consider whether less drastic responses had been exhausted by those who make war on terrorism.

Card then raises the question of whether it would not make better sense for an international agency to capture and try in an international court those accused of international terrorism, or of complicity in it, instead of leaving victim nations to take matters into their own hands, just as it would have made better sense to capture and try the man repeatedly accused of battering Hughes and the men accused of raping García, rather than leaving these women to defend themselves by whatever means necessary. Card thinks that an affirmative answer to this question means nations of the world have serious work to do, collectively, regarding intervention policies where terrorism and fear of terrorism loom. The conclusion she draws here is not that nations defending themselves against terrorism militarily are necessarily wrong. Rather, they should not be left in the position of having to make that decision. Meanwhile, making war on terrorism may put leaders of nations doing so at risk of becoming justifiably liable to inquests or hearings, if not trials for war crimes, by international tribunals, just as Hughes and García became liable to trial for murder.

It would also seem that Card's analogies between the war on terrorism and the two cases from U.S. domestic law serve to support the cosmopolitan, international law approach to terrorism favored by Pojman, Archibugi and Young, and myself.

In his contribution to this volume, Richard W. Miller evaluates the moral legitimacy of the war against the Taliban and the war against Saddam Hussein. He finds the first morally defensible and the second morally indefensible. According to Miller, the war against the Taliban was defensible because to limit ourselves to police action, foreign policy, and specifically targeted military attacks (the sort of approach favored by a number of contributors to this volume) would, he thinks, have significantly increased the risks of large-scale terrorism in the United States and elsewhere, although he does not give any evidence for this conclusion. And evidence is surely required here. As one commentator has put it, the 9/11 terrorist cells were less functionally dependent on Al Qaeda bases in Afghanistan than they were on flight schools in Florida.[30]

At the same time, Miller claims that the United States has a large postwar responsibility to improve the well-being of the people of Afghanistan, not only because of the consequences of the war just waged there, but also because the United States shares responsibility for the political turmoil in Afghanistan that brought the Taliban to power.

With respect to a war against Saddam Hussein, Miller points out that the UN's chief arms inspector, Scott Ritter, claims that inspections for weapons of mass destruction have worked in Iraq in the past and that they can reasonably be expected to do so again in the future. Miller further argues that Saddam Hussein and his regime are also different from bin Laden and his followers in that the former, unlike the latter, strongly prefer continued survival and control over their country to death in a conflagration, even if the conflagration is part of a disaster for the United States. Moreover, if the United States did go to war against Saddam Hussein, Miller points out, it would have reason to prevent Iraq from achieving too much democracy, since its secessionist consequences in the Kurdish north would appall Turkey and Syria, while its consequences in the Shiite south would threaten to shift the balance of power in the Persian Gulf in favor of Iran. The likely outcome, therefore, is a new strongman or repressive clique in Baghdad, friendly to U.S. interests, that might control Iraq less viciously than Hussein. This outcome, Miller thinks, would not justify undermining traditional norms of nonintervention at such grave risk to human life.

In my own contribution to this volume, I approach the question of how we should think about terrorism from the perspective of just war pacifism. According to this view, the few wars and large-scale conflicts that meet the stringent requirements of just war theory are the only wars and large-scale conflicts to which anti-war pacifists cannot justifiably object. Moreover, this view, as I defend it, does not impose an absolute prohibition on intentionally harming innocents. Specifically, it allows that harm to innocents can be justified if it is greatly outweighed by the consequences of the action. Using both hypothetical and historical examples as analogies, I argue that if the Israelis have the ultimate goal of confining most Palestinians to a number of economically nonviable and disconnected reservations, similar to those on which the United States confines American Indian nations, then the use by Palestinians of suicide bombers against Israeli civilians can be morally justified. I also argue that according to just war pacifism, neither the actions taken by the Israeli government with respect to the Palestinians nor those actions undertaken by the U.S. government with respect to the Al Qaeda network are morally justified because neither government has exhausted its nonbelligerent correctives before engaging in a military response. I further point out that the United States has arguably itself engaged in terrorist acts by (1) bombing a pharmaceutical plant in Sudan with respect to which we compensated the owner, but not the thousands of victims who were thereby deprived of drugs; (2) sponsoring sanctions against Iraq that kill an estimated three thousand to five thousand children in Iraq each month; (3) and supporting with $4 billion a year Israel's illegal occupation of Palestinian lands, which has resulted in many thousands of deaths. Given that these acts of terrorism and support for terrorism have served at least partially to motivate terrorist attacks on the United States itself, the United States surely needs to take steps to radically correct its own wrongdoing if it is to respond justly to the related wrongdoing of bin Laden and his followers. Last, I argue that the United States has to do more to be a good world citizen. It must stop being a conspicuous holdout with respect to international treaties, and it must do its fair share to redistribute resources from the rich to the poor as international justice requires.

In "Compassion and Terror," Martha C. Nussbaum argues that the events of 9/11 make vivid a philosophical problem that has been debated from the time of Euripides straight on through much of the history of the Western philosophical tradition. It is the question of what do to about compassion, given its obvious importance in shaping the civic imagination, but given, too, its obvious propensity for self-serving narrowness. Frequently, she claims, we get a compassion that is not only narrow, failing to include distant peoples, but also polarizing, dividing the world into an "us" and a "them." Nussbaum further rejects the Stoic view of dealing with this problem, which denies the importance of special relationships and external goods to human *eudaimonia*. Instead, Nussbaum proposes that we educate our children to recognize common human weakness and vulnerability. To be successful, she claims, that education needs to take place in a culture of ethical criticism and especially self-criticism, in which ideas of equal respect for humanity will be active players in the effort to curtail the excesses of the greedy self.

Nussbaum argues that the narrowness of our compassion and other emotions is a perfectly general problem, not a problem new in the context of the "war on terrorism." Terrorism, she claims, does make us pay attention to distant peoples for a while. Yet once things return to normal, we stop taking distant peoples and their problems into account. Moreover, she notes that most of the preventable suffering and death in the world is not caused by terrorism. Rather, it is caused by malnutrition, lack of education, and all the ills connected to poverty. She sees an even greater danger in the idea that there should be an ongoing "war on terrorism" In that it will fail to connect us to the daily sufferings of ordinary people. Nussbaum worries that the experience of terror and grief for our towers might be just that, an experience of terror and grief for our towers. Even worse, it could be a stimulus for blind rage and aggression against all our enemies. To counter this, Nussbaum claims we need to cultivate a culture of critical compassion that is constrained by respect for human dignity and by a vivid sense of the real losses and needs of others.

While Nussbaum is surely correct that most of the preventable suffering and death in the world is not caused by terrorism, these and other failures of international justice do provide a breeding ground for terrorism, and so must be addressed if we seek to do what we can to reduce the threat to terrorism in our times.

The contributions to this volume cover a broad range of topics with regard to terrorism and international justice. Some raise questions of definition, consistency of usage, and approach: French, Kapitan, Chomsky, and Card. Others raise questions concerning the evaluation of relevant narratives, conceptions of the good, and moral and religious frameworks: Burrell, Phillips, Kassam, Archibugi and Young, Nussbaum, and myself. And some others are concerned with the questions of how to evaluate particular actions and policies: Chomsky, Pojman, Archibugi and Young, Miller, and myself. Of course, all of these questions are interconnected, as the contributions to this volume clearly demonstrate. So we must try to answer all of these questions together if we hope really to answer any of them at all.

NOTES

1. See Jeffrey Simon, *The Terrorist Trap* (Bloomington: Indiana University Press, 2001), pp. 26–27.

2. David Rappoport, "Religion and Terror: Thugs, Assassins and Zealots," in *International Terrorism*, ed. Charles Kegley (New York: St. Martin's Press, 1990), pp. 147–149.

3. Daniel Gerould, *Guillotine, Its Legend and Lore* (New York, Blast Books, 1992), p. 13.

4. See Simon, pp. 27–28.

5. See Walter Laqueur, *New Terrorism* (New York: Oxford University Press, 1998), Chapter 1; Walter Laqueur, *The Age of Terrorism* (Boston: Little, Brown, 1987), Chapter 1.

6. Laqueur, *The Age of Terrorism*, Chapter 1.

7. Laqueur, *The Age of Terrorism*, Chapter 1.

8. Martha Crenshaw, "The Logic of Terrorism," in *Origins of Terrorism* ed. Walter Reich (New York: Cambridge University Press, 1990), p. 15; Simon, p. 43.

9. Simon, pp. 40–41.

10. Page Smith, *America Enters the World*, Vol. 7: *A People's History of the Progressive Era and World War I* (New York: McGraw-Hill, 1985), pp. 252–260.

11. Carl Wellman, "On Terrorism Itself," *Journal of Value Inquiry* 13 (1990):250–258.

12. See Jay Robert Nash, *Terrorism in the 20th Century* (New York: M. Evans and Company, Inc., 1998), Chapter 4.

13. Laqueur, *The Age of Terrorism*, Chapter 1.

14. See Simon, pp. 44–45.

15. Dan Kulzman, *Genesis 1948* (New York: World, 1970) p. 148.

16. Ian Bickerton and Carla Klausner, *A Concise History of the Arab-Israeli Conflict* (Upper Saddle River, NJ: Prentice-Hall, 2002), pp. 103–104; Kameel Nasr, *Arab and Israeli Terrorism* (London: McFarland, 1997), pp. 21–22; J. Bowyer Bell, *Terror Out of Zion* (New York: St. Martin's Press, 1977).

17. Bickerton and Klausner, p. 104.

18. Laqueur, *Age of Terrorism*, Chapter 1; Harry Henderson, *Terrorism* (New York: Facts on File, 2001), pp. 58–59.

19. Quoted in Christoph Rojahn, "Left-Wing Terrorism in Germany," *Conflict Studies* 313 (1998):3.

20. Nash, Chapter 8; Rojahn, pp. 1–25.

21. Nash, Chapter 9.

22. Nasr, p. 57.

23. David Tucker, *Skirmishes at the Edge of Empire* (London: Praeger, 1997), Chapter 1; Nasr, Chapter 5; Bickerton and Klausner, pp. 166–168.

24. Nasr, Chapter 13; Bickerton and Klausner, Chapter 9.

25. Bickerton and Klausner, Chapter 9; Henderson, pp. 42–45.

26. Robert Malley and Hussein Agha, "A Reply to Ehud Barak," *New York Review*, June 13, 2002, p. 68.

27. Nasr, Chapter 5; Bickerton and Klausner, Chapters 10 and 11; Henderson, pp. 42–45.

28. Henderson, pp. 33–34; Laqueur, *New Terrorism*, Chapter 1.

29. It is worth noting that Kapitan criticizes Paul Wilkinson and Igor Primoratz for claiming that terrorists target "innocent civilians" or "innocents" generally. It is possible, however, that Wilkinson and Primoratz only mean by those labels what Kapitan means by "civilians" or "noncombatants." Although with respect to warfare, combatants are not always morally guilty and noncombatants are not always morally innocent, there remains a sense of "being innocent" which is the same as that of "being a noncombatant."

30. Carl Conetta, "Strange Victory: A Critical Appraisal of Operation Enduring Freedom and the Afghanistan War," *Project on Defense Alternatives*, January 30, 2002.

PART I

What Is the Nature and Rhetoric of Terrorism?

CHAPTER 1

Murderers, Not Warriors

The Moral Distinction Between Terrorists and Legitimate Fighters in Asymmetric Conflicts

SHANNON E. FRENCH

In 1943, Paramount Pictures released the unashamedly patriotic and pro-war film *So Proudly We Hail!* chronicling the lives of eight U.S. Army nurses stationed in the Pacific during World War II. Halfway through the film, the women are trapped behind enemy lines because of the botched evacuation of a field hospital on the island of Bataan. They are terrified of capture, which is understandable given the tendency of the Japanese military at the time to abuse prisoners. The women have one possible avenue of escape, but it is blocked by a small patrol of Japanese soldiers. One of the nurses, played in the film by screen siren Veronica Lake, decides to sacrifice her life for the safety of the others. She hides a grenade inside her shirt and approaches the soldiers. When the men gather around the beautiful blonde she pulls the pin, killing them and herself. The other women seize the opportunity and flee the area.

Filmgoers on the 1940s homefront were meant to view Veronica Lake's character in *So Proudly We Hail!* as noble and heroic. No one would have thought of condemning her as a "terrorist." Yet her actions in many respects resemble those of modern suicide bombers— or "homicide bombers," as President Bush would have us call them— who are commonly described as "terrorists" and "murderers." Is it mere hypocrisy that we see an American nurse in World War II as one of the "good guys" fighting on the right side in what so many have called "The Good War"? Are we automatically blinded by the fact that she looks like many of us, talks like us, and shares our values and way of life, or can we objectively distinguish—on moral grounds—between her actions and those of the men (and women) currently decried as "terrorists"?

31

Drawing careful lines dividing what appear to be similar actions into various categories of praiseworthiness and blameworthiness can seem like an empty academic exercise—mere sophistry. When the actions in question concern the taking of human lives, however, those lines—however thin—become critically important. The difference between murder and killing in self-defense matters in the real world. It matters to the person who caused the death, and to all those affected by the death. As I have argued elsewhere,[1] understanding the distinction between warriors and murderers is vital for the preservation of the moral character of the men and women who fight our wars and of the nations and communities they are called to defend. The victims of a serial killer, an air raid, a sniper's bullet, and a terrorist's bomb are equally worthy of our pity, but those who caused their deaths may not be subject to equal moral censure.

Especially since the horrific events of September 11, 2001, there has been a great deal of debate concerning the morality of what are seen as terror tactics. A term that has come to the foreground is "asymmetric conflict"—one in which the two sides are dramatically mismatched, such that the strength, influence, and resources of one utterly dwarf the other. The world is not presently arranged in such a way that conflicts are likely to arise among great powers with fairly even distributions of military might. America is frequently termed "the sole remaining Superpower," and she is presently at peace or even allied with all of her former or potential near-future rivals, such as Russia, Great Britain, and China, in her "War on Terror." Therefore, all conflicts involving the United States are asymmetric in nature. Another asymmetric conflict that has been much in the news lately is that between the state of Israel and the Palestinian Authority. The Israeli Defense Force (IDF) is an organized, disciplined, and well-funded modern army trained to use advanced technology and weapons, while most of those who fight for the Palestinian cause are poorly funded, ill equipped, and under no effective centralized control.

Asymmetric conflicts are by no means a recent phenomenon. As long as there have been great powers, there have been smaller powers willing to challenge their dominance. Many such conflicts have been attempts by an inferior force to oust a superior, occupying force from its territory. Examples of asymmetric conflicts in this category could include the Celtic rebellion led by Queen Boudicca against the Roman occupation of Britain, the struggles by Native Americans to reclaim tribal lands seized by white settlers, and the efforts of French resistance fighters against the Nazis in World War II. Closely akin to these would be asymmetric attempts to repel the initial invasion of a colonizing, imperial power. Some asymmetric conflicts are seen more as internal insurgencies rather than the removal of an occupying force. Revolutionary wars are nearly always asymmetric, since they involve fledgling powers bent on either replacing (as in the case of the French Revolution) or splitting off from (as in the American Revolution) an established power.

Without the lessons of history, one might expect most asymmetric conflicts to end with the weaker side crushed by the stronger one. This has been the reality in many instances. To cite just a few examples: The Roman Empire reasserted its control over ancient Britain, bringing an end to the Celtic uprising and maintaining its occupation until approximately 400 C.E.; centuries later, the British Empire finally conquered fierce Zulu resistance and in 1887 annexed the Zululand territory in South Africa; China decisively suppressed a Tibetan revolt in 1959; and aboriginal people from the Americas to Australia have been pushed to the margins by waves of European invasions. However, history also offers innumerable examples of triumphs by the apparent "underdogs" in asymmetric conflicts. Rome eventually fell to undisciplined barbarian hordes that were once thought no match for the well-oiled war machine of the Roman legions. The rag-tag American revolutionaries defeated the British redcoats. The U.S. lost the Vietnam War, and an army of Islamic "holy warriors" sent the mighty Soviet Army scurrying out of Afghanistan.

This irrefutable evidence that the results of an asymmetric conflict are by no means a foregone conclusion bolsters the hopes of "Davids" everywhere who have stones already on their slings, ready to nail their respective "Goliaths" right between the eyes. The question is, should the asymmetry of a conflict affect the rules that govern it? Is the disadvantaged party in a lopsided battle obliged to obey the same *jus in bello* restrictions as its enemies? Does holding both sides in an asymmetric conflict to the same standards further stack the deck in favor of the dominant force, to the extent that having to fight fair is an unfair burden to place on the underdog?

When two nations with similar strength and resources battle one another, it is relatively easy for their leaders to establish mutually beneficial rules of engagement. It is rational for them to reach agreements about such matters as the use of particular weapons and tactics and the treatment of prisoners of war, because doing so will serve the interests of both parties without giving a disproportionate advantage to either one. On the other hand, when weaker forces take on stronger ones, any restrictions on the conduct of war that the former accept can only limit their arsenal of potential means to overcome their opening handicap.

Asymmetric conflict, like all warfare, is deadly serious business. However, considering the features of a less grave asymmetric contest may be instructive by analogy. Picture a boxing match between a heavyweight champion in peak physical condition and the stereotypical "ninety-pound weakling" of sand-in-the-face fame. In a fair fight, the underdog will get pulverized. Therefore, if he has any interest in winning, he should not agree to a set of rules that will limit his options in the ring. His best hope is to find a way to "fight dirty." The only way the champion will hit the mat first is if the underdog can, for instance, smuggle in a hypodermic filled with a strong sedative and inject the champ before his first swing.

It could be argued that even in such a mismatch, the underdog has a motive to endorse at least minimal restrictions on the combatants' conduct. After all, the underdog might well want there to be a rule against the champion beating him to death just for fun. Might not the weaker party voluntarily give up the chance to use underhanded tactics if it meant he could guarantee his own survival in the event of his defeat?

The answer is that it depends on the stakes. It may be hard to picture a boxer so devoted to winning that he would willingly risk death just to hold on to the slim possibility that he might be able to defeat a more powerful opponent if there are no holds barred. However, there are many people in conflicts around the world who are sufficiently dedicated to their side of an asymmetric struggle that they would sooner see themselves martyred than surrender the slightest edge.

The clearest defense for the underdog's use of unconventional or "out of bounds" tactics is the argument that doing so is not seeking an unfair advantage; rather, it is an attempt to counteract the unfair advantage that favors his opponent. It is simply leveling the playing field. If holding both parties to the same rules puts victory out of reach for the weaker side, warriors on the weaker side will be forced to choose between moral censure and defeat, regardless of the justice of their causes.

To avoid the charge of duplicity, the disadvantaged party need not make any pretense about accepting the conventional *jus in bello* restraints. Its members can be upfront about the fact that they prefer their odds in a "street fight" to those in a more formal "boxing match." However, if they make the choice to fight outside the rules, they forfeit their right to demand that their opponents fight within the rules. One cannot offer no quarter to one's enemies, then turn around and insist that one's own fighters be given full Geneva Convention protections whenever they are captured.

Legal disputes about the rights of Al Qaeda and Taliban prisoners held by the United States at Guantanamo Bay, Cuba, have highlighted the fact that prisoner of war (POW) status (and the attending standards for POW treatment) is not automatically conferred on all captured combatants. Specific criteria must be met, and forfeiture is possible. Current standards exclude not only those classified as "terrorists," but also members of most "underground" and insurgent forces. As John Mintz observed in a January 2002 article for the *Washington Post* ("Most Experts Say Al Qaeda Members Aren't POWs but Taliban Fighters Might Be"), in 1949 the international community decided that the anti-Nazi partisans of France, regardless of the obvious merits of their cause, "did not qualify for POW classification."[2] "Illegal combatants" in asymmetric conflicts do not play by the rules of war, nor are they protected by them.

It may be morally permissible for the weaker force in an asymmetric conflict to fight with *fewer* restraints, particularly if they openly acknowledge their intention to fight outside the usual conventions of war and they do not insist on enjoying the protection of those rules they have chosen to ignore. It is not morally permissible, however, for such a force—or any force, for that matter—to fight with absolutely *no restraints* whatsoever. There are rules unique to the context of warfare that may not restrain all types of combatants, but there are fundamental moral laws that are not context-dependent and cannot be suspended even in times of war. Our judgment against those who violate these laws in the "heat of battle" or the "fog of war" may be more merciful or forgiving than if the same violations were committed in less extreme circumstances. The violations themselves, however, cannot be converted by circumstances into morally permissible actions.

Recall the description of an imaginary underdog boxing against a heavyweight champion. If the underdog had never agreed to play by the rules, we would be hard pressed to fault him for overcoming the champ with that clever sedative-in-a-hypodermic trick. The higher we make the stakes for our fictional boxing match, the more we may allow the disadvantaged boxer to do inside the ring in order to give himself a chance of winning. If he is boxing for his life, his freedom, and the lives of his loved ones, we may even permit him to use more permanently damaging or perhaps lethal tricks to take down his opponent.

On the other hand, we could quite rightly find a great deal of fault with the underdog if he tried to overcome his disadvantage by kidnapping the champion's child and lighting the infant on fire just outside the boxing ring in order to destroy his opponent's concentration and will to fight (a horrific act of terror). The reason why torching the infant is far beyond the pale can be found by reviewing the reason why we do permit some forms of killing in war without regarding them as acts of murder.

Murder is broadly defined as the intentional killing of an innocent person. By participating in the fighting, combatants forfeit their status as "innocents" in the relevant sense. The combatants on one side of a conflict are threats to the lives of the combatants on the other side, and vice versa. Therefore, killing in war is more akin to killing in self-defense than to murder.

Following in the tradition of Michael Walzer, Robert Fullinwider explains this point well in "Terrorism, Innocence, and War":

> In war, . . . the notion of "innocence" has nothing to do with lack of blameworthiness. Rather, it divides individuals into two classes: those who may be directly targeted by military force and those who may not. The former includes uniformed armed forces (combatants), the latter ordinary civilians (noncombatants). This division derives not from the imperatives of crime and punishment but from the imperatives of self-defense. In resisting aggression, a state may direct lethal force against the agency endangering it, and that agency is the military force of the aggressor.[3]

Although Fullinwider refers to "uniformed armed forces," the principle he suggests that connects being a combatant with being a *threat* does not necessarily limit combatants to just those conventional military personnel who wear recognizable uniforms. This principle allows us to consider guerilla and "underground" forces that try to blend in with or hide among ordinary citizens as combatants. If they are fighters, they are a threat. In Walzer's words, they have become *dangerous*:

> [T]he soldier has already been forced to fight. . . . He can be personally attacked only because he already is a fighter. He has been made into a dangerous man, and though his options may have been few, it is nevertheless accurate to say that he has allowed himself

to be made into a dangerous man. For that reason, he finds himself endangered.[4]

At the same time, Fullinwider helps us avoid the trap of associating combatant and noncombatant status with guilt or innocence understood in terms of willing association with a particular cause:

> *From the point of view of moral-wrongdoing and just punishment*, many of the aggressor's military personnel may be innocent; they may be reluctant conscripts with no sympathy for their nation's actions. Likewise, among ordinary civilians, many may actively support and favor their country's criminal aggression. They are not innocent. But *from the point of view of self-defense*, the moral quality of the conscript's reluctance and the civilian's enthusiasm is not relevant. What matters is that the former is a combatant, the latter not.[5]

This is intuitively satisfying and provides a nice parallel to smaller-scale distinctions between legitimate and illegitimate claims of self-defense. Consider that if some woman attacks you and tries to kill you, you are permitted to kill her in self-defense. However, you cannot use the same self-defense grounds to justify going on to kill the woman's husband and children, who have made no move against you themselves but who were back at home cheering on their mother/wife's decision to kill you and perhaps baking her snacks to eat in celebration of her victory over you. Noncombatants in wartime may cheer on their soldiers and send them homemade cookies, but that does not make them legitimate targets of lethal force. Nor would your right to kill the woman in self-defense be revoked if it were discovered that she acted against you only under duress. You might then have cause to pity her and regret her death at your hands, but you were never required to let her kill you simply because she did not really *want* to kill you.

Even in time of war, if you intentionally kill someone who is no threat to you, such as an unarmed civilian or a secured POW, you are a murderer (morally, if not legally). Yet in the hell that is war, some number of noncombatants who are indeed nonthreatening always do get killed. There never was a war with no noncombatant casualties. Does that destroy the distinction between legitimate combatants (warriors) and murderers?

The "easy" cases are those like the My Lai massacre, in which unarmed Vietnamese villagers were intentionally lined up and shot by American soldiers. Such intentional slaughter of nonthreatening noncombatants can and should be labeled a war crime and an atrocity.

Nor can such actions be justified on the grounds that the villagers represented potential *future* threats. Any child born could potentially try to kill someone one day, but that does not justify strangling him or her in their cradles. Tragically, some groups do arm children, turning innocents into combatants. A child combatant can be legitimately targeted, just like any conscript who represents a present threat, even if he is unwilling, insane, brainwashed, or mentally incompetent. But a noncombatant of any age cannot be targeted merely because he or she *might become* a combatant.

More difficult to judge are cases of so-called collateral damage, where those who are not present threats are killed in the process of getting to those who are. In such cases, it is tempting to pin everything on intentionality. If combatants cause noncombatant casualties only *unintentionally*, does that get them off the moral hook?

In "The Ethics of Retaliation," Judith Lichtenberg embraces Fullinwider's line of reasoning that threateningness is the key to the combatant/noncombatant distinction:

> "[W]e can draw the line between legitimate and illegitimate targets via the notion of a threat. Combatants are ordinarily armed and threatening, noncombatants are not. (There will, of course, be borderline and unclear cases.)"[6]

This then raises for her the concern about collateral damage. For a solution, she turns, as nearly all military ethicists do sooner or later, to St. Thomas Aquinas and the Doctrine of Double Effect. The Doctrine of Double Effect (DDE) applies to situations in which it may be necessary or unavoidable to take an action that will cause the loss of innocent life in order to achieve some greater good:

> The principle holds that such an action should be performed only if the intention is to bring about the good effect and the bad effect will be an unintended or indirect consequence. More specifically, four conditions must be satisfied:
> 1. The action itself must be morally indifferent or morally good.
> 2. The bad effect must not be the means by which the good effect is achieved.
> 3. The motive must be the achievement of the good effect only.
> 4. The good effect must be at least equivalent in importance to the bad effect.[7]

Lichtenberg encapsulates the doctrine's usual application in war: "Whereas intending to kill civilians is never permissible, according to the doctrine of double effect, foreseeing civilian deaths as an effect of a permissible action (such as aiming at a military target) is not prohibited."[8]

Note that the initial statement of the doctrine stresses the importance of the *intention* behind the action: "if the *intention* is to bring about the good effect and the bad effect will be an *unintended or indirect consequence*. . . ." In addition, the third requirement of the DDE deals with the *motive* or intention behind the action. Judging intentionality, however, is no easy task. More contemporary work on moral responsibility may help to provide additional criteria by which to identify valid appeals to the DDE in collateral damage cases.

In "Three Ways of Spilling Ink," twentieth-century philosopher of language J. L. Austin offers valuable insights into the complex nature of intentionality through a close examination of the words we use to describe it. Austin distinguishes "between acting *intentionally* and acting *deliberately* or on *purpose*"[9] via the following thought experiment:

> I am summoned to quell a riot in India. Speed is imperative. My mind runs on the action to be taken five miles down the road at the Residency. As I set off down the drive, my cookboy's child's new gocart, the apple of her eye, is right across the road. I realize I could stop, get out, and move it, but to hell with that: I must push on. It's too bad, that's all: I drive right over it and am on my way. In this case, a snap decision is taken on what is essentially an *incidental* matter. I did drive over the gocart deliberately, but not intentionally—nor, of course, unintentionally either. It was never part of my intention to drive over the gocart. At no time did I intend to drive over it. It was incidental to anything I intended to do, which was simply to get to the scene of the riot in order to quell it. However "odd" it may sound, I feel little doubt that we should say here that we did run over the gocart deliberately *and* that we should not care to say we ran over it intentionally. We never intended to run over it.[10]

If we compare it to a collateral damage situation in wartime, what Austin's case suggests is that, for the purposes of moral accountability, asking about *intentions* may not be enough. If soldiers destroy civilian homes in an attempt to eliminate potential hideouts for terrorists, the soldiers may honestly assert that it was not their purpose or intention to harm or displace any noncombatants. Nevertheless, they did destroy the homes deliberately. Should such deliberate actions be considered "unintended or indirect consequences" for the purposes of an appeal to the DDE?

Responding to the work of J. L. Mackie and Donald Davidson on questions of responsibility and agency, Peter A. French addresses a further concern about intentionality that may also be relevant to the correct application of the DDE: that it may be appropriate to hold agents morally responsible for consequences of their intentional actions that they did not intend but were *willing* to allow. To illustrate this point, French draws on the classic case of Hamlet's stabbing of Polonius in Shakespeare's tragic play. While in his mother's (Queen Gertrude's) bedroom, Hamlet discerns that someone is hiding behind the arras. He assumes, mistakenly, that the hidden person is the king, whom he wishes dead. He stabs his sword through the tapestry, killing the man behind it. Hamlet's victim turns out to be the king's elderly advisor, Polonius, the father of Hamlet's girlfriend Ophelia and friend Laertes. French comments:

> [W]e are regularly held accountable for things we were willing to have happen when we do things we intend. One way to describe what Hamlet did in Gertrude's room is to say that he orphaned Ophelia. He most certainly had no intention of doing that, but it seems reasonable to say that he was willing to do that, as he was also willing to stab Polonius, if, as it happened, Polonius rather than the King was the person hiding behind the arras. The idea that being willing to do something does not entail intending to do it is embedded in the concept of negligence.[11]

A comparable situation in wartime would be bombing a target with the intention of killing enemy combatants without first securing sufficient intelligence to determine with some reasonable degree of certainty whether the persons at the target are in fact enemy combatants and not civilians. Although the intention may be to take out a legitimate target, failing to "look behind the arras" constitutes a *willingness* to strike an inappropriate target. Such willful negligence seems clearly to violate the spirit of the DDE.

In her discussion of the DDE, Lichtenberg does not shy away from addressing the possibility of forces abusing the doctrine in order to excuse acts that have more in common with murder than killing in self-defense. She turns to *Just and Unjust Wars* and finds that Walzer argues, too, that to not intend to kill noncombatants is, by itself, not to show enough restraint:

> Simply not to intend the death of civilians is too easy; most often, under battle conditions, the intentions of soldiers are focused narrowly on the enemy. What we look for in such cases is some sign of a positive commitment to save civilian lives. . . . And if saving

civilian lives means risking soldiers' lives, the risk must be accepted. But there is a limit to the risks that we require. . . . We can only ask soldiers to minimize the dangers they impose [on civilians].[12]

The efforts that might be made "to minimize the dangers" to non-combatants would include measures such as ensuring proper intelligence-gathering about targets and not deliberately destroying the homes of noncombatants just because leaving them standing makes it more difficult to access military targets. Beefing up the DDE in this way seems to satisfy Lichtenberg:

> Walzer's proviso saves the doctrine of double effect from abuse and trivialization. Properly understood, the doctrine does not allow people to escape responsibility for the fatal effects of their actions simply by averting their minds. It's not enough not to try to kill civilians; you have to try *not* to kill them.[13]

Walzer's proviso also entails that what has been dubbed "virtual war" by commentators such as journalist Michael Ignatieff (author of *Virtual War: Kosovo and Beyond*) is not morally acceptable. "Virtual war" occurs when the *superior* side in an asymmetric conflict uses advanced technology and weapons to fight from such a distance that the risk to its own combatants is minimal but the risk to noncombatants on the enemy side may be increased. Ignatieff warns modern warriors against the "moral danger" they face if they allow themselves to become too detached from the reality of war:

> Virtual reality is seductive. . . . We see war as a surgical scalpel and not a bloodstained sword. In so doing we mis-describe ourselves as we mis-describe the instruments of death. We need to stay away from such fables of self-righteous invulnerability. Only then can we get our hands dirty. Only then can we do what is right.[14]

Minimizing the danger to noncombatants must be the concern of forces on *both* side of an asymmetric struggle. As Lichtenberg stresses, "it is crucial to see that [Walzer's] proviso requires *our* soldiers taking risks to protect *their* civilians."[15] In some cases, this may mean ordering pilots to fly low enough to clearly identify targets or sending ground troops into harm's way. Recent improvements in martial technology have included the development of more precision weaponry to reduce collateral damage, which demonstrates the "positive commitment to save civilian lives" that Walzer demands. Intelligence-gathering to identify legitimate targets has also improved. In the Vietnam War, there was a twelve-to-one ratio of "shooters" (those actually targeting the weapons) to sources of intelligence and reconnaissance on the U.S. side. When the United States conducted Operation Enduring Freedom in Afghanistan as part of the "war on terror" that began in the fall of 2001, the ratio of intelligence platforms (which now include satellites, Unmanned Aerial Vehicles (UAVs), Special Forces units on the ground, etc.) to shooters had been reduced to one-to-one. Clearly, we have come a long way from the carpet-bombing days of the past.

Application of a more robust conception of the DDE can help distinguish murderers and terrorists from legitimate fighters in asymmetric conflicts. However, the first requirement of the DDE—that "the action itself must be morally indifferent or morally good" is problematic in the context of war. On the small scale, if we maintain the analogy between killing in war and killing in self-defense, "morally permissible" seems a better description than "morally indifferent or morally good." Taking a human life should never be a matter of moral indifference, nor does killing out of necessity seem aptly termed a "moral good."

On a larger scale, the issue becomes one of just cause; that is, striking even what is indisputably a military target would only qualify as "morally indifferent or morally good" if the force making the strike is fighting in a just cause. This would seem to imply that no appeal to the DDE to excuse noncombatant deaths as collateral damage could be made by combatants not fighting in a just cause. Initially, this is appealing. It could support an argument that would permit us to label fighters who cause any noncombatant deaths in the service of an unjust cause "murderers."

The problem is that determination of just cause is often far from obvious. Philosophers, statespersons, political scientists, lawyers, and theologians worldwide hotly debate various aspects of just war theory. If experts such as these cannot agree, are we prepared to condemn ordinary soldiers as murderers if we determine (perhaps with hindsight or information not universally available) that their cause is (or was) not just? Was every German pilot who caused a civilian death in World War II a murderer? What about American soldiers in Vietnam?

It is likely more just of us to set the issues of *jus ad bellum* aside when judging the combatants themselves. It is enough to restrict them in the area of *jus in bello* to permit only those noncombatant deaths that can be accounted for as collateral damage under the most demanding form of the DDE. Fighting in an evenly matched or asymmetric conflict, for a just or unjust cause, a combatant who targets only other combatants (who are a threat to him) and does not intentionally (or deliberately, on purpose, or through willful negligence) target noncombatants (who are not a threat to him) is a warrior, not a murderer.

Our attention through all of this discussion of intentionality and the combatant/noncombatant distinction has been on targets, not tactics. In the context of war, the focus must be on whom one kills, not how one kills them. I will not attempt here to scale the relative morality of shooting someone in the chest versus bayoneting him in the stomach versus bombing or burning him to death. A quick death is kinder than a slow one, but whether they kill quickly or slowly cannot be what distinguishes legitimate fighters from terrorists and warriors from murderers. We cannot excuse disadvantaged fighters in an asymmetric conflict from the moral necessity of minimizing noncombatant casualties. Where we can offer them some leeway to level the playing field is in the employment of unsavory tactics against enemy combatants.

Consider two separate strikes against the United States by the Al Qaeda network: the bombing of the *U.S.S. Cole* and the September 11 attacks. Both have been labeled acts of terrorism by the media and others. The 9/11 hijackers clearly targeted civilians. The World Trade Center towers were filled with noncombatants, as were the planes that hit them and the plane that crashed in Pennsylvania. It could be argued that the Pentagon is a legitimate military target, but there is no way to twist the DDE in such a way as to produce the verdict that it is morally permissible to intentionally, deliberately, and on purpose use a group of noncombatants as a weapon against combatants, which is what the hijackers did. Therefore, the hijackers were murderers (mass-murderers, in fact), not warriors.

On the other hand, it is no stretch to call the *U.S.S. Cole* a legitimate military target. It was—and thankfully now is again—a seaworthy military vessel armed for war and manned by uniformed members of the U.S. Navy. The men who struck and severely wounded the *Cole* with a zodiac full of explosives, killing themselves in the process, should be regarded as warriors in an asymmetric struggle (albeit a horribly misguided one), not terrorists. And the seventeen American sailors who died in the attack should be honored as war dead.

A challenge that might be made to the notion of labeling the Al Qaeda operatives who attacked the *U.S.S. Cole* legitimate warriors in an asymmetric conflict centers on the fact that the men were not representatives of a nation-state, but rather were "nonstate actors" and members of an international criminal organization. After all, if a member of the Mafia shot a uniformed Marine, it would be an act of murder, not an act of war. Addressing this point, Fullinwider cites the fact that according to the international community (see the 1977 UN International Convention for the Suppression of Terrorist Bombings), "No cause however good warrants a violent response if the actor is an individual or group, not a state."[16] This idea stems from the *jus ad bellum* requirement that wars be declared only by legitimate authorities.

Al Qaeda makes no claim to be the military arm of a state, although its members often do describe themselves as defenders of the *dar al Islam*, or the Islamic World. This lack of identification with a state places their status as warriors in serious jeopardy. On the other hand, if we rule that any fighters who belong to a militant organization that does not represent a state do not qualify as legitimate combatants, we may once again delegitimize all rebels and insurgents, regardless of the merits of their cause, the human rights abuses they may have suffered, or the oppressive and unrepresentative nature of the governments targeted by their rebellions. This seems to side too much with current powers in defending the status quo.

Palestine is not yet a nation-state. The Kurds do not have a state of their own. Neither do the Tibetans. Do we really want to say prima facie that when and if these groups take up arms against Israel, Iraq, and China, respectively, they cannot be considered legitimate combatants, even if they scrupulously target only combatants on the other side?

Drawing a distinction between nonstate actors like Al Qaeda operatives and members of rebel organizations because the latter have *aspirations* to statehood may seem attractive at first blush. But that opens the doors too wide. The members of Al Qaeda may aspire to create an Islamic extremist state that covers the globe. Even members of the Mafia would probably aspire to statehood, if the suggestion were made to them. What seems more promising is to require that those who are fighting to form their own states be able to cite specific, sustained violations of fundamental human rights committed by their oppressors. If they fail to do so, yet continue to employ violence as a means to achieve their ends, we can fairly regard them as criminals and terrorists, not warriors.

This solution does, however, plunge us back into the morass of linking moral judgments about individual fighters to determinations of just cause. We thus may wish to withhold our full-blown condemnation of lower-ranking fighters who have been persuaded by their leaders that they are in fact struggling against perpetrators of gross violations of human rights, providing that those fighters do not cross the most critical moral line by targeting noncombatants. We may see this as similar to the decision not to condemn ordinary soldiers for following legal orders in an unjust war, yet to require them to disobey illegal orders (e.g., orders to murder nonthreatening civilians) even in a just war.

The larger the "gray area," the less meaningful these distinctions appear. Yet the lines we have drawn so far do allow us to categorize many complicated cases as examples of terrorism/murder on the one hand or legitimate war-fighting/self-defense on the other. For example, these distinctions do allow us to deny the legitimacy of the label "warrior" to suicide/homicide bombers who strike civilian targets such as bus stops, pizzerias, wedding receptions, and pool halls; to the September 11 hijackers; and to the FARC rebels in Colombia who kidnap and murder civilians.

Those who question that it is ever possible to distinguish terrorist acts from legitimate asymmetric warfare often cite historical examples of "good guys" who committed acts that seem comparable to the acts of terrorists today. Fingers are commonly pointed at the colonists in the American Revolution or members of resistance movements against the Nazis during World War II. The question that must be asked when such comparisons are drawn is, were the historical acts really comparable to modern terrorist acts, especially in terms of *targets* (not just tactics)? If the answer is no, then the issue is moot. If the answer is yes, the conclusion should not be that all asymmetric fighters are terrorists or that all terrorists are just asymmetric fighters. Rather, it should be that those "good guys" (and only those) who targeted noncombatants while fighting in asymmetric conflicts (even in the interest of noble causes) in the past were in fact terrorists and murderers. However, those who used the same tactics against combatants were not. They were warriors.

There is no need to tar everyone involved in a particular struggle with the same brush. Nor does having acts of terror in a nation's historical record rob its present-day citizens of the right—the obligation, rather—to condemn actions of terror and murder in any era. Americans can condemn slavery worldwide even though slavery was once practiced in the United States. The charge of hypocrisy is only valid if an attempt is made to excuse past examples of immoral actions because they were done by "us" while condemning current examples of the same actions because they are being done by "them."

The distinctions between legitimate fighters in an asymmetric conflict and terrorists and between warriors and murderers must be drawn consistently, even if it makes some of our enemies warriors and some of our ancestors terrorists. Luckily for Veronica Lake, her character in *So Proudly We Hail!* meets the criteria for a legitimate warfighter after all. She targets only Japanese soldiers, who are clearly combatants. She is a warrior, not a murderer. Of course, once she took up arms, Veronica's character herself became a combatant. Thus the Japanese soldiers also would have been warriors, not murderers, had they managed to shoot the blonde bombshell before she exploded. Even in Hollywood, war is hell.

NOTES

1. Shannon E. French, *The Code of the Warrior: The Values and Ideals of Warrior Cultures Throughout History* (New York: Rowman and Littlefield Publishers, 2002).

2. John Mintz, "Most Experts Say Al Qaeda Members Aren't POWs but Taliban Fighters Might Be," *Washington Post*, Sunday, January 27, 2002, p. A22.

3. Robert K. Fullinwider, "Terrorism, Innocence, and War," *Philosophy and Public Policy Quarterly* 21.4 (Fall 2001): 9.

4. Michael Walzer, *Just and Unjust Wars.* (New York: Basic Books Inc., 1977), p. 145.

5. Fullinwider, p. 9.

6. Judith Lichtenberg, "The Ethics of Retaliation," *Philosophy and Public Policy Quarterly* 21.4 (Fall 2001): 6.

7. Ronald Munson, "An Overview of Aquinas' Natural Law Theory," reprinted in George R. Lucas et al., *Ethics for Military Leaders* (Boston: Simon and Schuster Custom Publishing, 1998), p. 397.

8. Lichtenberg p. 7.

9. J. L. Austin, *Philosophical Papers* (Oxford: Oxford University Press, 1979), p. 273.

10. Austin, p. 278.

11. Peter A. French, *The Spectrum of Responsibility* (New York: St. Martin's Press, 1991), p. 136.

12. Walzer, 155–156.

13. Lichtenberg, p. 7.

14. Michael Ignatieff, *Virtual War: Kosovo and Beyond* (New York: Picador USA [Metropolitan Books, Henry Holt and Company], 2000), pp. 214–215.

15. Lichtenberg, p. 8.

16. Fullinwider, p. 10.

CHAPTER 2

The Terrorism of "Terrorism"

TOMIS KAPITAN

Any intelligent discussion of terrorism must have some way of identifying the phenomenon under scrutiny. Only then is it possible to devise criteria for describing a given action, agent, or organization as "terrorist," to investigate the causes and objectives of terrorism, and to set parameters for a legitimate response to what some regard as a fundamental challenge to world peace. Scholars have long recognized these points, but the same is not true of more prominent forces shaping contemporary Western perceptions. In the United States, the mainstream media (newspapers, television, cinema), the independent "think tanks," and the main sectors of the government have sponsored a public discourse about terrorism devoid of any serious inquiry into, or concern about, the nature, origins, and goals of terrorist actions. The rhetoric with which they assail popular consciousness deflects attention away from a critical examination of these issues, and thereby contributes to the increasing spiral of hatred and atrocity. This happens because the use of "terror" and its cognates obscures the causes of political unrest and, consequently, impedes the development of rational policies for dealing with underlying grievances.

The rhetoric of "terror" is not always innocent; there are those who employ it deliberately in pursuit of specific political objectives. This is especially true in the popular discourse about political tensions in the Middle East, particularly concerning the Israeli-Palestinian conflict. The result has been disastrous, not only for the lives and well-being of individual Palestinians and Israelis, but, increasingly, for the entire world. Unless we diminish the use of emotive language in describing the circumstances, actions, and tendencies constituting this and similar such conflicts, we risk multiplying the amount of terrorist violence

47

in the world and moving even further from just and peaceful resolutions of pressing political problems.

THE SEMANTICS AND PRAGMATICS OF "TERRORISM"

There is little agreement on the meaning of "terrorism."[1] Often an explicit definition is not even attempted, and when the matter is broached, it is routinely admitted that there is no single universally accepted definition of the term—even the various agencies of the U.S. government are not united.[2] This might not be a problem for rhetorical purposes, but scholarship, policy-making, and law enforcement require some sort of definition in order to identify the phenomenon and to justify ascriptions.

To avoid lengthy debate over the merits of competing definitions, a standard description of "terrorism" will be adopted herein:

> Terrorism is the deliberate use of violence, or the threat of such, directed upon civilians in order to achieve political objectives.[3]

A few clarifications are in order. First, this definition is not only a stipulation indicating how "terrorism" will be used in this essay, but also a hypothesis about about the way the term is commonly, though perhaps not universally, understood in English discourse. In this latter sense, it can be viewed as a reportive definition. Second, the occurrence of "deliberate" suggests that the perpetrator is intentionally using or threatening violence to achieve political objectives *and* is identifying the targets as civilians. Some go further and insist that the targets are also to be described as "innocent."[4] While this might seem to have the advantage of revealing what is wrong with terrorism, it has the disadvantage of making classification of a particular act as "terrorist" more controversial. This drawback is even more evident if a definition requires that the perpetrator himself or herself *identifies* the targets as "innocents."[5] Such a requirement is likely to make terrorism exceedingly rare given that political violence is often committed by those who act from outrage over perceived injustices and who do not think their targets to be "innocent" of these injustices. Third, an act is not "terrorist" solely because of its results or the sources of its motivation, for example, revenge killings are not "terrorist" even if political conflict caused the desire for revenge.[6] Similarly, violence against military targets are not "terrorist" on the standard definition, despite government and media descriptions to the contrary. The perpetrator must have a political objective and identify the targets *as* civilians—allowing that in some cases an off-duty soldier can be classified as a civilian. Fourth, unlike the characterization favored by the U.S. State Department,[7] the standard definition allows any kind of person or organization to be an agent of terrorism, including states, even though there is little acknowledgment of this subcategory in popular discourse.

While we might spar over semantics, there are two points of particular importance in understanding the contemporary usage of "terrorism." One undeniable fact is that whether or not terrorism is illegitimate by definition, terms like "terrorism" and "terrorist" have acquired an intensely negative connotation in contemporary discourse.[8] The reasons behind this are complex, but part of the explanation is the perception that terrorism targets people who should not be targeted and involves methods that should not be employed, for example, the taking and killing of hostages. As such, quite apart from considerations of just cause, it violates some of the standard rules of *jus in bello*, specifically the principle of discrimination that rules out intentional attacks upon civilians and the principle of legitimate means (proportionality) that prohibits acts of treachery, wanton destruction, and massacre. Accordingly, the perpetrators of terrorist acts are commonly viewed as morally depraved, even when they are willing to go the extreme ends of sacrificing their own lives.

A further point is that "terrorism," as typically employed, has an *indexical* character bearing an implicit reference to the speaker's point of view, so that, for practical purposes, "terrorism" is coextensive with the phrase "terrorism against us." In this way, it behaves much like the phrase "the enemy," though without the same semantic backing since "enemy" is relational in a way that "terror," "terrorism" and "terrorist" are not. Several writers have pointed out this speaker-oriented bias,[9] and occasionally, media representatives have been candid about it. For example, in March 2002 the Public Editor of the *Chicago Tribune*, Don Wycliff, pointed out that while his paper routinely refers to the attacks of September 11 as acts of terrorism, it withholds that designation from actions in other places where some argue it is warranted. He explained the *Tribune*'s policy:

> [T]he *Tribune* is an American newspaper written principally for an American audience. . . . Our perspective is inescapably American (which is not to say it is necessarily the same as that of the U.S. government). Inevitably, as the news of Sept. 11 is reported and interpreted, that perspective is reflected in the product. Indeed, it al-

most has to be if we are to speak intelligibly on those events to our audience.[10]

Neither the *Tribune*, the American media in general, nor the U.S. government, is unique in this regard. Given the speaker-oriented bias, who receives the "terrorist" label depends on where you are and to whom you are listening. As Wycliff points out, it is generally agreed that those who flew hijacked planes into the World Trade Center towers were engaged in terrorist activity. But one effect of speaker-bias is that many actions and agents that would qualify as terrorist under the most definitions—certainly under the standard definition—have not been described as such in the U.S. media or government reports. For example, the killing of over three thousand civilians in Nicaragua by the U.S.-supported Contra rebels of the 1980s was not generally classified as "terrorism."[11] Again, the massacre of over two thousand Palestinian civilians in the Sabra and Shatilla refugee camps in Beirut in 1982 is not referred to as "terrorist" activity, nor are the alleged perpetrators of that massacre, and their allies in the Israeli military, called "terrorists."

At the level of overt actions committed by states are numerous examples that are not usually labeled as "terrorist," although they qualify as such under those definitions that allow for state terrorism. These include the destruction of Grozny by Russian forces during the Chechnya war of 1999; the U.S. bombing of Tripoli, Libya, in April 1986; the U.S. naval bombardment of Lebanese villages in the Chouf mountains in October 1983; and the Israeli aerial and land bombardment of Beirut in the summer of 1982 that resulted in the deaths of five thousand to six thousand civilians.[12] This is to say nothing about more large-scale military campaigns, like the U.S. bombing of North Vietnam and Cambodia during the Vietnam War, or the bombings of German and Japanese cities near the end of World War II.

State-terrorism can take other forms. One example is the institutionalized violence exercised against Palestinian civilians during Israel's thirty-five-year occupation of the West Bank and Gaza Strip. The occupation has featured torture, deportations, collective punishment, economic strangulation, destruction of property, confiscation of land, and firing upon unarmed civilians, actions that are routinely designed to intimidate a civilian population in order to secure political objectives. Yet this brand of structural violence against civilians is not referred to as "terrorism." The same can be said about the U.S.-led campaign against Iraq, including both the bombing of Iraqi technological infrastructure in 1991 and the subsequent policy of sanctions that have led to the deaths of over a million Iraqis.[13]

At the opposite extreme, some actions are routinely labeled "terrorist" that do not qualify as such under the standard definition. For example, throughout the 1990s, the Israeli and U.S. media were replete with references to "terrorist" actions by the Lebanese group Hezbollah against the Israeli military in southern Lebanon, or by Palestinians against Israeli soldiers in the occupied territories, targets that hardly qualify as civilians or noncombatants. Apart from the State Department's idiosyncratic definition of "noncombatant" to include off-duty soldiers, the same can be said for actions directed against the U.S. military, say, the bombing of the *U.S.S. Cole* in Yemen in October 2000 or of the U.S. Marine barracks in Beirut in October 1983.[14]

These few examples illustrate that, in the American context at least, widely-shared conceptions about the types of individuals and groups engaged in terrorist activity are not based on semantic considerations alone. Instead, they are fashioned by the speaker-oriented bias that permeates the rhetoric of "terror" used to describe contemporary political violence. When adding to the negative connotation, this rhetoric becomes a shaper—and perhaps, a distorter—of both value judgments and the actions to which such judgments give rise.

THE POLITICAL USE OF "TERRORISM" AND ITS EFFECTS

The discriminatory applications of the terms "terrorism" and "terrorist" by the American government and mainstream media reveal that these terms are not used with any real concern for scientific precision, consistency, or completeness. If they were so used, and if the government really meant what it says it means when it proclaims a "war on terrorism," then the United States would be declaring war on itself, or, at the very least, upon its allies that have practiced or supported violence against civilians for political ends. Instead, in the popular American discourse, "terrorism" and its derivatives are used selectively to depict those who resort to force in opposing U.S. government policies or the policies of its allies. This development is not entirely surprising. We might expect that the U.S. State Department would be selective in its catalog of terrorist incidents and organizations since it is an arm of a government pursuing its own political agenda. It is a bit more difficult to understand why a free press should follow the government's lead, but some have tried to explain this phenomenon by pointing out that the American media "support the existing social, political, and economic order in which they operate because they are part of and benefit from that order, and the views they convey rarely stray far from the norm."[15]

The American situation is not unique. Other countries, including Israel, Great Britain, Russia, India, and Egypt, routinely do the same, and so might any state in describing militant insurgents opposed to its policies, for example, as the Nazis did in describing resistance fighters in the Warsaw ghetto.[16] There is a definite political purpose in so doing. Because of its negative connotation, the "terrorist" label automatically discredits any individuals or groups to which it is affixed. It dehumanizes them, places them outside the norms of acceptable social and political behavior, and portrays them as people who cannot be reasoned with.[17] By delegitimizing any individuals or groups described as "terrorist," the rhetoric

- Erases any incentive an audience might have to understand their point of view so that questions about the nature and origins of their grievances and the possibility legitimacy of their demands will not even be raised.
- Deflects attention away from policies that might have contributed to their grievances.
- Repudiates any calls to negotiate with them.
- Paves the way for the use of force and violence in dealing with them and, in particular, gives a government "freedom of action" by exploiting the fears of its own citizens and stifling any objections to the manner in which it deals with them.[18]
- Fails to distinguish between national liberation movements and fringe fanatics.

The general strategy is nothing new; it is part and parcel of the war of ideas and language that accompanies overt hostilities; "terrorism" is simply the current vogue for discrediting one's opponents before the risky business of inquiry into their complaints can even begin. If individuals and groups are portrayed as irrational, barbaric, and beyond the pale of negotiation and compromise, then asking why they resort to terrorism is viewed as pointless, needlessly accommodating, or, at best, mere pathological curiosity.

The language of "terror" thereby fosters an unfortunate attitude, especially among those who are oblivious to its propagandistic employment. Obviously, to point out the causes and objectives of particular terrorist actions is to imply nothing about their legitimacy and justification—that is an independent matter—nor is it any sort of capitulation to terrorist demands. To ignore these causes and objectives, on the other hand, is to seriously undermine attempts to deal intelligently with terrorism, since it leaves untouched the factors motivating recourse to this type of violence. Far from contributing to a *peaceful* resolution of conflict, the rhetoric of "terror" prepares the uncritical person to sanction a violent response.

More dramatically, the "terrorist" rhetoric actually increases terrorism in four distinct ways. First, it magnifies the effect of terrorist actions by heightening the fear among the target population. If we demonize the terrorists, if we portray them as arbitrary irrational beings with a "disposition toward unbridled violence," then we are amplifying the fear and alarm generated by terrorist incidents. Second, those who succumb to the rhetoric contribute to the cycle of revenge and retaliation by endorsing terrorist actions of their own government, not only against those who commit terrorist actions, but also against those *populations* from whose ranks the terrorists emerge, for the simple reason that terrorists are frequently themselves civilians, living amid other civilians not so engaged. The consequence has been an increase in terrorist violence under the rubric of "retaliation" or "counter-terrorism"[19] Third, short of genocide, a violent response is likely to stiffen the resolve of those from whose ranks terrorists have emerged, leading them to regard their foes as people who cannot be reasoned with, as people who, because they avail themselves so readily of the "terrorist" rhetoric, know only the language of force. As long as they perceive themselves to be victims of intolerable injustices and view their oppressors as unwilling to arrive at an acceptable compromise, they are likely to answer violence with more violence. Fourth, and most insidiously, those who employ the rhetoric of "terrorism" for their own political ends are encouraging actions that they understand will generate or sustain further violence directed against civilians. Inasmuch as their verbal behavior is intended to secure political objectives through these means, then it is an *instance* of terrorism just as much as any direct order to carry out a bombing of civilian targets. In both cases, there is purposeful verbal action aimed at bringing about a particular result through violence against civilians.[20]

The Rhetoric of "Terror" in the Israeli-Palestinian Conflict

Politically motivated violence has accompanied the Israeli-Palestinian conflict since its inception in the late nineteenth century. In 1920s and 1930s, numerous incidents resulted in casualties to hundreds of

Arab and Jewish civilians battling over the future of British-governed Palestine. Each side had its ideologues and heroes. Among the first Palestinian Arabs to raise the banner of jihad was Sheikh Izzeddin Al-Qassim, whose followers included Arab peasants forced off farmlands that had been sold by absentee landlords to immigrant Jews. His death at the hands of British forces in 1935 sparked a three-year revolt that resulted in the deaths of over 450 Jews and 5,000 Arabs. In the process, the British demolished Palestinian homes, executed Palestinian leaders, and employed tanks, armored cars, and aircraft against Palestinian rifles.[21]

Within the Jewish community at the time were those who followed the lead of Vladimir Jabotinsky (1880-1940), who argued that it was folly to expect the Arabs to acquiesce peacefully to the establishment of a Jewish state in Palestine. Since the end of Zionism is moral, Jabotinsky contended, so are the means necessary to achieve it, even if this requires an "iron wall" of military might to prevail against Arab opposition. Jabotinsky advocated "retaliating" against Arabs who had targeted Jews and Jewish property and denied that there was a choice between pursuing "bandits" and punishing a hostile population. Instead, the choice is between "retaliating against the hostile population or not retaliating at all."[22]

In 1935, Jabotinsky's "Revisionist" party established the underground militia Irgun Zwei Leumi. In the 1940s, under the leadership of Menachem Begin, the Irgun, together with the Stern Gang, warred against British forces with the objective of making Palestine ungovernable. Threatening to "turn Palestine into a bloodbath," their tactics included bombings, kidnappings, assassinations, and letter bombs.[23] During the 1947–1949 war between Jews and Arabs, the *Irgun* went beyond "retaliation" in its effort to induce Palestinian Arabs to flee from territory the UN had designated for the Jewish state. Through a few well-timed massacres of civilians, most notoriously, at the Palestinian village of Deir Yassin in April 1948, over three hundred thousand Palestinians fled from their homes in areas that eventually became part of Israel, paving the way for the establishment of a decisive Jewish majority in the nascent Jewish state.[24] Afterward Begin wrote, "Of the about 800,000 Arabs who lived on the present territory of the State of Israel, only some 165,000 are still there. The political and economic significance of this development can hardly be overestimated."[25]

After the establishment of Israel and the dismantling of large segments of the Palestinian community, organized struggle against Israel took time to develop among the Palestinian refugees. It was not until after the 1967 War and the occupation of the remaining portions of Palestine that Palestinian resistance fighters began to make international news. In the late 1960s, Palestinian militants, working within groups like Al-Fatah, were described in the international press as "guerrillas," "commandos," and *fedayeen* (sacrificers). It was not until after the September 1970 civil war in Jordan that the Israeli designations of Palestinian fighters as "murderers," "saboteurs," and "terrorists" became more widespread, at least in the Western media. This was partly due to notorious actions by some of the militants themselves, for example, airplane hijackings by Popular Front for the Liberation of Palestine (PFLP) members in 1968–1970 and the attempted kidnapping of Israeli athletes at the Munich Olympics in 1972 that led to the deaths of eleven Israelis and five Palestinians.

The world was horrified by what had happened at Munich, especially because the operation occurred at the Olympic Games, one of the foremost symbols of global unity and cooperation. But the operation succeeded in drawing attention to the cause of dispossessed Palestinians who had been largely ignored in the first two decades after the loss of their homeland. The Al-Fatah leader, Abu Iyad, said the following:

> The sacrifices made by the Munich heroes were not entirely in vain. They didn't bring about the liberation of any of their comrades imprisoned in Israel . . . but they did obtain the operations' other two objectives; world opinion was forced to take note of the Palestinian drama, and the Palestinian people imposed their presence on an international gathering that had sought to exclude them.[26]

It is estimated that over 500 million people witnessed these events on television.[27] As another Palestinian spokesman put it, the Munich operation was like "painting the name of Palestine on the top of a mountain that can be seen from the four corners of the earth."[28]

The Palestinian's recourse to terrorism succeeded in placing Palestinian grievances and aspirations on the world's agenda. But, too often, their complaints were lost in the sensationalism of the deed. In the minds of many, disgust with the means outpaced sympathy with plight of Palestinian refugees and trumped the patience needed to understand core grievances. As the 1970s wore on and various left-wing groups in Europe and elsewhere made headlines with similar sorts of violence, the "terrorists" came to be viewed as a new type of barbarians whose willingness to hijack airplanes, to take hostages, and especially, to carry their struggle into foreign lands, placed them outside the bounds of civilized behavior. When the Reagan administration came into power in January 1981, combating this brand of "international terrorism" emerged as a foremost goal of U.S. foreign policy.

None of this has been lost upon those who employ the rhetoric of "terror" as a propaganda device, not only to discredit their opponents, but also to obfuscate and to deflect attention away from their own controversial policies. A prime example relevant to the Middle East is a book edited by Benjamin Netanyahu entitled *Terrorism: How the West Can Win*, published in 1986. While it offers a standard definition of "terrorism," the editor and the contributors apply the term selectively, and argue that the only way to combat terrorism is to "to weaken and destroy the terrorist's ability to consistently launch attacks," even at the "risk of civilian casualties."[29] Throughout, very little is said about the possible causes of terrorist violence beyond vague allusions to Islam's confrontation with modernity,[30] or passages of this calibre:

> The root cause of terrorism lies not in grievances but in a disposition toward unbridled violence. This can be traced to a worldview that asserts that certain ideological and religious goals justify, indeed demand, the shedding of all moral inhibitions. In this context, the observation that the root cause of terrorism is terrorists is more than a tautology.[31]

One is tempted to pass off these comments as pure rant, except that the book has reached a large audience, especially since its contributors include not only academics and journalists but also important policy-makers. Netanyahu himself went on to become the Israeli prime minister, and among the American contributors were the Secretary of State George Schultz, UN Ambassador Jeanne Kirkpatrick, and Senators Daniel Moynihan and Alan Cranston, each of whom voiced sentiments similar to those of Netanyahu. The upshot was that a terrorist is portrayed as a carrier of "oppression and enslavement," having "no moral sense," "a perfect nihilist,"[32] and whose elimination is the only rational means for the West to "win."[33]

Netanyahu's book conceals an unspoken agenda. Coming straight out of Jabotinsky's brand of Zionism, Netanyahu believes the Occupied Territories must stay under Israeli control. Since this is inconsistent with granting Palestinians statehood in those territories, the legitimacy of the Palestinian claim to self-determination must be ignored or undermined. By classifying Palestinian resistance to Israeli policies as "terrorism" and by portraying "terrorists" as some sort of monsters unworthy of moral dialogue, the effect of his book, if not its intent, is to shift political focus away from Israeli designs, policies, and actions in the occupied territories, for example, its land confiscations, settlement building, and human rights violations, and towards the more sensational reactions by the Palestinians.

The language typified in Netanyahu's book provides a paradigm of how the rhetoric of "terror" has generated only more terrorism. Its principle that the only way to deal with terrorism is with counter-terrorist violence, has been the policy of successive Israeli governments since the early 1950s.[34] The result has not reduced but *increased* the amount of terrorism in the Near East. There has been a steady increase in terrorist-related fatalities over the past quarter-century. For example, during the ten-year period from 1978 to 1987, eighty-two Israelis were killed in terrorist attacks perpetrated by Palestinians, a rate of a little more than eight Israelis per year, including both civilians and security personnel. Within the next ten-year period, 1988–1997, that figure had jumped to 421, that is, to an average of 42 Israeli deaths per year. During the same period, at least 1,385 Palestinians in the Occupied Territories were killed by Israeli security forces (all but eighteen of these were civilians). In the first twenty months of the second Intifada (September 29, 2000, to May 28, 2002) approximately 470 Israelis lost their lives—a rate of 282 Israeli deaths per year—whereas at least 1,400 Palestinians were slain. The Israeli Defense Force (IDF) availed itself of tanks, attack helicopters, and F-16 fighter jets during this period, while Palestinians increasingly resorted to suicide bombings. The vast bulk of the fatalities on both sides were civilians.[35]

Figures like these can be used to show several things. They illustrate how the Israeli "reprisal" killings of Palestinians have not deterred Palestinian violence directed at Israelis. They disprove Netanyahu's claim that terrorists will rarely engage in terror tactics if the risks to their own survival are too great, and they go directly against his argument that deterrence will put a stop to terrorism and protect innocent civilians from terrorist violence.[36] They show that despite Israel's policy of counterterrorism, Israelis are less secure today than they were ten years ago, and certainly less than twenty years ago. If any causal claim is to be made, Israeli attacks against Palestinian leaders, institutions, towns, villages, and camps have only intensified Palestinian anger and stiffened Palestinian resolve. Because honor, and its offspring, revenge, can override fear of death, the average Israeli lives in greater trepidation than ever before.

Yet in terms of sheer numbers, Palestinians have been even more victimized by the rhetoric of "terror." The most devastating uses of "terrorism" in the Israeli-Palestinian conflict have been to justify actions by the IDF against Palestinians in refugee camps. In September 1982, for example, after the evacuation of Palestine Liberation Organization (PLO) fighters from Beirut, Israeli officials contended that some "2,000 terrorists" remained in the refugee camps Sabra and Shatilla in southern Beirut, a claim repeated in the Israeli press. On September 15, Israeli Defense Minister Ariel Sharon authorized entry of what were presumed to be members of the Lebanese militia into the camps that were then sealed off by Israeli tanks. The only resistance they encountered came from a few lightly armed boys. For the next thirty-eight hours, aided by Israeli flares at night, the militiamen raped, tortured, mutilated, and massacred over two thousand civilians under the eye of IDF personnel.[37]

An Israeli commission of inquiry ridiculed the claim that a massacre was not forseen by Israeli officials and concluded that "indirect responsibility" rested on the shoulders of Sharon and other Israeli leaders. Presumably, the qualifier "indirect" was based on the assumption that Israeli soldiers did not actually do the killing. Yet allowing the revenge-seeking Lebanese militia into the camps under the fiction that they would clean out "terrorists" suggests complicity if not outright instigation. In other circumstances, those responsible—directly or indirectly—would have been charged with war crimes. But Israel was the victor in the Lebanon war, and memories are often short. Within four years, Ariel Sharon carried his chutzpah into the pages of the *New York Times*, arguing that the "civilized world" must form an alliance to wage a "war on terrorism" and stage "pre-emptive attacks on terror bases" in order to "eliminate" terrorists.[38]

As prime minister of Israel since March 2001, Sharon, once again, has been able to act on his ambitions, refusing to negotiate with the Palestinian leadership, intensifying settlement building in the West Bank,[39] and adopting an iron fist approach to Palestinian resistance. After the ongoing battles of the Al-Aqsa Intifada led to a rash of suicide bombings in Israel in March 2002, Sharon sent IDF troops, tanks, and helicopter gunships into the Palestinian-controlled areas of the West Bank, vowing to destroy the Palestinian "terrorist infrastructure." From April 4 to 13, the IDF besieged the Jenin refugee camp, home to fourteen thousand residents, meeting fierce resistance from some

160 Palestinian militants. IDF helicopters fired missiles into the camp, often striking civilian homes where no Palestinian fighters were present, and used armored bulldozers to penetrate the center of the camp, destroying many buildings in the process. After thirteen Israeli soldiers died fighting in the Hawashin district of the camp, bulldozers proceeded to raze homes in that area even after most of the fighting had ended. The number of Palestinian casualties has yet to be determined, but according to Human Rights Watch, the "extensive, systematic, and deliberate leveling of the entire district was clearly disproportionate to any military objective that Israel aimed to achieve."[40]

The assault of the Jenin refugee camp was the most devastating attack on a Palestinian population center in the West Bank during thirty-five years of Israeli occupation. As with Sabra and Shatilla, the Israelis claimed to be fighting terrorism, but the principal result was the destruction of civilian property, institutions, and lives. That the Israeli government could succeed in convincing people that it was eliminating the "terrorist infrastructure" of the Palestinians illustrates how the rhetoric of "terror" is a causal factor in generating even more terrorism. On one side, the bulk of the Israeli public and the American Congress were led to endorse Sharon's actions, giving a green light for a continuation of his offensive against "terrorism." On the other side, the flames of outrage and revenge were fanned, once again, among Palestinians and their sympathizers.

Moving Beyond the Rhetoric of "Terror"

In the absence of a negotiated settlement, the continuation of tit-for-tat violence between Israelis and Palestinians has long been foreseen. Already in 1956 UN Secretary-General Dag Hammarskjold informed Israeli Prime Minister David Ben-Gurion that Israel's retaliatory actions against Palestinians would postpone indefinitely peaceful coexistence between Israelis and Arabs.[41] Hammarskjold's advice went unheeded as successive Israeli governments added retaliation to retaliation, with deterrence offered as the standard justification.[42] As Hammarskjold predicted, the effect has been the very opposite. Raymond Close summarized the situation accurately as follows:

> The state of Israel has been committed for 50 years to a policy of massive and ruthless retaliation—deliberately disproportional. "Ten eyes for an eye," the Israeli like to say. And still their policy fails, because they have not recognized what the thoughtful ones among them know to be true—that terrorism will thrive as long as the

Palestinian population is obsessed with the injustice of their lot and consumed with despair.[43]

The United States has edged ever closer to mimicking Israeli strategy in its confrontation with terrorism. For example, the State Department has developed just "four basic policy tenets" for dealing with terrorism:

1. Make no concession to terrorists and strike no deals.
2. Bring terrorists to justice for their crimes.
3. Isolate and apply pressure on states that sponsor terrorism to force them to change their behavior.
4. Bolster the counterterrorist capabilities of those countries that work with the United States and require assistance.[44]

Nowhere does the State Department call for investigating the *causes* of persistent terrorist violence, or for any sort of policy review. This is surprising given that the State Department is a policy-making sector of the U.S. government—unlike the law enforcement agencies for whom these guidelines are more understandable. Its refusal to deal squarely with the *political* origins of terrorism has led it to adopt a position of dealing with the symptoms while ignoring the causes. The rhetoric of "terror" might not have caused the development of this curious stance, but it has paved the way for its acceptance by the general public.[45]

There are legitimate ways of responding *to* terrorist actions without responding *with* terrorism. Granting that terrorism is wrongful and intolerable, law enforcement agencies must make every effort to identify, apprehend, and prosecute individuals and organizations responsible for specific terrorist actions. A resort to force should occur only after the appropriate legal channels have been exhausted, and here one must be careful to target only those for whom one has firm evidence of terrorist activity. But it is a mistake to think of all terrorism merely as a problem of criminal offense and law enforcement. Persistent terrorism stemming from a given population is indicative of a serious political disorder. As long as the members of that population are outraged over perceived injustices and decide that terrorism is the *only* viable form of redress, then mere police action, coupled with a repeated failure to address their grievances, will solve nothing, and certainly, indiscriminate retaliation will only intensify hatred and resolve.

The solution to a particular problem of terrorism requires, at the very minimum, *examining* the circumstances wherein violence against civilians is seen as the only emotional outlet or route of resistance. Only then can intelligent moral responses be crafted. To reach this stage, it is imperative that the rhetoric of "terror" be recognized for what it is. Its practitioners are serving a political agenda, unwittingly or not. Its victims are innocents, civilians, noncombatants, whose plight is ignored and whose communities suffer from reprisals because some of their members have found violence to be the only way to react in a desperate hope that somehow, someone with enough sense and power, will realize that these grievances must be addressed. Perhaps they are wholly misguided, but when the rhetoric of "terror" succeeds in discrediting them before rational inquiry into the causes of their grievances and behavior can begin, then it is itself a cause of terrorism. If its practitioners anticipate this sort of result, they are guilty of knowingly furthering terrorism. Should they *intend* to bring that result, then they are themselves guilty of terrorist actions.

Language moulds thought, and thought precipitates action. The pejorative bias that infects the current employment of "terrorism" and "terrorist" discourages a clear moral assessment of political conflicts like that between Israelis and Palestinians. If these words cannot be used in a consistent and unprejudiced manner, then they are obstacles in the path towards the resolution of such conflicts and stimulators of further violence against civilians. Consequently, if terrorism has no place in a civilized world, then the rhetoric of "terror" has no place in the civilized discourse of today.

NOTES

Discussions with Robert Ashmore, Orayb Najjar, Roy Pearson, Louis P. Pojman, and Erich Schulte have helped stimulate my thoughts on terrorism, and I wish to express my gratitude to Raja Halwani, Rima-Magdalen Fakhry, and Herman Stark for helpful remarks on an earlier version of this essay.

1. The Jacobins first employed the term during the French Revolution, applying it to the actions of the revolutionary government in eradicating its enemies. By the mid-nineteenth century, it was used to signify anti-government activities, for example, the campaigns of Irish dissidents in the 1860s and of Russian revolutionaries of the 1880s [see Walter Laqueur, *The Age of Terrorism* (Boston: Little, Brown, and Company, 1987), Chapter 1; Jonathan R. White, *Terrorism* (Belmont, CA: Wadsworth, 2002), Chapter 5].

2. See the definitions of the State Department in its *Patterns of Global Terrorism* at www.state.gov, the FBI at www.fbi.gov/publish/terror/terrusa. html, and the Department of Defense at www.periscope.usni.com/demo/ termst0000282.html. While the UN operates with its own definition (www. inlink.com/~civitas/mun/res9596/terror.html) it has been unable to agree on workable criteria for ascribing "terrorism." See Thalif Deen, "Battle Rages over UN Anti-Terror Treaty." *Online Asia Times.* www.atimesocom/front/ CK30Aa02.html.

3. References to "political objectives"—those concerning control over certain regions or organizations—is typical of most definitions of "terrorism," for example, those of Noam Chomsky, who uses "terrorism" to refer to "the threat or use of violence to intimidate or coerce (generally for political ends)" [Jay M. Shafritz et al., *Almanac of Modern Terrorism* (New York: Facts on File, 1991), p. 264)], and Paul Wilkinson, who describes terrorism as "the systematic use of coercive intimidation, usually to service political ends" that commonly targets "innocent civilians" [Paul Wilkinson, *Terrorist Targets and Tactics* (London: Research Institute for the Study of Conflict and Terrorism, 2000), pp. 12–13]. The occurrence of "deliberate" in my definition suggests that the perpetrator is intentionally using or threatening violence to achieve political objectives and is identifying the targets as civilians or noncombatants. Wilkinson's insistence that the targets are also to be described as "innocent civilians" might seems to have the advantage of revealing what is wrong with terrorism, but it has the disadvantage of making classification of a particular act as "terrorist" more controversial. This drawback is even more evident if a definition requires that the perpetrator himself or herself identifies the targets as "innocents" [Igor Primoratz, "What Is Terrorism?" *Journal of Applied Philosophy* 7 (1990): 129–138.] Such a requirement is likely to make terrorism exceedingly rare given that political violence is often committed by those who act from outrage over perceived injustices and who do not think their targets to be "innocent" of these injustices.

4. For example, Wilkinson.

5. Primoratz.

6. In this sense, the usage of "terrorist" is somewhat broader than what the standard definition permits. That is, the common media practice is to classify acts as "terrorist" if there is a suspicion that they stem from political grievances, regardless of whether the motive is accompanied by any definite political objectives. See Auishai Margalit, "The Terror Master," *New York Times Review of Books*, October 5, 1995, pp. v17–22.

7. The U.S. State Department describes "terrorism" as "premeditated, politically motivated violence perpetrated against noncombatant targets by *subnational groups or clandestine state agents,* usually intended to influence an audience" (my emphasis, Yonah Alexander and Donald J. Musch, *Terrorism: Documents of International and Local Control* (Dobbs Ferry, NY: Oceana Publications Inc., 2001), p. 5). This definition is contained in Title 22 of the United States Code, Section 2656f(d).

8. While the Jacobins used "terrorist" with a positive connotation (see note 1), a negative sense was associated with the term in the writings of Edmund Burke (see Laqueur, p. 11). Geoffrey Nunberg has noted that "the word terrorism led a double life—a justified political strategy to some, an abomination to others. The Russian revolutionaries who assassinated Tsar Alexander II in 1881 used the word proudly. And in 1905, Jack London described terrorism as a powerful weapon in the hands of labor, though he warned against harming innocent people." As late as 1947, the Jewish Stern Gang in Palestine referred to themselves as "terrorists" and Ben Hecht wrote approvingly of the Jewish "terrorists of Palestine" in their attacks upon British targets in Palestine. See David Hirst, *The Gun and the Olive Branch* (London: Faber and Faber, 1984), p. 119.

9. See, for example, C. C. O'Brien, "Liberty and Terrorism, *International Society* 2 (1977): 91; and Annemarie Oliverio, *The State of Terror* (Albany, NY: SUNY Press, 1998) Chapter 1. Robert Picard writes that it "has become an axiom that terrorism describes acts of violence committed by others, and the similar violence committed by one's own nation or by those with whom one sympathizes, is legitimate" (*Media Portrayals of Terrorism* [Ames: Iowa State University Press, 1993], p. 3). Noam Chomsky points out that there is a "propagandistic usage" in which "the term "terrorism" is used to refer to terrorist acts committed by enemies against us or our allies" (from Interview Number 5 with Chomsky on Znet at www.znet.com). I thank Erich Schulte for calling this point to my attention.

10. Don Wycliff, "Sorting Out Usage of the T-word," *The Chicago Tribune*, March 21, 2002.

11. Edward Herman and Gerry O'Sullivan, *The Terrorism Industry* (New York: Pantheon Books, 1989), p. 46.

12. The failure to recognize such instances of state terrorism is pointed out by several writers, including Noam Chomsky, *The Culture of Terrorism* (Boston: South End Press, 1988); Chomsky, "Middle East Terrorism and the American Ideological System," in *Blaming the Victims: Spurious Scholarship and the Palestinian Question*, ed. Edward Said and Christopher Hitchens (London: Verso, 1988), pp. 97–148; Edward Herman, *The Real Terror Network: Terrorism in Fact and Propaganda* (Boston: South End Press, 1982); Richard Falk, "The Terrorist Foundations of Recent U.S. Policy," in *Western State Terrorism*, ed. Alexander George (New York: Routledge, 1991), pp. 102–120; Robert Ashmore, "State Terrorism and Its Sponsors," in *Philosophical Perspectives on the Israeli–Palestinian Conflict*, ed. Tomas Kapitan (Armonk, NY: M.E. Sharpe, 1997), pp. 105–132; and Oliverio.

13. Documentation concerning both cases can be found on the Web sites of several human rights organizations, including Human Rights Watch, Amnesty International, Voices in the Wilderness, The World Health Organization, and the Israeli human rights organization, B'tselem. Then Secretary of State Madeline Albright responded affirmatively when asked whether the

UN sanctions on Iraq were "worth" the deaths of a half-million Iraqi children (*60 Minutes* interview, aired May 12, 1996).

14. See for example, the U.S. State Department, "Patterns of Global Terrorism." In it, Hezbollah's attacks on the Israeli targets are described as "terrorist" despite the fact that these attacks were directed upon the Israeli military in southern Lebanon (p. 39). Needless to say, Hezbollah is on the State Department's list of terrorist organizations. Again, the actions of Palestinian groups Hamas and Islamic Jihad are described as "terrorist" even when directed against Israeli occupying forces, whereas Israel's undercover assassinations of Palestinian figures were not so described (pp. 41–45). That the bombing of the *U.S.S. Cole* was taken as a terrorist action is implicit in the descriptions given on pp. 47 and 76.

15. Picard, p. 121. The collusion of interests between the U.S. government and the mass media is also documented in Herman, Chapter 4; Herman and O'Sullivan, Chapter 8; Chomsky, *Culture of Terrorism*, Chapter 11; and Chomsky, Middle East Terrorism."

16. Herman and O'Sullivan, p. 261.

17. Picard, p. 13. See also the description of terrorists in Benjamin Netanyahu, *Terrorism: How the West Can Win* (New York: Farrar, Straus, and Giroux, 1986), pp. 7–15.

18. A case in point is the debate that took place early in 2002 over the status of the Al Qaeda prisoners captured in the U.S.-Afghan war. The U.S. administration determined that, as "terrorists," these prisoners are not governed by the Third Geneva Convention that deals with the treatment of those detained in wartime.

19. See, for example, the U.S. bombings in Lebanon and Libya cited earlier. Again, ever since the early 1950s, Israeli "reprisals" for violence against Israelis committed by Palestinians has routinely resulted in the deaths of more Arab civilians; for example, after the operation at the Munich Olympics in 1972, the Israeli air force killed between two hundred and five hundred people, mainly civilians, in bombing raids in Lebanon and Syria. (see Hirst, p. 314).

20. A recent instance of an incitement to terrorist violence on the pretext of combating terrorism can be found in an article by Alan Dershowitz, "A New Way of Responding to Palestinian Terrorism," *The Jerusalem Post*, March 18, 2002. In describing his proposal to end the current Israeli-Palestinian violence, Dershowitz called for the organized destruction of a single Palestinian village in retaliation for every terrorist attack against Israel. "It will be a morally acceptable trade-off even if the property of some innocent civilians must be sacrificed in the process."

21. Hirst, pp. 75–97.

22. Joseph Schechtman, *Fighter and Prophet: The Last Years* (New York: Yoseloff, 1961), p. 474.

23. Edgar O'Ballance, *The Language of Violence* (San Rafael, CA: Presidio Press, 1979), pp. 24–25.

24. See Erskine Childers, "The Other Exodus," *The Specator*, May 12, 1961, pp. 672–675; Benny Morris, *The Birth of the Palestinian Refugee Problem, 1847–1949* (Cambridge: Cambridge University Press, 1987); and Simha Flapan, *The Birth of Israel* (New York: Pantheon, 1987).

25. Menachem Begin, *The Revolt* (London: W. H. Allen, 1951), p. 164.

26. Abu Iyad, with Eric Rouleau, *My Home, My Land: A Narrative of the Palestinian Struggle* (New York: Times Books, 1981), pp. 111–112.

27. Michael Wierinka, *The Making of Terrorism* (Chicago: University of Chicago, 1993), p. 43.

28. Hirst, p. 311.

29. Netanyahu, *Terrorism*, pp. 202–205.

30. Netanyahu, *Terrorism*, p. 82.

31. Netanyahu, *Terrorism*, p. 204.

32. Netanyahu, *Terrorism*, pp. 29–30.

33. Given that the overwhelming number of examples of terrorism are identified as coming from the Arab and Islamic worlds, and that "retaliation" against terrorists is repeatedly urged even at the expense of civilian casualties, one can easily agree with Edward Said's assessment of the book as nothing short of "an incitement to anti-Arab and anti-Moslem violence" (Edward Said, "The Essential Terrorist," in *Blaming the Victims*, ed. Said and Hitchens, p. 157).

34. See Hanon Alon, *Countering Palestinian Terrorism in Israel: Toward a Policy Analysis* (Santa Monica, CA: Rand Corporation, 1980), pp. 68–81, which mentions that the Israeli policy of combating "international terrorism" included the proviso that civilian populations that "shelter anti-Israeli terrorists" will not be immune from punitive action. For additional discussion of Israeli policy, see Noemi Gal-Or, "Countering Terrorism in Israel," in *The Deadly Sin of Terrorism*, ed. David A. Charters (Westport, CT: Greenwood Press, 1994), pp. 137–172, and Barry Blechman, *The Consequences of Israeli Reprisals: An Assessment* (Ph.D. diss., Georgetown University, 1971).

35. The estimate of Israeli fatalities comes from the Israeli Embassy in the United Kingdom, at www.israel-embassy.org.uk/web/pages/fatal.htm, and from the Israeli human rights group B'tselem, at www.btselem.org. The figures on the Palestinians are from B'tselem and from the Palestine Monitor at www.palestinemonitor.org/factsheet/Palestinian_killed_fact_sheet.htm. According to their estimates, civilians constituted approximately 70 percent of the Israelis killed and 85 percent of the Palestinians killed in the period from September 29, 2000, to May 14, 2002. The figures show an approximate ratio of one dead Israeli for three dead Palestinians during the Al-Aqsa Intifada, whereas in the first year and a half of the first Intifada, one Israeli was killed for every twenty-five Palestinians (see "In New Conflict, Narrowing Ratio of Dead Pressures Sharon," *New York Times*, March 12, 2002). p. 1

36. Netanyahu, *Terrorism*, pp. 207, 211.

37. Hirst, pp. 422–429; Swee Hai Ang, *From Beirut to Jerusalem* (London: Grafton, 1989), pp. 53–72.

38. Ariel Sharon, "It's Past Time to Crush the Terrorist Monster," *New York Times*, September 30, 1986. p. 35

39. Sharon has persistently advocated the ongoing settlement of the Occupied Territories by Jewish citizens of Israel. In May 2002, B'tselem reported that in the first year of his tenure as prime minister, thirty-four new settlements were begun in the West Bank. B'tselem also reported that 41.9 percent of the West Bank is under the direct control of the settlers and that since 1993, the population of West Bank settlers had doubled.

40. See the Human Rights Watch report issued in May 2002 on the IDF's siege of the Jenin camp at www.hrw.org/press/2002/05/jenin0503-prin. Related reports by Human Rights Watch reports can be found at their Web site, www.hrw.org. Amnesty International and B'tselem published similar reports at the same time. It should be noted that the IDF closed off the camp to the media and humanitarian organizations until April 19, and the Israeli government refused to allow a UN investigation team to visit the area in the aftermath of the siege.

41. Brian Urquhart, *Hammarskjold* (New York: Alfred K. Knopf, 1972), p. 157.

42. See Moshe Dayan, "Why Israel Strikes Back," in *Under Fire: Israel's Twenty Year Struggle for Survival*, ed. Donald Robinson (New York: Norton, 1968); and Benjamin Netanyahu, *Fighting Terrorism* (New York: Farrar, Straus, and Giroux, 1993). Blechman suggests that Israeli governments have also resorted to the strategy of reprisals in an attempt to satisfy public rage, frustration, and anxiety by providing "a counterfeit form of redress" (p. 286).

43. Raymond Close, "How Not to Fight Terrorism," *Washington Post National Weekly Edition*, September 7, 1998.

44. U.S. State Department, pp. 1–2.

45. The State Department's exclusion of any evaluation of policy or examination of causes is echoed in a recent publication from the Center for Strategic and International Studies, *To Prevail: An American Strategy for the Campaign Against Terrorism*. This study is summarized in "Defeating Terrorism: New Strategy for the Campaign Against Terrorism," November 27, 2001, at http://www.csis.org/press/pr01_69.htm. Wilkinson 2000, pp. 233–234, advocates a similar tough line in dealing with terrorists, although he cautions that the "response of the liberal democratic state" should always remain within the rule of law. In the opposite direction, Raymond Close writes that for America to adopt the Israeli model would "weaken our leadership position in the world" and undermine the most effective defenses we have against terrorism, namely, "a commitment to the rule of law, dedication to the fairness and evenhandedness in settling international disputes, and a reputation as the most humanitarian nation in the world." Former Assistant Secretary of State George Ball argued in the same manner in *New York Times* on December 16, 1984, emphasizing our "prime objective should clearly be to correct, or at least mitigate, the fundamental grievances that nourish terrorism rather than engage in pre-emptive and retaliatory killing of those affected by such grievances."

PART II

Who Are the Terrorists, and Why Do They Hate?

CHAPTER 3

Terror and Just Response

NOAM CHOMSKY

September 11 will surely go down in the annals of terrorism as a defining moment. Throughout the world, the atrocities were condemned as grave crimes against humanity, with near-universal agreement that all states must act to "rid the world of evildoers," that "the evil scourge of terrorism"—particularly state-backed international terrorism—is a plague spread by "depraved opponents of civilization itself" in a "return to barbarism" that cannot be tolerated. But beyond the strong support for the words of the U.S. political leadership—respectively, George W. Bush, Ronald Reagan, and his Secretary of State George Shultz[1]—interpretations varied: on the narrow question of the proper response to terrorist crimes, as well as on the broader problem of determining their nature.

On the latter, an official U.S. definition takes "terrorism" to be "the calculated use of violence or threat of violence to attain goals that are political, religious, or ideological in nature . . . through intimidation, coercion, or instilling fear."[2] That formulation leaves many questions open, among them the legitimacy of actions to realize "the right to self-determination, freedom, and independence, as derived from the Charter of the United Nations, of people forcibly deprived of that right . . . , particularly peoples under colonial and racist regimes and foreign occupation." In its most forceful denunciation of the crime of terrorism, the UN General Assembly endorsed such actions, by a vote of 153–2.[3]

Explaining their negative votes, the United States and Israel referred to the wording just cited. It was understood to justify resistance against the South African regime, a U.S. ally that was responsible for over 1.5 million dead and $60 billion in damage in neighboring countries in 1980–1988 alone, putting aside its practices within. And the resistance was led by Nelson Mandela's African National Congress, one of the "more notorious terrorist groups," according to a 1988 Pentagon report, in contrast to pro-South African RENAMO, which the same report describes as merely an "indigenous insurgent group" while observing that it might have killed one hundred thousand civilians in Mozambique in the preceding two years.[4] The same wording was taken to justify resistance to Israel's military occupation, then in its twentieth year, continuing its integration of the Occupied Territories and harsh practices with decisive U.S. aid and diplomatic support, the latter to block the longstanding international consensus on a peaceful settlement.[5]

Despite such fundamental disagreements, the official U.S. definition seems to me adequate for the purposes at hand,[6] although the disagreements shed some light on the nature of terrorism, as perceived from various perspectives.

Let us turn to the question of proper response. Some argue that the evil of terrorism is "absolute" and merits a "reciprocally absolute doctrine" in response.[7] That would appear to mean ferocious military assault in accord with the Bush doctrine, cited with apparent approval in the same academic collection on the "age of terror": "If you harbor terrorists, you're a terrorist; if you aid and abet terrorists, you're a terrorist—and you will be treated like one." The volume reflects articulate opinion in the West in taking the U.S.-U.K. response to be appropriate and properly "calibrated," but the scope of that consensus appears to be limited, judging by the evidence available, to which we return.

More generally, it would be hard to find anyone who accepts the doctrine that massive bombing is the appropriate response to terrorist crimes—whether those of September 11, or even worse ones, which are, unfortunately, not hard to find. That follows if we adopt the principle of universality: If an action is right (or wrong) for others, it is right (or wrong) for us. Those who do not rise to the minimal moral level of applying to themselves the standards they apply to others—more stringent ones, in fact—plainly cannot be taken seriously when they speak of appropriateness of response, or of right and wrong, good and evil.

To illustrate what is at stake, consider a case that is far from the most extreme but is uncontroversial, at least among those with some respect for international law and treaty obligations. No one would have supported Nicaraguan bombings in Washington when the United States rejected the order of the World Court to terminate its "unlawful use of force" and pay substantial reparations, choosing instead to escalate the international terrorist crimes and to extend them, officially, to attacks on undefended civilian targets, also vetoing a Security Council resolution calling on all states to observe international law and voting alone at the General Assembly (with one or two client states) against similar resolutions. The United States dismissed the International Court of Justice (ICS) on the grounds that other nations do not agree with us, so we must "reserve to ourselves the power to determine whether the Court has jurisdiction over us in a particular case" and what lies "essentially within the domestic jurisdiction of the United States"—in this case, terrorist attacks against Nicaragua.[8]

Meanwhile Washington continued to undermine regional efforts to reach a political settlement, following the doctrine formulated by the administration moderate, George Shultz: The United States must "cut [the Nicaraguan cancer] out" by force. Shultz dismissed with contempt those who advocate "utopian, legalistic means like outside mediation, the United Nations, and the World Court, while ignoring the power element of the equation." "Negotiations are a euphemism for capitulation if the shadow of power is not cast across the bargaining table," he declared. Washington continued to adhere to the Shultz doctrine when the Central American presidents agreed on a peace plan in 1987 over strong U.S. objections: the Esquipulas Accords, which required that all countries of the region move toward democracy and human rights under international supervision, stressing that the "indispensable element" was the termination of the U.S. attack against Nicaragua. Washington responded by sharply expanding the attack, tripling CIA supply flights for the terrorist forces. Having exempted itself from the Accords, thus effectively undermining them, Washington proceeded to do the same for its client regimes, using the substance—not the shadow—of power to dismantle the International Verification Commission (CIVS) because its conclusions were unacceptable, and demanding, successfully, that the Accords be revised to free U.S. client states to continue their terrorist atrocities. These far surpassed even the devastating U.S. war against Nicaragua that left tens of thousands dead and the country ruined perhaps beyond recovery. Still upholding the Shultz doctrine, the United States compelled the government of Nicaragua, under severe threat, to drop the claim for reparations established by the ICJ.[9]

There could hardly be a clearer example of international terrorism as defined officially, or in scholarship: operations aimed at "demonstrating through apparently indiscriminate violence that the existing regime cannot protect the people nominally under its authority," thus causing not only "anxiety, but withdrawal from the relationships making up the established order of society."[10] State terror elsewhere in Central America in those years also counts as international terrorism, in the light of the decisive U.S. role and goals, sometimes frankly articulated, for example, by the Army's School of the Americas, which trains Latin American military officers and takes pride in the fact that "Liberation Theology . . . was defeated with the assistance of the U.S. Army."[11]

It would seem to follow, clearly enough, that only those who support bombing of Washington in response to these international terrorist crimes—that is, no one—can accept the "reciprocally absolute doctrine" on response to terrorist atrocities or consider massive bombardment to be an appropriate and properly "calibrated" response to them.

Consider some of the legal arguments that have been presented to justify the U.S.-U.K. bombing of Afghanistan; I am not concerned here with their soundness, but their implications, if the principle of uniform standards is maintained. Christopher Greenwood argues that the United States has the right of "self-defense" against "those who caused or threatened . . . death and destruction," appealing to the ICJ ruling in the Nicaragua case. The paragraph he cites applies far more clearly to the U.S. war against Nicaragua than to the Taliban or Al Qaeda, so if it is taken to justify intensive U.S. bombardment and ground attack in Afghanistan, then Nicaragua should have been entitled to carry out much more severe attacks against the United States. Another distinguished professor of international law, Thomas Franck, supports the U.S.-U.K. war on grounds that "a state is responsible for the consequences of permitting its territory to be used to injure another state"; fair enough, and surely applicable to the United States in the case of Nicaragua, Cuba, and many other examples, including some of extreme severity.[12]

Needless to say, in none of these cases would violence in "self-defense" against continuing acts of "death and destruction" be considered remotely tolerable acts, not merely "threats."

The same holds of more nuanced proposals about an appropriate response to terrorist atrocities. Military historian Michael Howard proposes "a police operation conducted under the auspices of the United Nations . . . against a criminal conspiracy whose members should be hunted down and brought before an international court, where they would receive a fair trial and, if found guilty, be awarded an appropriate sentence." Reasonable enough, although the idea that the proposal should be applied universally is unthinkable. The director of the Center for the Politics of Human Rights at Harvard argues that "The only responsible response to acts of terror is honest police work and judicial prosecution in courts of law, linked to determinate, focused and unrelenting use of military power against those who cannot or will not be brought to justice."[13] That too seems sensible, if we add Howard's qualification about international supervision, and if the resort to force is undertaken after legal means have been exhausted. The recommendation therefore does not apply to 9/11 (the United States refused to provide evidence and rebuffed tentative proposals about transfer of the suspects), but it does apply very clearly to Nicaragua.

It applies to other cases as well. Take Haiti, which has provided ample evidence in its repeated calls for extradition of Emmanuel Constant, who directed the forces responsible for thousands of deaths under the military junta that the United States was tacitly supporting (not to speak of earlier history); these requests the United States ignores, presumably because of concerns about what Constant would reveal if tried. The most recent request was on September 30, 2001, while the United States was demanding that the Taliban hand over Osama bin Laden.[14] The coincidence was also ignored, in accord with the convention that minimal moral standards must be vigorously rejected.

Turning to the "responsible response," a call for implementation of it where it is clearly applicable would elicit only fury and contempt.

Some have formulated more general principles to justify the U.S. war in Afghanistan. Two Oxford scholars propose a principle of "proportionality": "The magnitude of response will be determined by the magnitude with which the aggression interfered with key values in the society attacked"; in the U.S. case, "freedom to pursue self-betterment in a plural society through market economics," viciously attacked on 9/11 by "aggressors . . . with a moral orthodoxy divergent from the West." Since "Afghanistan constitutes a state that sided with the aggressor," and refused U.S. demands to turn over suspects, "the United States and its allies, according to the principle of magnitude of interference, could justifiably and morally resort to force against the Taliban government."[15]

On the assumption of universality, it follows that Haiti and Nicaragua can "justifiably and morally resort to" far greater force against the U.S. government. The conclusion extends far beyond these two cases, including much more serious ones and even such minor escapades of Western state terror as Clinton's bombing of the al-Shifa pharmaceutical plant in Sudan in 1998, leading to "several tens of thousands" of deaths according to the German ambassador and other reputable sources, whose conclusions are consistent with the immediate assessments of knowledgeable observers.[16] The principle of proportionality therefore entails that Sudan had every right to carry out massive terror in retaliation, a conclusion that is strengthened if we go on to adopt the view that this act of "the empire" had "appalling consequences for the economy and society" of Sudan so that the atrocity was much worse than the crimes of 9/11, which were appalling enough, but did not have such consequences.[17]

Most commentary on the Sudan bombing keeps to the question of whether the plant was believed to produce chemical weapons; true or false, that has no bearing on "the magnitude with which the aggression interfered with key values in the society attacked," such as survival. Others point out that the killings were unintended, as are many of the atrocities we rightly denounce. In this case, we can hardly doubt that the likely human consequences were understood by U.S. planners. The acts can be excused, then, only on the Hegelian assumption that Africans are "mere things," whose lives have "no value," an attitude that accords with practice in ways that are not overlooked among the victims, who may draw their own conclusions about the "moral orthodoxy of the West."

One participant in the Yale volume (Charles Hill) recognized that September 11 opened the second "war on terror." The first was declared by the Reagan administration as it came to office twenty years earlier, with the rhetorical accompaniment already illustrated; and "we won," Hill reports triumphantly, though the terrorist monster was only wounded, not slain.[18] The first "age of terror" proved to be a major issue in international affairs through the decade, particularly in Central America, but also in the Middle East, where terrorism was selected by editors as the lead story of the year in 1985 and ranked high in other years.

We can learn a good deal about the current war on terror by inquiring into the first phase, and how it is now portrayed. One leading academic specialist describes the 1980s as the decade of "state terrorism," of "persistent state involvement, or 'sponsorship,' of terrorism, especially by Libya and Iran." The United States merely responded, by adopting "a 'proactive' stance toward terrorism." Others recommend the methods by which "we won": The operations for which the United States was condemned by the World Court and Security Council (absent the veto) are a model for "Nicaragua-like support for the Taliban's adversaries (especially the Northern Alliance)." A prominent historian of the subject finds deep roots for the terrorism of bin Laden: in South Vietnam, where "the effectiveness of Vietcong terror against the American Goliath armed with modern technology kindled hopes that the Western heartland was vulnerable too."[19]

Keeping to convention, these analyses portray the United States as a benign victim, defending itself from the terror of others: the Vietnamese (in South Vietnam), the Nicaraguans (in Nicaragua), Libyans and Iranians (if they had ever suffered a slight at U.S. hands, it passes unnoticed), and other anti-American forces worldwide.

Not everyone sees the world quite that way. The most obvious place to look is Latin America, which has had considerable experience with international terrorism. The crimes of 9/11 were harshly condemned, but commonly with recollection of their own experiences. One might describe the 9/11 atrocities as "Armageddon," the research journal of the Jesuit university in Managua observed, but Nicaragua has "lived its own Armageddon in excruciating slow motion" under U.S. assault "and is now submerged in its dismal aftermath." Others fared far worse under the vast plague of state terror that swept through the continent from the early 1960s, much of it traceable to Washington. A Panamanian journalist joined in the general condemnation of the 9/11 crimes, but recalled the death of perhaps thousands of poor people (Western crimes, therefore unexamined) when the president's father bombed the barrio Chorillo in December 1989 in Operation Just Cause, undertaken to kidnap a disobedient thug who was sentenced to life imprisonment in Florida for crimes mostly committed while he was on the CIA payroll. Uruguayan writer Eduardo Galeano observed that the United States claims to oppose terrorism, but actually supports it worldwide, "in Indonesia, in Cambodia, in Iran, in South Africa, . . . and in the Latin American countries that lived through the dirty war of the Condor Plan," instituted by South American military dictators who conducted a reign of terror with U.S. backing.[20]

The observations carry over to the second focus of the first "war on terror": West Asia. The worst single atrocity was the Israeli invasion of Lebanon in 1982, which left some twenty thousand people dead and much of the country in ruins, including Beirut. Like the murderous and destructive Rabin-Peres invasions of 1993 and 1996, the 1982 attack had little pretense of self-defense. Chief of Staff Rafael ("Raful") Eitan merely articulated common understanding when he announced that the goal was to "destroy the PLO as a candidate for negotiations with us about the Land of Israel,"[21] a textbook illustration of terror as officially defined. The goal "was to install a friendly regime and destroy Mr. Arafat's Palestinian Liberation Organization," Middle East correspondent James Bennet writes: "That, the theory went, would help persuade Palestinians to accept Israeli rule in the West Bank and Gaza Strip."[22] This may be the first recognition in the mainstream of facts widely reported in Israel at once, previously accessible only in dissident literature in the United States.

These operations were carried out with the crucial military and diplomatic support of the Reagan and Clinton administrations, and therefore constitute international terrorism. The United States was also directly involved in other acts of terror in the region in the 1980s, including the most extreme terrorist atrocities of the peak year of 1985: the CIA car-bombing in Beirut that killed 80 people and wounded 250; Shimon Peres's bombing of Tunis that killed 75 people, expedited by the United States and praised by Secretary of State Shultz, unanimously condemned by the UN Security Council as an "act of armed aggression" (United States abstaining); and Peres's "Iron Fist" operations directed against "terrorist villagers" in Lebanon, reaching new depths of "calculated brutality and arbitrary murder," in the words of a Western diplomat familiar with the area, amply supported by direct coverage.[23] Again, all international terrorism, if not the more severe war crime of aggression.

In journalism and scholarship on terrorism, 1985 is recognized to be the peak year of Middle East terrorism, but not because of these events: rather, because of two terrorist atrocities in which a single person was murdered, in each case an American.[24] But the victims do not so easily forget.

This very recent history takes on added significance because leading figures in the re-declared "war on terror" played a prominent part in its precursor. The diplomatic component of the current phase is led by John Negroponte, who was Reagan's Ambassador to Honduras, the base for the terrorist atrocities for which his government was condemned by the World Court and for U.S.-backed state terror elsewhere in Central America, activities that "made the Reagan years the worse decade for Central America since the Spanish conquest," mostly on

Negroponte's watch.[25] The military component of the new phase is led by Donald Rumsfeld, Reagan's special envoy to the Middle East during the years of the worst terrorist atrocities there, initiated or supported by his government.

No less instructive is the fact that such atrocities did not abate in subsequent years. Specifically, Washington's contribution to "enhancing terror" in the Israel-Arab confrontation continues. The term is President Bush's, intended, according to convention, to apply to the terrorism of others. Departing from convention, we find, again, some rather significant examples. One simple way to enhance terror is to participate in it, for example, by sending helicopters to be used to attack civilian complexes and carry out assassinations, as the United States regularly does in full awareness of the consequences. Another is to bar the dispatch of international monitors to reduce violence. The United States has insisted on this course, once again vetoing a UN Security Council resolution to this effect on December 14, 2001. Describing Arafat's fall from grace to a position barely above bin Laden and Saddam Hussein, the press reports that President Bush was "greatly angered [by] a last-minute hardening of a Palestinian position . . . for international monitors in Palestinian areas under a UN Security Council resolution," that is, by Arafat's joining the rest of the world in calling for means to reduce terror.[26]

Ten days before the veto of monitors, the United States boycotted—thus undermined—an international conference in Geneva that reaffirmed the applicability of the Fourth Geneva Convention to the occupied territories, so that most U.S.-Israeli actions there are war crimes—and when "grave breaches," as many are, serious war crimes. These include U.S.-funded Israeli settlements and the practice of "wilful killing, torture, unlawful deportation, wilful depriving of the rights of fair and regular trial, extensive destruction and appropriation of property . . . carried out unlawfully and wantonly."[27]

The Convention, instituted to criminalize formally the crimes of the Nazis in occupied Europe, is a core principle of international humanitarian law. Its applicability to the Israeli-occupied territories has repeatedly been affirmed, among other occasions, by UN Ambassador George Bush (September 1971) and by Security Council resolutions: 465 (1980), adopted unanimously, which condemned U.S.-backed Israeli practices as "flagrant violations" of the Convention, and 1322 (October 2000), by a vote of 14–0, United States abstaining, which called on Israel "to abide scrupulously by its responsibilities under the

Fourth Geneva Convention," which it was again violating flagrantly at that moment. As High Contracting Parties, the United States and the European powers are obligated by solemn treaty to apprehend and prosecute those responsible for such crimes, including their own leadership when they are parties to them. By continuing to reject that duty, they are enhancing terror directly and significantly.

Inquiry into the U.S.-Israeli-Arab conflicts would carry us too far afield. Let's turn further north, to another region where "state terror" is being practiced on a massive scale; I borrow the term from the Turkish State Minister for Human Rights, referring to the vast atrocities of 1994, and from sociologist Ismail Besikci, who returned to prison after publishing his book *State Terror in the Near East*, having already served fifteen years for recording Turkish repression of Kurds.[28] I had a chance to see some of the consequences firsthand when visiting the unofficial Kurdish capital of Diyarbakir several months after 9/11. As elsewhere, the crimes of September 11 were harshly condemned, but not without memory of the savage assault the population had suffered at the hands of those who appoint themselves to "rid the world of evildoers," and their local agents. By 1994, the Turkish State Minister and others estimated that 2 million had been driven out of the devastated countryside, many more later, often with barbaric torture and terror described in excruciating detail in international human rights reports, but kept from the eyes of those paying the bills. Tens of thousands were killed. The remnants—whose courage is indescribable— live in a dungeon where radio stations are closed and journalists imprisoned for playing Kurdish music and students are arrested and tortured for submitting requests to take elective courses in their own language; there can be severe penalties if children are found wearing Kurdish national colors by the omnipresent security forces, and the respected lawyer who heads the human rights organization was indicted shortly after I was there for using the Kurdish rather than the virtually identical Turkish spelling for the New Year's celebration; and on, and on.

These acts fall under the category of state-sponsored international terrorism. The United States provided 80 percent of the arms, peaking in 1997, when arms transfers exceeded the entire Cold War period combined before the "counterterror" campaign began in 1984. Turkey became the leading recipient of U.S. arms worldwide, a position it retained until 1999 when the torch was passed to Colombia, the leading practitioner of state terror in the Western Hemisphere.[29]

State terror is also "enhanced" by silence and evasion. The achievement was particularly notable against the background of an unprecedented chorus of self-congratulation as U.S. foreign policy entered a "noble phase" with a "saintly glow," under the guidance of leaders who for the first time in history were dedicated to "principles and values" rather than narrow interests.[30] The proof of the new saintliness was their unwillingness to tolerate crimes near the borders of NATO—only within its borders, where even worse crimes, not in reaction to NATO bombs, were not only tolerable but also required enthusiastic participation, without comment.

U.S.-sponsored Turkish state terror does not pass entirely unnoticed. The State Department's annual report on Washington's "efforts to combat terrorism" singled out Turkey for its "positive experiences" in combating terror, along with Algeria and Spain, worthy colleagues. This was reported without comment in a front-page story in the *New York Times* by its specialist on terrorism. In a leading journal of international affairs, Ambassador Robert Pearson reports that the United States "could have no better friend and ally than Turkey" in its efforts "to eliminate terrorism" worldwide, thanks to the "capabilities of its armed forces" demonstrated in its "anti-terror campaign" in the Kurdish southeast. It thus "came as no surprise" that Turkey eagerly joined the "war on terror" declared by George Bush, expressing its thanks to the United States for being the only country willing to lend the needed support for the atrocities of the Clinton years—still continuing, although on a lesser scale now that "we won." As a reward for its achievements, the United States is now funding Turkey to provide the ground forces for fighting "the war on terror" in Kabul, although not beyond.[31]

Atrocious state-sponsored international terrorism is thus not overlooked: It is lauded. That also "comes as no surprise." After all, in 1995 the Clinton administration welcomed Indonesia's General Suharto, one of the worst killers and torturers of the late twentieth century, as "our kind of guy." When he came to power thirty years earlier, the "staggering mass slaughter" of hundreds of thousands of people, mostly landless peasants, was reported fairly accurately and acclaimed with unconstrained euphoria. When Nicaraguans finally succumbed to U.S. terror and voted the right way, the United States was "United in Joy" at this "Victory for U.S. Fair Play," headlines proclaimed. It is easy enough to multiply examples. The current episode breaks no new ground in the record of international terrorism and the response it elicits among the perpetrators.

Let's return to the question of the proper response to acts of terror, specifically 9/11.

It is commonly alleged that the U.S.-U.K. reaction was undertaken with wide international support. That is tenable, however, only if one keeps to elite opinion. An international Gallup poll found only minority support for military attack rather than diplomatic means.[32] In Europe, figures ranged from 8 percent in Greece to 29 percent in France. In Latin America, support was even lower: from 2 percent in Mexico to 16 percent in Panama. Support for strikes that included civilian targets was very slight. Even in the two countries polled that strongly supported the use of military force, India and Israel (where the reasons were parochial), considerable majorities opposed such attacks. There was, then, overwhelming opposition to the actual policies, which turned major urban concentrations into "ghost towns" from the first moment, the press reported.

Omitted from the poll, as from most commentary, was the anticipated effect of U.S. policy on Afghans, millions of whom were on the brink of starvation even before 9/11. Unasked, for example, is whether a proper response to 9/11 was to demand that Pakistan eliminate "truck convoys that provide much of the food and other supplies to Afghanistan's civilian population," and to cause the withdrawal of aid workers and a severe reduction in food supplies that left "millions of Afghans . . . at grave risk of starvation," eliciting sharp protests from aid organizations and warnings of severe humanitarian crisis, judgments reiterated at the war's end.[33]

It is, of course, the assumptions of planning that are relevant to evaluating the actions taken; that too should be transparent. The actual outcome, a separate matter, is unlikely to be known, even roughly; crimes of others are carefully investigated, but not one's own. Some indication is perhaps suggested by the occasional reports on numbers needing food aid: 5 million before 9/11, 7.5 million at the end of September under the threat of bombing, 9 million six months later, not because of lack of food, which was readily available throughout, but because of distribution problems as the country reverted to warlordism.[34]

There are no reliable studies of Afghan opinion, but information is not entirely lacking. At the outset, President Bush warned Afghans that they would be bombed until they handed over people the United States suspected of terrorism. Three weeks later, war aims shifted to overthrow of the regime: The bombing would continue, Admiral Sir Michael Boyce announced, "until the people of the country themselves recognize that this is going to go on until they get the leadership changed."[35] Note that the question of whether overthrow of the miserable Taliban regime justifies the bombing does not arise, because that did not become a war aim until well after the fact. We can, however, ask about the opinions of Afghans within reach of Western observers about these choices—which, in both cases, clearly fall within the official definition of international terrorism.

As war aims shifted to regime replacement in late October, one thousand Afghan leaders gathered in Peshawar, some exiles, some coming from within Afghanistan, all committed to overthrowing the Taliban regime. It was "a rare display of unity among tribal elders, Islamic scholars, fractious politicians, and former guerrilla commanders," the press reported. They unanimously "urged the U.S. to stop the air raids," appealed to the international media to call for an end to the "bombing of innocent people," and "demanded an end to the U.S. bombing of Afghanistan." They urged that other means be adopted to overthrow the hated Taliban regime, a goal they believed could be achieved without death and destruction.[36]

A similar message was conveyed by Afghan opposition leader Abdul Haq, who was highly regarded in Washington. Just before he entered Afghanistan, apparently without U.S. support, and was then captured and killed, he condemned the bombing and criticized the United States for refusing to support efforts of his and of others "to create a revolt within the Taliban." The bombing was "a big setback for these efforts," he said. He reported contacts with second-level Taliban commanders and ex-Mujahiddin tribal elders, and discussed how such efforts could proceed, calling on the United States to assist them with funding and other support instead of undermining them with bombs. But the United States, he said, "is trying to show its muscle, score a victory and scare everyone in the world. They don't care about the suffering of the Afghans or how many people we will lose."[37]

The plight of Afghan women elicited some belated concern after 9/11. After the war, there was even some recognition of the courageous women who have been in the forefront of the struggle to defend women's rights for twenty-five years, the Revolutionary Association of the Women of Afghanistan (RAWA). A week after the bombing began, RAWA issued a public statement (October 11) that would have been front-page news wherever concern for Afghan women was real, not a matter of mere expediency. They condemned the resort to "the monster of a vast war and destruction" as the United States "launched a vast aggression on our country," that will cause great harm to innocent Afghans. They called instead for "the eradication of the plague of Taliban and Al Qaeda" by "an overall uprising" of the Afghan people themselves, which alone "can prevent the repetition and recurrence of the catastrophe that has befallen our country."

All of this was ignored. It is, perhaps, less than obvious that those with the guns are entitled to ignore the judgment of Afghans who have been struggling for freedom and women's rights for many years and to dismiss with apparent contempt their desire to overthrow the fragile and hated Taliban regime from within without the inevitable crimes of war.

In brief, review of global opinion, including what is known about Afghans, lends little support to the consensus among Western intellectuals on the justice of their cause.

One elite reaction, however, is certainly correct: It is necessary to inquire into the reasons for the crimes of 9/11. That much is beyond question, at least among those who hope to reduce the likelihood of further terrorist atrocities.

A narrow question is the motives of the perpetrators. On this matter, there is little disagreement. Serious analysts are in accord that after the United States established permanent bases in Saudi Arabia, "Bin Laden became preoccupied with the need to expel U.S. forces from the sacred soil of Arabia" and to rid the Muslim world of the "liars and hypocrites" who do not accept his extremist version of Islam.[38]

There is also wide, and justified, agreement that "Unless the social, political, and economic conditions that spawned Al Qaeda and other associated groups are addressed, the United States and its allies in Western Europe and elsewhere will continue to be targeted by Islamist terrorists."[39] These conditions are doubtless complex, but some factors have long been recognized. In 1958, a crucial year in postwar history, President Eisenhower advised his staff that in the Arab world, "the problem is that we have a campaign of hatred against us, not by the governments but by the people," who are "on Nasser's side," supporting independent secular nationalism. The reasons for the "campaign of hatred" had been outlined by the National Security Council a few months earlier: "In the eyes of the majority of Arabs the United States appears to be opposed to the realization of the goals of Arab nationalism. They believe that the United States is seeking to protect its interest in Near East oil by supporting the status quo and opposing political or economic progress." Furthermore, the perception is accurate: "[O]ur economic and cultural interests in the area have led not unnaturally to close U.S. relations with elements in the Arab world whose primary interest lies in the maintenance of relations with the West and the status quo in their countries."[40]

The perceptions persist. Immediately after 9/11, the *Wall Street Journal*, and later others, began to investigate opinions of "moneyed Muslims": bankers, professionals, managers of multinationals, and so on. They strongly support U.S. policies in general, but are bitter about the U.S. role in the region: about U.S. support for corrupt and repressive regimes that undermine democracy and development, and about specific policies, particularly regarding Palestine and Iraq. Although they are not surveyed, attitudes in the slums and villages are probably similar, but harsher; unlike the "moneyed Muslims," the mass of the population has never agreed that the wealth of the region should be drained to the West and local collaborators, rather than serving domestic needs. The "moneyed Muslims" recognize, ruefully, that bin Laden's angry rhetoric has considerable resonance, in their own circles as well, even though they hate and fear him, if only because they are among his primary targets.[41]

It is doubtless more comforting to believe that the answer to George Bush's plaintive query, "Why do they hate us?," lies in their resentment of our freedom and love of democracy, or their cultural failings tracing back many centuries, or their inability to take part in the form of "globalization" in which they happily participate. Comforting, perhaps, but not wise.

Although shocking, the atrocities of 9/11 could not have been entirely unexpected. Related organizations planned very serious terrorist acts through the 1990s, and in 1993 came perilously close to blowing up the World Trade Center, with much more ambitious plans. Their thinking was well understood, certainly by the U.S. intelligence agencies that had helped to recruit, train, and arm them from 1980 and continued to work with them even as they were attacking the United States. The Dutch government inquiry into the Srebrenica massacre revealed that while they were attempting to blow up the World Trade Center, radical Islamists from the CIA-formed networks were being flown by the United States from Afghanistan to Bosnia, along with Iranian-backed Hezbollah fighters and a huge flow of arms, through Croatia, which took a substantial cut. They were being brought to support the U.S. side in the Balkan wars, while Israel (along with Ukraine and Greece) was arming the Serbs (possibly with U.S.-supplied arms), which explains why "unexploded mortar bombs landing in Sarajevo sometimes had Hebrew markings," British political scientist Richard Aldrich observes, reviewing the Dutch government report.[42]

More generally, the atrocities of 9/11 serve as a dramatic reminder of what has long been understood: With contemporary technology, the rich and powerful no longer are assured the near monopoly of violence that has largely prevailed throughout history. Although terrorism is rightly feared everywhere, and is indeed an intolerable "return to barbarism," it is not surprising that perceptions about its nature differ rather sharply in the light of sharply differing experiences, facts that will be ignored at their peril by those whom history has accustomed to immunity while they perpetrate terrible crimes.

NOTES

1. Bush cited by Rich Heffern, *National Catholic Reporter*, January 11, 2002. Reagan, *New York Times*, October 18, 1985. Shultz, U.S. Dept. of State, *Current Policy* 589, June 24, 1984; 629, October 25, 1984.

2. *US Army Operational Concept for Terrorism Counteraction*, TRADOC Pamphlet No. 525-37, 1984.

3. Resolution 42/159, 7 December 1987; Honduras abstaining.

4. Joseba Zulaika and William Douglass, *Terror and Taboo* (New York, London: Routledge, 1996), p. 12. 1980–1988 record, see Inter-Agency Task Force, Africa Recovery Program/Economic Commission, *South African Destabilization: The Economic Cost of Frontline Resistance to Apartheid* (UN, 1989), New York: p. 13, cited by Merle Bowen, *Fletcher Forum* Winter 1991. On expansion of U.S. trade with South Africa after Congress authorized sanctions in 1985 (overriding Reagan's veto), see Gay McDougall and Richard Knight, and in *Sanctioning Apartheid*, ed. Robert Edgar (Trenton, NJ: Africa World Press, 1990).

5. For review of unilateral U.S. rejectionism for thirty years, see my Introduction to *The New Intifada*, ed. Roane Carey (London, New York: Verso, 2000); see sources cited there for more detail.

6. It is, however, never used. On the reasons, see Alexander George, ed., *Western State Terrorism* (Cambridge: Polity-Blackwell, 1991).

7. Strobe Talbott and Nayan Chanda, "Introduction," in *The Age of Terror: America and the World After September 11* (New York: Basic Books and the Yale University Center for the Study of Globalization, 2001).

8. Abram Sofaer, "The United States and the World Court," U.S. Dept. of State, *Current Policy* 769 (December 1985). The vetoed Security Council resolution called for compliance with the ICJ orders, and, mentioning no one, called on all states "to refrain from carrying out, supporting or promoting po-

litical, economic or military actions of any kind against any state of the region." Elaine Sciolino, "The U.S. Media: Courting (Over) Nicaragua," *New York Times*, July 31, 1986.

9. Shultz, "Moral Principles and Strategic Interests," April 14, 1986, U.S. Dept. of State, *Current Policy* No 820. Shultz Congressional testimony, see Jack Spence, in *Reagan Versus the Sandinistas*, ed. Thomas Walker (Boulder, CO, London: Westview, 1987). For review of the undermining of diplomacy and escalation of international state terror, see my *Culture of Terrorism* (Boston: South End, 1988); *Necessary Illusions* (Boston: South End, 1989); *Deterring Democracy* (London, New York: Verso, 1991). On the aftermath, see Thomas Walker and Ariel Armony, eds., *Repression, Resistance, and Democratic Transition in Central America* (Wilmington, DE: Scholarly Resources, 2000). On reparations, see Howard Meyer, *The World Court in Action* (Lanham, MD, Oxford: Rowman & Littlefield, 2002), Chapter 14.

10. Edward Price, "The Strategy and Tactics of Revolutionary Terrorism," *Comparative Studies in Society and History* 19.1 (1977); cited by Chalmers Johnson, "American Militarism and Blowback," *New Political Science* 24.1 (2002).

11. SOA, 1999, cited by Adam Isacson and Joy Olson, in *Just the Facts* (Washington: Latin America Working Group and Center for International Policy, 1999), p. ix.

12. Greenwood, "International Law and the War Against Terrorism,'" *International Affairs* 78.2 (2002), appealing to par. 195 of *Nicaragua v. USA*, which the Court did not use to justify its condemnation of U.S. terrorism, but surely is more appropriate to that than to the case that concerns Greenwood. Franck, "Terrorism and the Right of Self-Defense," *American Journal of International Law* 95.4 (October 2001).

13. Howard, *Foreign Affairs*, January/February 2002; talk of October 30, 2001 (Tania Branigan, *Guardian*, October 31). Ignatieff, *Index on Censorship* 2 (2002).

14. *New York Times*, October 1, 2001.

15. Frank Schuller and Thomas Grant, *Current History* (April 2002).

16. Werner Daum, "Universalism and the West," *Harvard International Review* (Summer 2001). On other assessments, and the warnings of Human Rights Watch, see my *9-11* (New York: Seven Stories, 2001), pp. 45ff.

17. Christopher Hitchens, *Nation*, June 10, 2002.

18. Talbott and Chanda, "Introduction."

19. Martha Crenshaw, Ivo Daalder, James Lindsay, and David Rapoport, *Current History, America at War*, December 2001. On interpretations of the first "war on terror" at the time, see George, *Western State Terrorism*.

20. Envio (UCA Managua), October; Ricardo Stevens (Panama), NACLA *Report on the Americas* November/December; Galeano, *La Jornada* (Mexico City), cited by Alain Frachon, in *Le Monde,* November 24, 2001.

21. For many sources, see my *Fateful Triangle* (Boston: South End, 1983; updated 1999 edition, on South Lebanon in the 1990s); *Pirates and Emperors* (New York: Claremont, 1986; Pluto, London, Black Rose Press, 2000); *World Orders Old and New* (New York: Columbia University Press, 1996).

22. Bennet, *New York Times,* January 24, 2002.

23. For details, see my essay in George, *Western State Terrorism.*

24. Crenshaw et al., *Current History.*

25. Chalmers Johnson, *Nation*, October 15, 2001.

26. Ian Williams, *Middle East International*, December 21, 2001, January 11, 2002. John Donnelly, *Boston Globe*, April 25, 2002; the specific reference is to an earlier U.S. veto.

27. Conference of High Contracting Parties, *Report on Israeli Settlement* (Washington: Foundation for Middle East Peace). On these matters see Francis Boyle, "Law and Disorder in the Middle East," *The Link* 35.1 (January–March 2002).

28. For some details, see my *New Military Humanism* (Monroe, ME: Common Courage, 1999), Chapter 3, and sources cited there. On evasion of the facts in the State Department Human Rights Report, see Lawyers Committee for Human Rights, *Middle East and North Africa* (New York: 1995), p. 255.

29. Tamar Gabelnick, William Hartung, and Jennifer Washburn, *Arming Repression: U.S. Arms Sales to Turkey During the Clinton Administration* (New York and Washington: World Policy Institute and Federation of Atomic Scientists, October 1999). I exclude Israel-Egypt, a separate category. On state terror in Colombia, now largely farmed out to paramilitaries in standard fashion, see particularly Human Rights Watch, *The Sixth Division* (September 2001) and Colombia Human Rights Certification III, February 2002. Also, among others, Me'dicos Sin Fronteras, *Desterrados* (Bogota: 2001).

30. For a sample, see *New Military Humanism* and my *A New Generation Draws the Line* (London: Verso, 2000).

31. Judith Miller, *New York Times*, April 30, 2000. Pearson, *Fletcher Forum* 26.1 (Winter/Spring 2002).

32. http://www.gallup.international.com/terrorismpoll-figures.htm; data from September 14–17, 2001.

33. John Burns, *New York Times*, September 16, 2001; Samina Amin, *International Security* 26.3 (Winter 2001–2002). For some earlier warnings, see *9/11*. On the postwar evaluation of international agencies, see Imre Karacs, *Independent on Sunday* (London), December 9, 2001, reporting their warnings that over a million people are "beyond their reach and face death from starvation and disease." For some press reports, see my "Peering into the Abyss of the Future," Lakdawala Memorial Lecture, Institute of Social Sciences, New Delhi, November 2001, updated February 2002.

34. Ibid., for early estimates. Barbara Crossette, *New York Times,* March 26, 2002, and Ahmed Rashid, *Wall Street Journal,* June 6, 2002, reporting the assessment of the UN World Food Program and the failure of donors to pro-

vide pledged funds. The WFP reports that "wheat stocks are exhausted, and there is no funding" to replenish them (Rashid).

The UN had warned of the threat of mass starvation at once because the bombing disrupted planting that provides 80 percent of the country's grain supplies (AFP, September 28; Edith Lederer, AP, October 18, 2001). Also Andrew Revkin, *New York Times,* December 16, 2001, citing U.S. Department of Agriculture, with no mention of bombing.

35. Patrick Tyler and Elisabeth Bumiller, *New York Times,* October 12, quoting Bush; Michael Gordon, *New York Times* October 28, 2001, quoting Boyce; both p. 1.

36. Barry Bearak, *New York Times,* October 25, 2001; John Thornhill, and Farhan Bokhari, *Financial Times,* October 25, October 26, 2001; John Burns, New York Times, October 26; Indira Laskhmanan, *Boston Globe,* October 25, October 26, 2001.

37. Interview with Anatol Lieven, *Guardian,* November 2, 2001.

38. Ann Lesch, *Middle East Policy* IX.2 (June 2002). Also Michael Doran, *Foreign Affairs,* January–February 2002; and many others, including several contributors to *Current History,* December 2001.

39. Sumit Ganguly in *Current History.*

40. For sources and background discussion, see my World Orders Old and New, pp. 79, 201ff.

41. Peter Waldman et al., Wall Street Journal, September 14, 2001; also Waldman and Hugh Pope, Wall Street Journal, September 21, 2001.

42. Aldrich, *Guardian*, April 22, 2002.

CHAPTER 4

Narratives Competing
for Our Souls

DAVID B. BURRELL

Children love stories; parents carefully choose which ones to read to them, knowing the power stories have to shape our lives. Advertisers know this as well, designing episodes calculated to let our fantasies spin out the rest. And like advertisements, many stories have the goal of persuading us to see the world in a certain way, or even to become this kind of person. So we all learn to develop, early on, what Norman Mailer said every erstwhile writer needed: a "built-in crap detector." Sensing the power of rhetoric, we need to protect ourselves from its blandishments so that we can "make up our own mind," as we put it, about the situation at hand. When we encounter two sets of stories, each vying for our allegiance, the pull we feel to "take sides" can activate that critical sense: "Let's hear the other side." Philosophy courses today might well focus on developing the skills we need to adjudicate between "conflicting narratives," as they try to counter our culture's lazy injunction simply to *choose*. In matters of import, choosing won't do; we need to understand. Yet as Socrates reminded us, the only reliable path to understanding matters of human worth must wend its way through competing narratives. These reflections document my struggle to do just that with the Israeli-Palestinian conflict, offering some suggestions how to monitor the narratives told, as well as how to supply narratives where snapshots pretend to do the job. Yet assessment of this sort can never be a solitary endeavor, so I need to thank all the friends to whom I have listened and with whom I have argued. Indeed, this task of weighing competing narratives—which can absorb one's life and may well have to do so in the world in which we live—requires friends as none other does, for only friendship allows us to stay the course through recurring disagreements to reach a yet more discriminating understanding.

History gives invaluable perspective, but histories also take the form of stories, as Americans divide on the very titles: for example, "civil war" or "war between the states." An attempt to sketch the background of the Palestinian-Israeli conflict will amply illustrate this point. Best begin with what Europeans call "the great war," in which the Ottomans ("Turks" for short) had been aligned with Germany and the Austro-Hungarian Empire against the "Allies." The recently constructed railroad from Istanbul to Mecca, as able to carry troops as pilgrims, veered perilously close to the Suez Canal, a critical supply line for the prolonged western front. So the British chose a mercurial "Lawrence" to divert the Bedouin from intertribal warfare to sabotage the railroad, frustrating Turkish efforts to attack the canal. This strategy played into a fledgling Arab nationalism, spurred by Lebanese literary societies focusing on the intrinsic merits of Arabic, the language of the Holy Quran. In return for this critical role, their leaders received vague promises of self-determination after the war. Yet while the victors carved up Europe into proper nation-states (with some notable and dire exceptions, like Yugoslavia), the "Arabs" (so-called, since the Ottoman Empire had relied on Islam itself to divert attention from nation-centered enclaves) were deemed not yet ready for that, so the same victors imposed a constructed *mandate* status on what we call the Middle East, with France responsible for Syria and Lebanon and the British for Iraq, Jordan, and Palestine—each of which had been administrative units under the Ottomans.

While Lawrence was enlisting the services of the Bedouin to save the canal, the Jewish elite in England were soliciting support from the Foreign Office for Zionist ambitions in Palestine. Lord Balfour managed to elicit a document endorsing (in suitably ambiguous diplomatic prose) "the establishment in Palestine of a national home for the Jewish people, . . . it being clearly understood that nothing shall be done which may prejudice the civil and religious rights of the existing non-Jewish communities. . . ." (Citing this declaration in his *Exodus*, Leon Uris omits the limiting clause.) So conflicting orders from London fueled conflict between Jews and Arabs in the Holy Land, leaving those governing the British mandate with an impossible task. Early Zionist efforts dated from the end of the nineteenth century, in the wake of pogroms in czarist Russia, but the Balfour Declaration gave them fresh impetus in the twenties, spurred further by national socialism in Germany during the thirties. When the effect of the Nazis' "final solution" became clear to the world in 1945, Jewish exodus to

Palestine changed from a trickle to a flood, following a deluge of Western sympathy mingled with guilt. Meanwhile, the "indigenous people," who shared none of the guilt, were to bear the brunt of the genocide, as it affected the minds and hearts of Jews and non-Jews alike. What resulted was an effective colonization of Palestine by world Jewry that neatly escaped the label, executed as it was in the midst of efforts at decolonization, beginning in south Asia (with the partition of India in 1947) and soon assumed by African independence movements. The rise of Western sympathy readily armed Jewish fighters, effectively diverting attention from the disaster attending "the indigenous people" fighting for their homeland. Leon Uris's *Exodus* as well as Lapierre and Collins's *O Jerusalem* neatly dramatize this perspective, glorifying the Zionist struggle while eclipsing any Palestinian presence. So the stories attending nation-building (and the "desert blooming") effectively shaped the world's perception of the fledgling state of Israel, obscuring even the faces of the indigenous people—a mindset that prevails among American "anchor persons" on the evening news to this date, as lines of questioning simply presume that Israel is "us" and Palestine "them," no matter how "fair" they try to be.

When the Israeli state archives were opened (after fifty years) in 1998, a spate of "new histories" emerged to tarnish the myths and validate the Palestinian counterstory of a *Nakbah*: the "disaster" to the lives and livelihood of the "indigenous people" and countless of their villages.[1] Yet by this time the "Holocaust-industry," abetted by its most eloquent witness Elie Wiesel, had virtually muted any critique of Israel by Western Christians, giving Israeli leaders carte blanche to pursue the contradictory policies attendant upon the victories of 1967. Yet it was their own towering intellectual apologist, Yesheyahu Leibowitz, who turned from professor to prophet in the wake of that euphoria, to shout: "Give it back! I have had to argue with formidable protagonists, including Martin Buber and Judah Magnes, in favor of a Jewish state, to properly develop our culture. Yet we would cease to be a Jewish state demographically were we to assimilate the people in the land we have just occupied into our body politic; yet we will cease to be Jewish ethically if we try to rule over people whom we cannot admit to citizenship."[2] Other voices of clarity joined his in the crucial days following the "six-day war," but the dream of occupying "biblical Palestine" soon silenced them all, often reinforced by religious reminders that "God gave us the land"—a cry that would in time clearly divide Israel between "secular" and "religious" Jews. (We should urge evangelical Christians to look again at the Bible to register the gulf between God's unconditional promise that Israel will always be God's people—a promise unequivocally if belatedly endorsed by Vatican II; and the promise of the land, conditioned on countless fronts. Failure to keep the Torah or respect the stranger in their midst, and so on, will jeopardize Israel's capacity to live in the land peacefully.)

So we have finally come to the nub of the present conflict: a contradiction. We Americans know the truth of René Girard's contention that a contradiction at the heart of a body politic can elicit violence, as the declaration that "all human beings are created equal" confronted the stipulation that "slaves shall count as three-fifths of a person."[3] Seventy-five years later the nation was at war with itself, as efforts to suppress the contradiction generated by the compromise over slavery encountered first children's questions and then concerted religious campaigns. Indeed, the American debate over slavery has been mimicked by Israeli debate over the post-1967 occupation, so it is hardly surprising that American visitors to the Holy Land find the situation of Palestinians vis-à-vis Israel reminiscent of the way the "Negro-question" perdured for one hundred years after the war intending to eradicate slavery. For the past thirty-five years Israel has been pursuing policies of denial, even fabricating legalistic arguments that there has been no occupation, since the territory occupied did not properly belong to the sovereign states of Jordan or Egypt. Yet the Intifada of 1987 already made it clear: If it walks like an occupation, as well as feels and tastes like one, it's an occupation! The multiple subterfuges invented to escape the contradiction that Professor Leibowitz had identified were made even murkier by settlers able to co-opt biblical language for political advantage, together with the ritual invocation of "the Holocaust" to disarm Western critics. The result has been a baffling equivocation on ending the occupation: The strategy of "land for peace" announced at Oslo became a way to ensure Israeli hegemony, by relegating the tasks of civil administration of dense population areas to the Palestinian Authority, while settlement population doubled in the seven years following Oslo (1993–2000). So while the slogan of "land for peace" ostensibly presaged the end of occupation, Israeli hegemony was to continue by other means.

All of this happened under the umbrella of the "peace process," of course, which we in the Western media kept cheering, all the while blind to its underside. Indeed, the focus of our media on "media events," rather than on what may be taking place among the different peoples, helps to account for the demise of Camp David II during the summer of 2000, for neither the Israeli government nor the Palestinian Authority had encouraged the kind of people-to-people exchange that can make peace possible. So it is hardly surprising that fifteen people around a table could not bring themselves to take bold actions; indeed, the failure of Camp David II is increasingly seen to be the failure of "top-down" initiatives, and by the very people who had invested their expertise in such processes. And as the facts gather to neutralize the media hype, it has turned out that the parcel offered was so honeycombed that percentages were thoroughly misleading. As Rabbi Michael Lerner put it, my offer to you of 95 percent of my house is bound to fail when you find out I have kept the corridors![4] Why American media did not simply show us the maps is baffling, almost leading one to contrive a conspiracy theory about those intent on misleading us—but several years in the Middle East, rife with such theories, has led me to reject them on grounds of simplicity: It is hard to pull off a conspiracy.

There is another position, however, that stands in stark contrast to that of Yesheyahu Leibowitz and was articulated by another philosopher, Emil Fackenheim, in 1982, in the course of a Christian-Jewish dialogue group called "the Rainbow." Indeed, what he said was so startling that I remember the setting quite clearly, along with my walk home with a distinguished colleague from Hebrew University's Islamics faculty, Hava Lazarus-Yafe. (I had in fact invited Emil Fackenheim to Notre Dame as part of a Carnegie summer institute for philosophy teachers [in 1969] on the strength of his excellent study of the religious dimension of Hegel's thought, so we knew one another, although he had recently moved from Bloomington to Jerusalem to express his personal response to "the Holocaust.") The startling statement, imbedded in an impassioned argument, insisted that the survival of the Jewish people (after Auschwitz) justified any means.[5] With my blood turning cold, I tried to invoke Socrates (in Plato's *Apology*): Sheer survival counts for nothing if in the process I betray my humanity. But apparently Socrates no longer counted against what this philosopher now took to be the Torah. Yet we should be grateful to philosophers for stating things clearly, at least, for it allowed Hava to agree with me that she could never countenance such a statement, even if her very presence there testified that her mother had prevailed (in the thirties), persuading her father that his family was more important than his German synagogue, so inducing him to move them to Palestine. But Emil Fackenheim's assertion had forcibly reminded me of Socrates's argument (expanded in Plato's *Republic*) that unjust actions taken to save one's skin are in fact self-destructive, since those who survive by such means have rendered themselves rotten from within. Indeed, many a novel has orchestrated that argument. My argument here juxtaposes Fackenheim's crass assertion with Leibowitz's clear injunction, to expose daily media fabrications as just that: attempts to render acceptable policies generated to serve an inner contradiction, by continuing to mask it. For logicians remind us that anything follows from a contradiction, so attempts to mask a contradiction can only compound the illusion.

Yet that is the most effective way we can remove one set of conflicting stories from the competition: by showing how those stories serve a contradiction, which will emerge more clearly as we trace them to that original inconsistency. So if we are grateful to Professor Leibowitz for identifying the initial contradiction embodied in the continuing occupation, we should be equally indebted to Professor Fackenheim for unmasking what motivates those Israeli actions and policies that strike us as inhumane. Yet rather than endorse his contention—that the survival of the Jewish people justifies any means—we should protest those inhumane actions and policies out of love for the Jewish state that Leibowitz envisaged. For if Socrates is right, what survives will be rotten from within. And that is just what many Israelis and an increasing number of diaspora Jews are concluding. As Zachariah al-Haq, the Palestinian codirector of the Israeli-Palestinian Center for Research and Information (IPCRI), said of his partner Gershom Baskin's trenchant analyses opposing current Israeli policy: "Gershom understands the strategic interests of Israel."[6] In Socratic terms, well-being and integrity must trump mere survival. So whether they be labeled "secular" or "religious" makes little difference; one set of stories can nourish the soul of Israel while the other will destroy it. Michel Sabbah, the Latin Patriarch of Jerusalem, put it forthrightly in a recent letter:

> The conflict between Palestinians and Israelis is not basically a question of Palestinian terrorism that threatens security or the existence of Israel. It is a question of Israeli military occupation that started in 1967, which provokes Palestinian resistance, which then threatens the security of Israel. To go on speaking about Palestinian terrorism, without seeing the right of the Palestinians to their freedom and to end the occupation, is condemning oneself not to see reality, and to remain impotent in reaching a solution.[7]

So when Israelis attempt to deny the fact of occupation, by actions or even outright statements (like Sharon's insistence that "the occupation is a lie"), we should recognize a cover-up for what it is. Just as parents need to remind their children when trying to wean them away from the apparently self-protective habit of lying, nations too will find it to be cheaper in the long run to tell the truth, since it saves endless prevarication to cover the first. The Latin Patriarch is urging nothing more than that, while Israel's refusal to cooperate with the investigation team authorized by the United Nations Security Council cannot but elicit the inference that they must have something to hide.

So the case of Jenin brings us to the most difficult issue of all, which is not one of analysis. It emerges in response to reports of the subsequent depredations of the Israeli Defense Force (IDF) in their recent incursions into the Palestinian population centers of Ramallah and of Bethlehem, as well as the less publicized raids into surrounding villages. Many otherwise intelligent Israelis simply cannot hear these reports, and are quick to pass them off as "lies." It is as though anything negative about their country, and especially about the IDF, is insupportable. Any American who went through the painful process of self-education demanded by the Vietnam War can understand this reaction, for it took us some time to assimilate stories of atrocities committed by U.S. forces; although once we had done so, we became attuned to similar U.S. involvement with the Contras (via the notorious School of the Americas), preparing us for the current U.S. hesitancy to support an International Court. So there is a process of attrition, whereby a nation's actions destroy it founding myths, to move its citizens from innocence to experience, and so develop a critical attitude toward calls for patriotism. Nor need this critical turn deny that *patriotism* is a virtue; it rather demands that we incorporate such criticism into our refined sense of that virtue. As Israelis struggle with that "critical turn," aided by their "new historians," we can appreciate how difficult that must be for a nation so much younger and more vulnerable than the United States in the 1960s. Yet even that degree of appreciation will not suffice; we need to explore more sensitively the issue of vulnerability, especially to see how Ariel Sharon was able to divert attention from the "best offer Israel has ever received" in the Saudi peace plan: recognition of all the surrounding Arab states. It is not enough to see this as the cynical ploy of a prime minister opposed to peace, since losing the specter of "Arab nations surrounding Israel wanting to push us into the sea" would take the wind out of the militarists' sails by offering the IDF the chance to be just that—a defense force—and remove the motivation for adventures like Lebanon in 1982 and beyond. All this may well be true; indeed, no one (as we have seen) can reasonably expect the current Israeli government to bring peace. But the roots reach deeper than a Likud ideology; they reach to the hearts of Jews who have gathered in Palestine to form the state of Israel. A story may best reveal those roots.

A younger colleague of mine is the son of a man who had survived the genocide at Auschwitz by having been sent from Poland in the thirties to be with an uncle in New York. (Experience has shown that this kind of "survival" is the worst, as those who never experienced the trauma personally have been fated to wonder why they were spared what others suffered.) Although his father had died recently, the son had inherited much of the trauma, so I suggested he join me in Jerusalem during a sabbatical semester, which he did for three weeks. (Perhaps not the wisest invitation, as I came to see, yet I had hoped that our friendship could help him see with new eyes.) Following the usual pattern of our Notre Dame program in Jerusalem, we went everywhere to visit friends: Ramallah, Bethlehem, east (Arab) and west (Jewish) Jerusalem, Tel Aviv (to make contact with his relatives), and the Galilee, including Jenin. In short, I submitted him to the warp and woof of Israel/Palestine, in an effort to let him see it. One *shabbat* morning we tripped down the sloping entrance road to the Tantur Ecumenical Institute, crossing Hebron Road to await the ubiquitous *shirrut* (service taxi) to take us into east Jerusalem. We were waiting with a young Palestinian when a police car swung by, and two beefy men got out in half-uniform—it was the sabbath, after all—and shooed the young man back into Bethlehem, paying no attention at all to us.

As this was an ordinary enough experience for one who had seen what we had in the previous ten days, I turned to my friend and colleague to resume our conversation, only to see him looking aghast at the disappearing police car. As I tried to make light of the incident, he enlightened me: "You did not see what I saw: the fear in their faces was just like what I saw in my father's!" He was alluding not to the young man from Bethlehem but to the policemen, so I suddenly saw what I had known before but never felt: a people transfixed by fear. I was reminded of my friend Yehuda's telling me of his grandmother's warning as he set off for graduate school: "There are a lot of *goyim* out there." Can anyone who is not Jewish really feel this? And how do Jews whom we know who appear to have moved beyond this fear do it? These questions, triggered by what I saw through the eyes of my friend, introduced just the right amount of "unknowing" into my ceaseless endeavor to understand what is going on here. They also implicated me, of course, since that potent residue of fear is an understandable legacy of the marginalization (and worse) of eighteen centuries of Christendom, so it is hardly surprising that it be reflected over the short space of less than a century. Moreover, these policemen serve a nation founded in the wake of the *Shoah*, subject to two major wars shortly after the initial independence struggle, so the contours of such collective fear begin to reveal themselves, along with its potency, as well as the potency for politicians to pander to it with the code word "security." So now I knew what that term is designed to mean, and the strategic ways it can be used to manipulate an entire populace. Moreover, the more one reflects on this ingrained feature of what one might call "the Israeli psyche," the less hope one can muster for an end to the spiraling feuding (as Avishai Margalit has identified it) that we have witnessed over the past year and a half.[8]

Yet the upside of fear is indeed survival, and should that keen sense for survival that seems also to have been ingrained into this people be tempered with Socrates's salutary warnings, a sturdy majority may well opt for a realistic form of parallel existence, which in time could grow into genuine coexistence, as generations move into a future in which the clear dependence of one state on the other for "peace with security" could begin to bear fruit among select groups of persons. Here again, the role of societal groupings to encourage political breakthroughs will prove telling. Yet if hope can be salvaged, it will take a great deal of work by people on each side, among their own as well as jointly. Moreover, my suspicion is that these will have to be people of faith—Jews, Christians, and Muslims—for nothing but a sturdy faith can dissipate the smokescreens of ideology, especially those ideologies reinforced by a hard "religious" overlay. We have long been involved in such ventures at Tantur, located on the seam between Jerusalem and Bethlehem, Israel and Palestine, profiting from the efforts of Thomas Stransky, rector during the nineties, to create at Tantur a space in which Israelis and Palestinians, Jews and Arabs, could speak freely enough to respect disagreements. Indeed, any action presupposes preparations that have been undertaken in faith, the ground of hope, as we proceed into an unknown future. So we build on those who have gone before, notably on this venture of Tantur, which has gone through a number of metamorphoses, all of which have been animated by an original faith in the presence of the God of Abraham in this blessed and conflicted land.

If these be signs of hope, however, they are ever in danger of being eclipsed by a media intent on a "balanced view of the two sides," always reacting to violent events and characteristically tone-deaf to the human dimensions of this conflict, to say nothing of the operative contradiction we have identified as shaping Israeli policies. I am coming to the conclusion that television news is inherently misleading, when their preoccupation with a single event keeps them from reaching into their archives to place it in a wider context. So, for example, a suicide bombing in Kiryat ha-Yovel, a neighborhood of Jerusalem, featured shots of the carnage plus part of a video done by the young woman to explain her actions, yet without the complementary shots of Israeli tanks penetrating her refugee camp ten days before. The actions of the IDF in Daheshe camp, as reported by residents, displayed a callous disrespect for the homes of these poor persons, as young soldiers following orders to break through the contiguous walls of dwellings in their sweep through the camp would casually pass their hands over the shelves to smash the dishes on the floor. This is the type of report, of course, that Israelis cannot bear to hear, like the wanton destruction of the Palestinian Cultural Center in Ramallah, yet when a military operation is launched in terms as vague as "flushing out terrorists," mischief is bound to result. Now none of this can justify the young woman's actions, but a few archival photos would go a long way toward placing them in context—indeed, a context that could lead us rather quickly back to the originating contradiction: refugee camps, occupation, and all that. Yet as long as the media avoid any contextual moves or explanatory categories, playing out the scenario as though we have but "two sides at war," we can expect little illumination. There are alternative sources, which I shall list at the end of this article, but it is dismaying to have to work against the powerful networks, who seem quite blind to the difficulties inherent in photojournalism, and so are unable to summon the will or the resources to counteract what they fail to notice. So we are called to work overtime, as it were, to develop those critical capacities that our founders deemed indispensable to a working democracy.

A final word on the Palestinians, for this critical analysis has focused on Israel. I must invoke the ritual disclaimer of bias, however, for it is my contention that the Palestinians have less to do with the roots of this conflict than the Israeli penchant for demonizing them—and especially their symbolic leader Arafat—leads us to believe. In fact, as I have been suggesting, this is far more a matter of Israeli attitudes toward the "other" in their midst than it is those "others" themselves. (Again, drawing on the parallel of slavery in American history, our civil war was less over "the Negroes" than it was over the issue of slavery itself, and its effect on the body politic as a whole.) Here is where the Israeli "right" and "left" divides, often along lines which identify the *left* with "secular" and the *right* with "religious," although there are illustrative and heartening exceptions to that stereotypic division. Ambiguities in the descriptor of "Jewish state" lead some to emphasize the ethical heritage of Judaism to underscore their declaration of independence that guarantees freedom to all citizens, Jew or non-Jew; while others read it more ethnically (or tribally) to sustain an atmosphere in which administrative procedures regularly make life difficult if not noxious for "others" in their midst. But the empirical fact that this "other" need not be Palestinian suggests that the conflict is more one of self-definition than it is of endemic conflict between two peoples. Moreover, the standing policies of Zionist settlement from the beginning have reflected a heritage of separation, so that few Israeli Jews know very many Palestinians personally. So stereotypes are allowed to abound, reinforcing the contention that we are rather witnessing a war of attitudes among Israelis themselves than a head-on conflict with Palestinians—attitudes toward "the other" that reflect the different strands of Jewish history, notably the cultural gap between Jews from Muslim lands (Sephardim) and those from Western Christendom (Ashkenazi), working themselves out in the heated atmosphere of the Middle East.

That having been said, however, what can one reasonably say about "the Palestinians?" Again, snapshots of funerals in the wake of IDF killings portray an extremely volatile people, but anyone who has lived among them finds a people with nearly infinite patience and long-suffering. In fact, as Lucy Nuseibeh has argued, the most telling examples of nonviolence we have are Palestinian women making do in the midst of incredible obstacles and creating a foyer in which the nourishment and education of children are given priority over everything else.[9] How contrary to the manufactured canard that parents sent their children against firearms with stones, or the celebrated remarks of mothers praising their sons or daughter for destroying themselves in the cause of Palestine. Anyone who knows Palestinian family life, with its lasting and intimate bonds, would have to ask themselves what could have driven a mother to make such statements. Rather than take them as characterizing Palestinian attitudes toward their children, a sensitive hearer will try to identify the sources of such desperation, and may even trace them back to what we have called the original contradiction. But in the absence of personal exchange, and with little more than photojournalism to give the news, the number of such sensitive listeners will inevitably dwindle. So that leaves us but one constructive path to peace in this area, or any other, I suspect. Groups from different sectors of society, most notably faith groups, must continue to being people together, in an effort to efface stereotypes and to foster the kind of human exchange that alone can bring peace between peoples.

To keep our sanity in the mist of such taxing work, however, we will need analytic categories, like the ones suggested here, to disclose contradictions that will continue to operate, fueling violence until they are exposed and neutralized. So, for example, as we sought to explain (without ever attempting to justify) suicide missions by pointing to the continuing humiliation and violence perpetrated against innocent Palestinians, we can also get our bearings on ostensibly irrational Israeli actions by recalling the endemic fear we have identified, as well as the imperious demand to cover up the standing contradiction of the occupation. And irrational responses—like one political party's explicit renouncement of any future Palestinian state—will multiply as more and more Israeli supporters (like the writers of *New York Times* editorials) begin to recognize the occupation for the festering contradiction that it is. Those dedicated to the status quo have but one shopworn strategy: Continue the cover-up. So the last word will be one of hope, ironic as that may sound. For we must be grateful for the collapse of Camp David II, which showed up the hollowness of Oslo's attempt to keep the status quo in all but name; and even for Sharon's stroll on the Temple Mount, which triggered the Al-Aqsa Intifada and helped him become prime minister. That action, together with his subsequent policies, has brought the contradiction into evidence as never before, and will impel yet more draconian strategies of cover-up, until Israeli citizens and supporters in other countries will see clearly that different steps must be taken, the first of which must be to erase the contradiction of the occupation. Indeed, the call for that is increasingly clear, even while patterns of avoidance are slow to change.

NOTES

1. Benny Morris, *Righteous Victims* (New York: Knopf, 1999), also Yezid Sayigh, *From Armed Struggle to Statehood* (Oxford: Oxford University Press, 2000).

2. My references to Leibowitz are from oral conversation and current press reports, but see Yeshayahu Leibowitz, *Judaism, Human Values, and the Jewish State*, ed. Eliezer Goldman (Cambridge, MA: Harvard University Press, 1992), Chapter 21, "The Territories": "Out of concern for the Jewish People and its state we have no choice but to withdraw from the territories and their population on and a half million Arabs" (226).

3. René Girard, *Things Hidden from the Foundation of the World* (Stanford, CA: Stanford University Press, 1987); the American examples are taken from the Declaration of Independence and the Constitution, respectively.

4. For Michael Lerner's reflections, see his journal *Tikkun*: www.tikkun.org.

5. While this event was not recorded, similar sentiments can be found in his *To Mend the World* (New York: Schocken, 1982): see "Jewish Existence after the Holocaust," pp. 294–313.

6. For IPCRI communications, consult their Web site: www.ipcri.org.

7. "Perspectives on the Conflict between Palestinians and Israelis," *Pentecost* 8 (May 2002), available from nonviolence@writeme.com.

8. *New York Review of Books*, September 20, 2001.

9. "Palestinian Women and Nonviolence," January 12, 2002, MiddleEast-Wire.com, distributed by Common Ground News Service (cgnews@sfcg.org).

CHAPTER 5

The War Against Pluralism

ROBERT L. PHILLIPS

PART 1: PROBLEMS

Modern, or new age, terrorism can be dated to the 1960s, when, in the aftermath of a failed civil rights movement, a revived Irish Republican Army (IRA) began a campaign to oust the British from Northern Ireland. The decades of the '70s and '80s saw a proliferation of terrorist groups, mainly of a leftist persuasion, who operated within the ideological parameters of the Cold War. Some of these were state actors usually funded from communist or Middle Eastern sources. Colonel Mu'ammar Gadhafi, for instance, supplied arms and money to both sides in the Northern Ireland conflict. His arm: destablilization of the West. There was in this period a myriad of shifting causes and ideological manifestos, most of them incoherent. Students of these matters generally categorized terrorism as a form of low-intensity conflict. Terrorists, it was said, could do a limited amount of physical damage but not in excess of what we could live with. Hence, while we could expect sporadic terrorist incidents, there was no need to panic. This view made sense given the ephemeral character of terrorist ideology. Compared to the possibility of nuclear holocaust, the terrorist threat seemed minimal. Terrorist attacks against the West seemed of even less moment with the fall of the Soviet Union and the general demise of leftism. The "end of history" was duly declared and the two thousandth anniversary of the birth of Christ was celebrated as the apotheosis of secularism, liberalism, and capitalism with nothing but blue skies ahead.

This happy vision of the previous two years was devastated by the events of September 11. It would, I believe, be a grave error to regard what has happened as merely another episode in the long history of terrorism. To his credit, President Bush appears to understand this. This is so because, unlike the terrorist groups of the second half of the preceding century, Islamic fundamentalism represents a deep and coherent ideology stretching back fourteen centuries and that is interiorized into the souls of millions of people. It is, moreover, fueled by a great anxiety that a way of life is threatened with extinction. Islam is a religion in the fullness of that term—an all-encompassing commitment to what is ultimately real. Resurgent Islam is a challenge to Western interests not through the destruction of life and property as such but by undermining that consumerist morale essential to a "prosperous" economy. Modern capitalist life is founded not on producing essential goods but on producing advertising-driven products that people do not want or need. This state of mind presupposes a view of the world as essentially benign. In earlier times great disasters were seen as a divine reminder of our mortality and the essential futility of all purely human ends and as a spur to contemplation at the Last Things. Such thinking is fatal to consumerism, which depends upon treating as ends the goods of this world. Already, we are daily admonished to return as quickly as possible to mindless consumption lest the economy fall into recession. While the West faces nothing as remotely devastating as the Cold War threat of nuclear holocaust, there is the possibility of serious culture and economic shock.

Part of the stunning horror of the World Trade Center attack was the spectacle of an immense structure invested with the spirit of the age suddenly not there. It is rare that we so radically confront the nature of evil as nonbeing, as the absence or privation of good. The scope, rapidity, and finality of this event and its future portents naturally call for reflection. In particular, does this event mesh with larger historical forces, or is it merely the expression of the hatred of the few? Given the scope of the operation and the careful planning behind it stretching over many years, we must obviously think about this event in a larger explanatory framework.

In the *Republic*, Plato develops a theory of human nature that stipulates two fundamental facts.[1] The first is that human beings cannot fully flourish without truth. Man has a natural telos for his first cause. He needs to know the explanation of everything that is. For Plato, the philosopher is the highest form of human life precisely because he recognizes this natural unqualified eros toward truth. He cannot rest content in the shadows (rationalizations) of the cave but must work his way out into the sunlight of reality. It thus becomes his duty as a just man to return to the cave and liberate from ignorance his fellow men. This duty reveals the second main necessity of human nature.

Plato's philosopher cannot remain with his private vision of the good because human fulfillment is corporate. Complete human flourishing occurs only in the polis. While there is in persons a natural eros toward truth, societies as such do not naturally conform to the order of truth: The order of politics is not the order of Being. Hence, Plato's challenge is how to create a corporate order in which the philosopher can live, that is, in which man can perfect himself according to his nature. The *Republic* is Plato's answer: There will be no happiness until philosophers become kings and kings become philosophers. This powerful image of the good society united by its ordination to the transcendent dominates much of the history of philosophy and culture in the West.

While Plato was skeptical about the possibility of such a community ever actually existing (perhaps it is laid up in heaven, he says) the rise of Christian and Islamic monotheism saw attempts to create the holy state. For both these religions, the medieval period represented the high point of such endeavors. The purpose of the state for both these religions was to assist the salvation of souls. Enforced uniformity of belief was necessary to protect souls from those errors that might lead to the loss of heaven. Hence, laws enforcing belief were acts of charity, and heresy was seen as a kind of treason punishable by death. The Crusades were a clash of absolutes, opposed views of truth. But behind this clash was a profound mutual understanding that truth mattered. In a sense, these religions incorporated Plato's insight regarding the need of a transcendent foundation for the social order. Man is ordained to his first cause, which turns out to be the eternal God. This life is a vale of tears in which that soul formation occurs that determines our place in Heaven or Hell. Human choice, thus understood, has a cosmic significance.

The sixteenth century Protestant schism was, at its heart, about private judgment versus the infallible magisterium of the church. While Protestants retained the Bible as an objective standard of truth, private judgment inevitably relativized it. With truth relativized there was a natural progression to political pluralism.

The savage wars of religion that resulted from the break-up of Christendom culminated in the Peace of Westphalia, which sought social peace by setting aside the question of religious truth. The religion of each country would copy its monarch's faith. The stage was now set for getting God out of public life altogether. Eighteeth-century deism represented a rear-guard effort to retain some transcendent truth by making God a cosmic watchmaker who set the universe going and then promptly retired. Deism was a compromise between the perceived need for a transcendent standard and the wholesale abandonment of any effort to understand nature in theological terms. Darwin put the final seal on God's nonparticipation in the cosmos. It only remained for Nietzsche to announce that it was all over. But Nietzsche, prophetic as always, realized that this was not an unalloyed good. For if Christianity was a slave religion to which we should bid good riddance, we still had the problem of man's need for transcendence. This he found in the aesthetic concept of the Superman, an idea that led directly to the false transcendence of fascism and communism. Twentieth-century experiments in these ideologies proved devastating as they all sought to make immanent the transcendent in a pointless quest for the true polis. Marxism, especially, was a pale imitation of Christianity, mimicking its eschatology in a final revolution that would usher in heaven on earth.[2]

Although the post–Cold War announcement of the end of history was an exaggeration, that idea heralded an important insight: pluralism has outlasted all its enemies. Nowhere did pluralism take deeper root than in America, with its guarantees of free speech and its separation of church and state. While pluralism was born for essentially pragmatic reasons (social peace), an ideology of natural rights developed to give it a semblance of transcendence—freedom had now become an end in itself.

Because of the historical origins of pluralism as the search for social peace, foundational questions are denied serious consideration. That is, questions of the ultimate meaning of human life are made irrelevant to social change. Reason is thereby trivialized since ultimate truth is ruled as impossible of corporate attainment. Foundational questions are suppressed not in the sense that discussion of them is censored—far from it, free speech is central to pluralist ideology. Rather, pluralist society is immune from any formal modification in light of such discussions. Pluralism permits and encourages all points of view except its replacement. The question of a common truth by which all men shall live is effectively suppressed. People are free to seek their own meanings as long as these are compatible with others doing the same thing. The only overarching good is social peace. Pluralist ideology touts freedom of speech as a necessary condition in the search of truth, but then it turns out that the search is neverending, or, rather, the search is an end in itself.

As no society can be entirely bereft of shared values, pluralism does generate its own set of goods by default. One of these is not religion. Polls consistently report that 90 percent of Americans believe that God is the ultimate source of meaning. But in pluralist society religion is firmly privatized as especially threatening to social peace. Freedom of religion permits people to hold whatever beliefs they want as long as they are not imposed on the body politic. This has the effect of leaving us with a form of pragmatic atheism by default. For example, the prohibition of prayer in public schools means that a graduating class is forced to behave, as a corporate body, as if atheism were true. They are forced to declare in everything they say or do that their proceedings have no transcendent significance. Each member may pray (or not) privately, but the communal life of the group, which is after all what they are together to celebrate, must remain resolutely atheistical for all practical purposes. Hence, pluralism inexorably generates secularism. So, while 90 percent of Americans are theist, the remaining 10 percent dominate the public order.

What then are the values of secular pluralism? They are, at least, three in number. First, in the absence of a Platonic polis, or the aspiration to one, acquisition of power for its own sake assumes great urgency since the only social bond is the negative injunction to avoid harm to others. Any other aspiration is viewed as "mere opinion." In such a world maximization of individual autonomy becomes both an ideal and a precaution. Second, as serious proposals for a unifying social vision are precluded, pluralist societies will discover goods that all can agree upon at the level of the lowest possible common denominator. Traditional vices such as avarice, gluttony, lust, and envy come to be seen as rights. Pluralist society is necessarily consumerist. It is dominated by the economic question and its populations are regarded primarily as producers and consumers. Because this is a false and demeaning understanding of human life, it tends to break down when confronted by reality. In response to the attacks of September 11, bioterrorism, and the like, most Americans have become suddenly reflective with respect to the sufficiency of pluralist/ secularist goods. We face here Plato's challenge as to how to satisfy the ineluctable social dimension of human flourishing. For Plato is surely correct that such flourishing requires participation in common goods such as friendship, justice, and the pursuit of knowledge, all of which are impossible of attainment in the isolation of a pluralist society conceived as merely a loose collection of individuals united only in the pursuit of enlightened self-interest. This is why it is dismaying to hear our leaders exhorting us to return at once to a mindless consumerism lest the economy collapse and the very foundations of pluralism/secularism be undermined.

Third, a society based on consumerism creates a culture of infantilism wherein entertainment and sexual gratification become all-consuming. Tremendous resources are expended on entertainment understood as a creation of an ersatz reality. The chief form this takes is an obsession with sexual gratification entirely divorced from a communion of persons and the transmission of life. All the social pathologies of pluralist society are directly traceable to the chronic incapacity to achieve sexual self-mastery. Indeed, the aforementioned values play off each other—sex is used to fuel consumerism, power lies in possessions, entertainment drives us deeper into infantilism. In short, the failure of pluralist society to achieve a genuine order creates a permanent disjunction between public life and the eros to the transcendent. Hence, since the 1960s when pluralism emerged as triumphant there has been an ongoing culture war. The attacks of September 11 and subsequent terrorist episodes are part of what has now become the global dimension of that war. With the fall of the Soviet Union, Marxism was no longer a credible alternative to pluralism. This left the United States with its immense power, its omnipresence, and its seductive values as a triumphant threat to traditional societies. For good reason deeply conservative Islam fears America, the Great Satan. For what did Satan offer if not the illusion of freedom as autonomy? One deep irony of our situation is that Americans individually are the most religious of people—nine out of ten Americans declare themselves Christians—so it is interesting to see how religion has been forced into a pluralist mode. Perhaps most instructive is the case of the Catholic Church.[3] Traditional Catholicism shares with Islam the idea of a holy state. The Catholic position toward American pluralism was from the beginning that the church would take advantage of freedom of religion as a means of building up a Catholic society whose positive law would come eventually to reflect natural law and wherein Catholicism would be the predominant faith. Protestant suspicions of the compatibility of Catholicism with American pluralism were, in fact, entirely justified, as an examination of nineteenth- and early twentieth-century papal encyclicals will demonstrate.[4] By midcentury Catholics were well on their way to becoming the majority religion due to prolific childbearing. Living in self-organized enclaves with their own schools, hospitals, and colleges, Catholics began to construct a powerful alternative society. Look, for example, at how the Catholic Legion of Decency dictated the content of Hollywood movies from the '30s into the '60s. But the very success of Catholics in the post–World War II period took them out of their exile into Protestant suburbs, where they quickly assimilated the values of pluralism. The central symbol of the new Catholicism was JFK, the first Catholic president. But the price of this acceptance was a complete repudiation of traditional Catholic teaching on church-state relations. A case in point is JFK's famous assurance to a group of Baptist ministers that his Catholicism would have no bearing whatsoever on his decisions as president. The taming of the Catholic Church was completed by Vatican II, which produced a document on religious liberty that suppressed the ideal of a Catholic state.

The documents of Vatican II mark a historical power shift: If you want to live in the modern world, you will adapt to secular pluralism. The spectacle of the world's largest and only georeligion being humbled by the forces of modernity was certainly not lost on Islam, which itself had been battered by the forces of Western imperialism. Secular descriptions of Islamic societies as "medieval" and as bastions of backwardness and superstition draw the battle lines with great clarity from a Muslim perspective. Islamic hostility to the West is based primarily on a moral abhorrence of what they see as profound spiritual decadence—rampant consumerism, abortion, divorce, contraception, sexual perversion, the exploitation of women forced by subtle propaganda into the workforce leaving their children in the care of others, and the expulsion of religion from public life. Muslims are not alone here. These objections resonate with traditional Catholics and Protestants living within pluralist societies.

Hence, I would argue that what motivates radical Islam is not some traditional impulse to convert the world via jihad with hordes of the warriors of God but, rather, fear for the utter destruction of a traditional way of life. Such fear is certainly justified. Pluralism is immensely attractive. Pluralists sacrifice truth for social peace through the exaltation of human autonomy. For many people this may be a price worth paying. Indeed, it may seem to exact no cost at all. But we should be in no doubt what that price is, for in the end every substantive question, every deeply held religious or philosophical conviction is trumped by the (default) values of pluralism. These values as we have seen are base and unworthy of a full human life. The present reports on the liberation of Kabul describe the first actions of individuals to be watching TV and turning up their stereos to top volume. The *New York Times* describes hordes of Afghans, eyes glazed and mouths agape, mesmerized by a trashy Indian movie. These were the first fruits of their freedom.

There has been much controversy recently over whether the dominant intellectual categories of postmodernism and deconstruction are adequate to comprehend the attacks of September 11. According to the postmodernist story, we need to learn to live "lightly" in a present where the expressions "true and false, meaning and meaninglessness" have dropped from use.[5] What remains is the morally neutral aesthetic project of individual self-creation. It follows that on rational or moral grounds there is no difference between the September 11 victims and their killers. As the bodies that fell from the World Trade Center formed a most beautiful arc of descent, anyone preferring or embracing this perspective cannot be faulted. No event is truly good or evil; any event may be redescribed in an infinity of ways.

In fact, public reaction to the war on terrorism has been to return overwhelmingly to traditional values, especially religion. Does this portend a serious reappraisal of secularism? Postmodernism is the logical outcome of the (mistaken) Enlightenment belief that one can get rid of God and still have some use for the word "true." Insofar as the postmodernist critique of the Enlightenment yields a kind of moral nihilism it is inadequate to confront real evil. In light of our horror at the mass murder of three thousand innocent people, are we prepared to honestly reexamine other dimensions of the culture of death? It so happens that there are four thousand children killed every day in this country by abortion. Heretofore, the ruling elites have "redefined" this extermination under the pluralist banner of "choice." Will we continue to see this and similar issues as mere questions of personal opinion?

An illuminating example of pluralism in action is a recent article by columnist Ellen Goodman entitled "The Other Terrorism in America," in which she asserts a moral equivalence between the September 11 attackers and those who bomb abortion clinics. "Terrorists of both stripes shape the same intolerance. The Army of God and the soldiers of the jihad find support in the words of those who would never fly a plane into a tower or send anthrax to a senator. These are people who 'merely' provide a 'moral' framework for violence by labeling Americans as 'infidels' or doctors as 'murderers.' "

What makes this a classic pluralist statement is the charge that those who regard abortion as unjust killing and those who see America as a culture of death are morally culpable of aiding terrorism. That is to say, pluralism cannot accommodate its critics. One wonders, is the terrorist violence a product of criticisms of pluralist values or is it the result of a steadfast refusal to honestly confront the foundational question of what constitutes a good society?

If great evils are being tolerated in the name of social peace then admonishing critics to shut up will hardly discourage violence. It is only by assuming the absolute correctness, the inviolability, of pluralist arguments that such censorship could be justified.

That pluralism carries its own evaluative baggage must be confronted, and is being confronted by the continuing violence. It will no doubt continue until we are willing to grapple with substantive issues. This means more than simply permitting discussion about these issues but being committed to embrace alternative possibilities. That is, peace is not possible if we continue to sidestep substantive moral controversy by falling back on "choice."

In his discussion of perfect societies in the *Republic*, Plato ranks democracy low on the scale just adjacent to tyranny. By democracy Plato is not, of course, speaking of modern representational democracy as a political decision procedure, but rather as a culture of relative or nonexistent truth. Plato has many complimentary things to say about democracy thus understood.

He describes pluralism as the most attractive of all societies and compares its diversity to the different colors in a patterned dress. Most people he thinks would judge this to be the best form of society, like women and children who judge by appearances. It is an agreeable, somewhat anarchic kind of society that "treats all men as equal, whether they are equal or not."

Why does Plato speak in such a favorable way of pluralistic society? The answer I think lies in the final paragraph of Book 6. Plato doubts that the republic he has described will ever exist. And his ultimate pessimism about the social order is articulated in a powerful statement on the philosopher ruler. Only a small remnant will survive of all those who are worthy to be philosophers. And this small company when they have experienced the happiness of philosophy and seen the frenzy of popular life will live quietly and keep to themselves "like a man who stands under the shelter of a wall during a driving storm of dust and hail; they see the rest of the world full of wrongdoing and are content to keep themselves unspotted from wickedness in this life, and finally leave it with cheerful composure and good hope." It is for this reason that Plato finds something good to say about pluralist society. Precisely because pluralism does not care for any but the basest of goods, the philosopher can find a place to hide. As no one in pluralist society cares about fundamental questions (they live as if there are no such questions) the philosopher can persist in his own views as long as they are privatized. This is, of course, a deeply pessimistic conclusion and one that tacitly admits the impossibility of a truly human life, a life that on Plato's own reckoning is inseparable from the holy polis.

The seductive attractiveness of pluralism is its freedom understood as contentless, waiting to be filled with private visions of the good. As I have argued, this position embodies an intolerable contradiction on Plato's terms, and one that continues to explode in the violence of culture war locally and globally. We are made for transcendence. Goods latent in human nature cry out for realization in the form of a common good. The self is fulfilled only through forgetfulness of the self and the unconditional embrace of the good whereby the will seeks satiation. Pluralist society continually represses this eros by firmly privatizing all moral visions in the pursuit of social peace. Hence, transcendence is forever turned back upon itself. Such repression cannot forever be tolerated. For to deny transcendence is to deny our common humanity. If repressive contradictions are not defused by reason, they will explode in unreason. And so it becomes ever more difficult to find "the shelter of a wall."

PART II: PROSPECTS

Let us make it clear at the outset that any government, no matter what its past transgressions or cultural defects, has a duty to defend its people from being massacred. Hence, the robust military campaign in Afghanistan and elsewhere is morally necessary. One hopes that such operations now and in the future can be conducted according to the traditional principles of a just war. But obviously the elusiveness of the terrorists makes this difficult. The war against terrorism is more akin to the war against crime, and, therefore, the fighting will likely be long-term and sporadic. Victory will often be less than complete.

All the same, it is important to hold before us constantly the fact that we are involved in a culture war. Hence, attempts to placate the terrorists by, for example, distancing ourselves from Israel would not accomplish very much since Israel is seen by Islam as a pluralist/secular beachhead—most Israelis are, in fact, secular Jews.

My argument is that the Islamic critique of Western secular pluralism is cogent but not, of course, the employment of terrorism as a means of implementing the core vision of traditional Islam: a state wherein the positive law reflects the moral law and where religion is not privitized but rules over all things pertaining to salvation.

This being made completely clear, we may again ask if these terrible and ongoing events of the recent past might be the occasion for reflection and reconsideration of secular pluralism. While secular pluralism has a long evolutionary reach all the way back to the Reformation, its current dominant form emerged in the 1960s. Prior to that it could be said that America had pretensions to a moral order. Is it likely that Islam would have seen us as the Great Satan in 1950? Religion was not yet privatized and the churches played a central role in articulating the good life. Abortion, divorce, newborns denied the protection of committed parents, homosexuality, violence, pornography, recreational sex, suicide, and euthanasia and out-of-control STDs were socially repudiated or prohibited by law. I do not speak here of a "golden age" of morality. Rather, I make the point that there was a commitment to the ideal of objective moral truth and that religion played a big role in stipulating a metaphysical concept of human nature. Americans were intensely democratic but not yet pervasively secular. Transcendence was still an ideal however inadequately realized. One could still speak without blushing of America as a "Christian country." By the late 1960s happiness and fulfillment had become decidedly this-worldly.

The pluralist secular mentality has been strongly abetted by the rise of global capitalism. Capitalism is extremely destructive of traditional societies and of ideologies of transcendence. Recent violent protests against globalization have cut across the usual political lines, uniting such disparate figures as Ralph Nader and Pat Buchannan. Many of these protesters are environmentalists, new agers, animal rights activists, and others who share a conception of the natural order as something other than merely instrumental. In this respect they also reflect an ordination toward transcendence. They espouse meanings larger than those merely human pragmatic concerns that drive a consumerist based secular pluralism. The immense power and reach of global capitalism virtually guarantee that profit and loss will dominate the social order, thus converting nature into a mere object of use.

As disparate as these groups may be, they share an implicit quest for an objective order of meaning, a common belief in a greater than merely human signification, a quest that puts them at odds with pluralism, its base values, and "choice." If Plato is correct that pluralism cannot ultimately satisfy the urge toward transcendent meaning, we can expect the global culture wars to continue and intensify. While man cannot live a truly human life without transcendent meaning, pluralism requires that such meaning be subordinate to its requirements or be eliminated altogether. In the end postmodern nihilism is the only available philosophy for pluralism. This subordination means that subsidiary organizations such as church and family are fatally weakened as bearers of meaning because they know, at the end of the day, that they are merely another of the many "choices" that make up pluralist society. The immense energy of global capitalism splinters these frail structures, reducing their members to individual consumers, minds filled with advertising jingles.

In a recent article Salman Rushdie stated the issue most uncompromisingly from the perspective of pluralism: "The restoration of religion to the sphere of the personal, its depoliticization, is the nettle that all Muslim societies must grasp in order to become modern. The only aspect of modernity interesting to the terrorists is technology, which they see as a weapon that can be turned on its makers. If terrorism is to be defeated, the world of Islam must take on board the secularist-humanist principles on which the modern is based, and without which Muslim countries' freedom will remain a distant dream."[6] The hubris of this remark is breathtaking. It illustrates the degree to which secular pluralism reigns in the West as an unquestionable ideology. The secular pluralist believes that his is the position of neutral reasonableness above the clash of ideologies when, in fact, its demand for the privatization of the quest for transcendence in the name of an unctuous moral tolerance is as absolutist as any of the "religions" that it hates.

Plato's democratic man is happy and carefree because he thinks he *is* his freedom. He thinks he is free no matter what he chooses. But the philosopher knows that his freedom aims for the perfection of his nature by conforming it to the good, the true, and the beautiful. Within a pluralist society indifferent to truth the philosopher may perhaps hide and nurse his dreams. But unless pluralism is able to imagine its own demise, not all will choose to hide.

NOTES

1. See *Republic*. Book 8, 543–592.

2. For a full account of this history, see John C. Rao, *Americanism* (Norwalk, CT: Dietrich Von Hildebrand Institute, 1995).

3. See Rao, *Americanism*.

4. Pius XII, *Mortalium Animos*.

5. Richard Rorty, *Objectivity, Relativism and Truth* (Cambridge: Cambridge University Press, 1991).

6. *New York Times*, November 2, 2001.

CHAPTER 6

Can a Muslim Be a Terrorist?

ZAYN KASSAM

CAN A MUSLIM BE A TERRORIST?[1]

Sure, why not, I wonder, for so can a Jew, a Hindu, a Sikh, a Catholic, or, indeed, a member of any faith. The difficult question is whether the religion with which terrorists are aligned actually teaches, promotes, or requires them to engage in terrorism as their religious duty. Painfully, for the majority of the world's Muslims, many contemporary headlines and opinion pieces in the news announce the verdict: Islam teaches jihad and honors suicide bombings with a safe passageway to heaven replete with flowing rivers of milk and honey and the promise of doe-eyed virgins. Such a verdict contrasts with the view most Muslims themselves hold: They think of their religion as one of peace consequent upon the act of surrender (*islam*) to the divine being they consider synonymous with the God of the Hebrew Bible and the New Testament.

Despite the efforts of many academics who study Islam ("Islamologists" or "Islamicists") and journalists to show that the Quranic term "jihad" (literally, "struggle, effort") must be understood in its historical context, the term has come to signify a central tenet of the Islamic faith to the popular mind and conveys the notion that all Muslims are religiously predisposed to violence and hate. In a rhetorical gesture designed to replace Communism with Islam as the new other or enemy of Western civilization, the imaginary of the Muslim as unreasonable, rigid, and authoritarian continues to be projected in the popular media, whether through profiles of single Muslim men such as Saddam Hussein or Osama bin Laden or through characterizations of the entire faith of Islam, such as those articulated most recently by Franklin Graham, son of Reverend Billy Graham. In its seventh-century context, jihad was not directed against members of other monotheistic faiths but rather was to be conducted in response to the persecution visited upon the nascent Muslim community by the rulers

114

of Mecca, the Quraysh, who perceived in Muhammad a direct threat to their political and economic hegemony. As such, then, jihad, or armed struggle, was not to be initiated except in response to an attack, or when no other course was feasible; only when these conditions were met was it permissible to take another human life during jihad. Nor was armed struggle, according to the narratives (*hadith*, plural *ahadith*) recorded in historical memory as depicting the words and actions of the Prophet to be considered the best aspect of religiosity, for the "greater jihad" was identified as the internal jihad or struggle against one's soul in the practice of righteousness. In its subsequent historical development, jihad against those outside the boundaries of Muslim domains was considered to be one of the responsibilities of the caliph or ruler, again only to be undertaken when the other side struck first or in defense, and never to be initiated by an individual, only by the ruler of the Islamic polity. Self-immolation is denounced in the Quran; a soldier who died defending the early Islamic community, on the other hand, was declared a martyr for defending his faith. There are parallels here with nascent Christian communities whose members were martyred by non-Christian state officials. Is every war in which a Muslim finds himself (or herself) a jihad? No. Muslims, in their variety of languages, have developed a vocabulary for wars that are not undertaken in defense of their religion but rather in defense of their territory: the terms *jang* and *harb* are two such examples.

COLONIZATION AND ITS DISCONTENTS

Unfortunately, in the contemporary postcolonial world, such fine distinctions have been lost on Muslims currently engaged in struggling for their causes, whatever they may be. There are several reasons for the coupling of religious language with the language of struggle. First and foremost, the otherizing by colonial powers of their Muslim populations, a process that has been documented by Edward Said and others, facilitated a delineation of the difference between the colonizers and the colonized in terms that were set up as religious, since the religion of Islam was blamed by the colonizers as responsible for the backwardness of the subject peoples, especially exemplified in the segregation of women from the public sphere. Such a discourse served to justify to home constituencies the continued presence of colonial powers in the colonies, as well as the need to civilize—and indeed Christianize—the backward infidel (notwithstanding the efforts made to squash suffragette movements in the home countries). Such an attitude built upon a long history of distrust and repugnance toward Muslims, going back as far as the Crusades with respect to the *religion* of the Muslims, and to the Graeco-Persian wars with respect to the *ethnicities* of such Muslims. Colonizing discourses also laid the parameters of any resistance to those colonizing powers within the language of a religious struggle for self-determination and self-rule. Since adherence to Islam was made responsible for the perceived backwardness of the subject peoples, the counterargument produced by those peoples was precisely that Islam would rescue them from subordination.

Second, despite the rhetoric of delivery of civilizational tools to the subject peoples, the intensely poor quality of educational, health, and civic services provided to the populations while simultaneously draining the subject territories of their natural and labor resources resulted in either slow development or maldevelopment of the human resources among subject peoples, in addition to eroding traditional cultures.

Thus, formerly colonized Muslim nations entered the era of independence and self-rule beset with challenges that are likely to endure for some decades to come. The first of these challenges consists of the need to modernize given the fact that internal cultural processes of self-determination had lost much of their social and cultural, not to mention political, integrity in the intervention of the colonial powers. Such a historical intervention had introduced Western-style education and institutions, whether acquired at home or abroad, into the cultural frameworks of subject peoples, and newly emergent independent nations were well aware that their survival and ongoing viability as nations depended on their ability to be players in the Western hegemonic realm of economics and politics. The resulting agony over whether modernization entailed survival through a wholesale adoption of Western practices and ideologies or whether modernization was possible in a manner integrated into traditional cultural and religious praxis has been explored in the novels of Naguib Mahfouz, Yahya al-Haqqi, Cheikh Hamidou Kane, Salman Rushdie, Attiya Hossein, Ismat Chhughtai, Aziz Necin, Orhan Pamuk, and Sadegh Hedayat, to mention just a few. Kane, for instance, in his novel *Ambiguous Adventure* articulates the struggle thus: "It suddenly occurs to us that, all along our road, we have not ceased to metamorphose ourselves, and we see ourselves as other than what we were. Sometimes the metamorphosis is not even finished. We have turned ourselves into hybrids, and there we are left. Then we hide ourselves, filled with shame."[2] A distinction must be made between modernization understood as technologization, and modernization understood as Westernization. For many Muslims, enjoying the fruits of scientific progress is seen as a form of divine bounty; Westernization, on the other hand, is fraught with issues of power and domination and exemplifies societies that have lost their moral moorings. Modernization as Westernization connotes secularization or the separation of religion from public life, especially politics, and herein lies the crux of the debate between Muslim modernists, who argue that religion should be separated from what is in the best interests of society (itself a laudable religious aim), and Muslim conservatives, who argue that indeed the best interests of society lie in the re-Islamization of public institutions, including the law.

Connected to the challenge of modernization lies a second challenge, the challenge of identity. Does modernization necessitate imbuing Western culture along with Western technology? Boroujerdi, writing on Iranian intellectual life,[3] makes an observation that could well be extended to the entire formerly colonized Muslim world, that is, that all things Western are necessarily mediated through the lens of the (unhappily) remembered colonized experience. The search for an authentically local form of modernization was on, and resistance to Western forms of modernization formed part and parcel of the quest for a national identity that was struggling to be modern in its use of technology and ability to parlay at the economic table of emergent globalization, and yet culturally resonant with its own history, social institutions, and peoples.

The relationship between largely Muslim-populated nations and Western nations was an uneasy one during much of the twentieth century. The end of colonization certainly did not spell the end of first European, and then American, influence in Muslim regions. While others in this book and elsewhere have more substantively explored such relationships, suffice it here to draw attention to several factors that militate against harmonious relationships unless addressed. One such factor relates to the consequences of carving up Palestine in order to create the country of Israel. The lack of reparation to displaced Palestinians, the continued Palestinian refugee camps, the building of settlements and military roads through internationally agreed-upon Palestinian territories, the uneven distribution of water in the Occupied Territories, the withholding of taxes from Palestinian enterprises, and the international upholding of the fiction that there are two equal and opposite "countries" struggling against each other are some of the reasons underlying the violence that is, unfortunately, now not only characteristic of but also a daily occurrence in the region. The massive American fiscal support of Israel and the largely unflagging European and American moral support of Israeli policies toward the Palestinians—who, until recently, comprised also a sizeable Christian population—have led to the perception that the "West" is still Crusader-like, antagonistic toward its formerly colonized Muslim peoples, and that the Western civilized world's rhetoric of democracy, human rights, international conventions, and fair play do not matter when it comes to Palestine.

Another factor relates to the Cold War, in which several Muslim nations became pawns in a larger power struggle between the forces of capitalism and the forces of communism, and in smaller power struggles between Muslim nations. The case of Afghanistan is particularly poignant, as its ability to chart its own course after the departure of the British remained continually at risk given its strategic positioning between Soviet Central Asian territories and the Middle East. The training of Afghani Mujahiddin through American- and Saudi-funded[4] (via Pakistan's Interservices Intelligence Directorate, ISI) installations and personnel accomplished several objectives: It gave the Afghans a sense of purpose in removing the Soviets from their soil, dovetailing with larger American interests in limiting Soviet spheres of influence. However, at the same time, in order to impel the Mujahiddin to fight, a connection had to be made between the notion of jihad and the liberation of Afghanistan; whether credible or not, a *Washington Post* article suggests that USAID-funded "textbooks filled with violent images and militant Islamic teachings, part of covert attempts to spur resistance to the Soviet occupation" were developed at the University of Nebraska (Omaha)'s Center for Afghanistan Studies.[5] John K. Cooley chillingly suggests that American, Pakistani, and Saudi funding and collaboration in support of Islamist groups was based on "(t)he tacit consensus . . . that the Muslim religion, fundamentally anti-Communist, if translated into politics, could be harnessed as a mighty force to oppose Moscow in the Cold War, in a world growingly polarized by that war."[6] Further, the recruitment of Muslims from outside of Afghanistan to assist in the effort led to the internationalization of ideologically driven militants now ready to take on the task of engaging in vigilante military activity should the rationale, however irrational, demand it. Once the Soviets had been forced out of Afghanistan, the land was left to its own devices, and in disarray, hence fertile ground for the Islamist recruitment, especially in the Afghan refugee *madrasabs* (literally, "a place in which to study," that is, school or classroom) along the Afghan-Pakistani border and the subsequent establishment of the Taliban who, in turn, provided ready fodder for the likes of Osama bin Laden. The rest is history. The smaller power struggle between the Pakistani need to have a pliable neighbor to the north in order to safeguard its borders to the south ensured their preference for Islamists rather than left-leaning Afghan leadership, thereby providing logistical and government support and encouragement to a politicized form of Islam rather than to Muslims who sought to modernize their country and address the challenges facing development without drawing religious norms into the equation. While this author is by no means advocating leftist as opposed to capitalist forms of economy, the point is that the support needed to address the problems of rebuilding Afghanistan was directed toward a small group that saw the answer in religiously fundamentalist terms rather than in drawing upon the rich intellectual-, creative-, and social justice–oriented heritage of prior Islamic societies.

A third factor relates to the politics of access to oil. The establishment of military bases in oil-bearing regions and the propping up of governments and leaders friendly to American and European interests have been detrimental to the growth of democracy and institutions devoted to social welfare in the region. One might wonder whether the discovery of oil has been a curse as it has assured American and other foreign intervention in the politics of the region.

Thus, challenges to Western culture, perceived as rapacious and self-serving—despite the attempt of courses on Western civilization that paint it as glorious, humanistic, and universalistic in its hopes of rights and dignity for all humans—were given voice more than fifty years ago, long before the Mujahiddin were trained in Afghanistan largely to serve Western purposes. Iranian thinkers such as Jalal Al-i Ahmed (d. 1969) in Iran coined the term gharbzadegi, literally "born of the West," but commonly translated as "westoxification." Other thinkers such as Abu al-Ala Mawdudi (d. 1979) in Pakistan and Sayyid Qutb (d. 1966) in Egypt, along with Ibn al-Wahhab's (d. 1792) interpretation of Islam (regnant in Saudi Arabia), contributed toward forming totalizing conceptualizations of what it means to be Muslim in a

Muslim society governed by Muslim institutions. In all of these, the influence of the writings of the medieval Syrian jurist Ibn Taymiyya (d. 1328), who was left to languish in prison, are clearly apparent. Thinkers such as these, whose Shiite parallel may be found in Iran's Ayatollah Khomeini and his successors, defined their visions of an Islamic "orthodoxy" that is exclusivist, anti-Western, and highly shariah oriented in the hopes of inculcating pride in the Islamic tradition in an attempt to create Islamic nations that would provide an alternate model to Western nations. Drawing upon the ideologies provided by such orthodoxy creationists, innumerable groups have sprung up all over the Islamic, and now Western, world, in the hopes of garnering political power that would ensure the running of Muslim states in a Muslim manner as defined by such ideologues, and thereby able to resist Western control over minds, resources, culture, and politics while simultaneously reinstating pride in Islam and self-governance—hence the definition of an Islamist as one who holds that every aspect of a Muslim's life must be governed by Islam through shariah law and whose ultimate aim is to take over the reins of both public and private life and to regulate these according to the particular legal regime of the orthodoxy creator to whom they subscribe. While all Islamists are Muslim, all Muslims are not Islamists. Further, while all Islamists subscribe to versions of the ideology stated here, the majority of these do not believe in utilizing physically violent means in achieving their aims, although some Islamist groups do have an organizational arm devoted to that purpose. A case in point is Hamas, whose main body concerns itself with the delivery of social services, while its militant arm, 'Izz al-Din al-Qasim, is often cited as responsible for what it considers "acts of justice" or retaliation.

Debate, discussion, and rhetorical as well as legal and military struggles ensued through much of the Islamic world in the twentieth century regarding the extent to which Islamic praxis, institutions, and ideologies should play a role in civic life and societal organization. Efforts to "Islamize" already Muslim populations were thus carried out, for instance, in Pakistan, under the regime of General Zia ul-Haq (in command from 1976 to 1988), who placed a shariah bench in the law courts and moved to pass the Hudood Ordinances of 1979 (making rape and adultery practically synonymous), as well as the Shariat Bill in 1985 (passed in 1991), with their disastrous consequences for women. Similar efforts are also underway in Malaysia, the Sudan, and Nigeria, to name but a few. Perhaps the most obvious examples of an

attempt to Islamicize all aspects of social, political and cultural interaction are in Iran and Afghanistan, the first under Khomeini and the
second under the Taliban. While the two are by no means synonymous since Iran is Ithna Ashari or Twelver Shiite, whereas the Taliban
espoused an extreme form of Sunni Islam, they are similar in their attempt to totalize their discrete understandings of "correct" Islam and
Islamic praxis over all aspects of society and civic life.

THE REACH OF ISLAMISM

Why would Muslims seek to support such totalizing ideologies, such
narrow understandings of a rich, diverse, and intellectually and culturally vibrant tradition expressed in the many historically discrete
forms of Islam ("Islams," as dubbed by Aziz Al-Azmeh)[7] already present in the world? Part of the success experienced by Islamist groups
is because of the widespread educational efforts funded in many instances by oil wealth, which do not hesitate to utilize modern technological advances for the purpose of *da'wah*, or missionizing. Part
relates to the fact that religion is so deeply intertwined with cultural
life as to be inseparable from it, and piety is a valued characteristic.
Thus, many Muslims feel that they are advancing their piety through
knowledge (*'ilm*) about their faith, and the notion that piety is best
expressed through adherence to religious law (*shariah*) makes complete the hold of religion over every aspect of life. The lack of training in the humanities and in developing critical thinking skills in general education curricula means that religious instruction is virtually
uncritically accepted as being divine in origin, and hence not to be
questioned without earning the charge of being an infidel, perhaps
among the worst offenses a Muslim could commit. Part of the success
relies on the fact that many recruits to Islamist thinking are materially impoverished and feel that the slogan of the Islamists, that is, "Islam is the solution," will provide a panacea to their social discomfi-
ture. Others, those who flock from the rural areas to the cities in
pursuit of work opportunities or an education, deal with cultural dis-
location by resorting to an ideology that will keep them safe from the
cosmopolitan and uncertain nature of social relations in the city. Still
others, the upwardly mobile young, faced with the often corrupt, in-
efficient and authoritarian governments that cannot provide adequate
jobs, deliver social services, or political stability, let alone a presence
on the world stage politically or with respect to globalization, find in

the Islamist ideologies, varied as these are geographically, a platform on which to mount resistance both against their own regimes as well as at the hegemonic power of the West, especially the United States. And part of the success lies in the fact that many Islamist groups provide much-needed education (albeit through the religious schools, the *madrasahs*), social services, a sense of community, a sense of direction and purpose, and a projection of a worldwide Muslim *ummah* (community) that must work toward establishing socially just societies on earth. While all of these provisions assist in motivating the ordinary pious Muslim recruited to the Islamist cause to turn into activists, and while such activism is usually directed at local causes, it is not difficult to see how such ideologies could easily be turned toward causes that go beyond the borders of any specific region. Access to military training and arms completes the capability for making a perceived just cause sufficient reason to engage in armed activity: ideology coupled with perceived causes coupled with arms and training. It would be untrue to say that all Islamists are trained to engage in armed combat, for perhaps many stop at introducing piety through the shariah into all aspects of their lives, just as it would be untrue to say that all militant Islamists are necessarily shariah observant, for if they were, then the Quranic principles of tolerance, compassion, pluralism, and sanctions against killing might be taken far more seriously.

Another factor that complicates the relationship of religion to armed struggle in Muslim societies is that often the perceived cause for activism is by itself sufficient justification for militant activism, and the participant happens to be a Muslim, but does not necessarily consider such activism to be religiously derived or rooted. Such might be the case for adherents of the People's Democratic Party in Afghanistan, or the leftist parties such as the Popular Front for the Liberation of Palestine in the Occupied Territories. Unfortunately, while some of our academic investigations are aware of the diversity of ideologies and motivations underpinning such activism, in the media all acts of terrorist or resistance activity are labeled Muslim, with the implication that the acts are religiously motivated. Compounding this widespread assumption that all Muslims are piously motivated is that the very language of resistance is indistinguishable from religious language, since the latter is so deeply imbedded in linguistic norms—a resonant example might be found in our "goodbye" ("God be with ye"). Nor, indeed, does the media acknowledge the sometimes variegated religious base of the population; for instance, the large numbers of

Palestinian Christians who also might have participated or continue to participate in armed or militant struggle before their numbers dwindled to their present 10 percent have rarely been acknowledged by the media.

Several points must be made with respect to the reform and revivalist, and now Islamist, ideologies sweeping through the Muslim world and, given global migration patterns, through pockets of the Western world. First, it is not clear, despite the successes of such movements, what percentage these groups comprise in relation to the entire Muslim population (about 1.4 billion worldwide). Second, neither is it clear what percentage of these are militant or have access to arms. Our suspicion is that an overwhelming percentage simply remains within the boundaries of doing good works, on the one hand, and missionizing themselves and others to accept a narrowly defined, and shariah-bound form of Islam, on the other. Distressing as the latter is, it is not a militant threat but rather a social and civic threat, especially for women and for minorities, and has the capacity to engender mistrust and intolerance of the West, and further, of its sister monotheisms, not to mention geographically proximate polytheisms and atheisms, both of which run contrary to much of the history and spirit of Islam. With respect to militarization, the question is, where does one find armed Islamists? It appears that before September 11, 2001, armed Islamists largely fought other Muslims, whether in Algeria (post-independence), Iran (post-Khomeini), Afghanistan (the Taliban), or Egypt (against Sadat), or participated in liberation struggles fighting largely non-Muslims in Israel, Kashmir, and possibly the Philippines. It is not clear whether the Muslims fighting in the Philippines, Chechnya, Bosnia, Albania, and Lebanon are Islamist in ideology, although clearly Islam serves as a group marker for a common cause (as might Catholicism in Ireland). In all cases, increasingly Islamist ideology is being paired with an armed struggle for liberation from perceived hostile forces. That is to say, while not all pious Muslims, Islamist or not, are militant, it is likely that in cases where militancy is advocated, the pool of willing participants appears to be drawn from Islamists. September 11 marked the first truly large-scale expression of anti-American sentiment, and one has to wonder whether such attacks were restricted to the particular virulent form of the ideology espoused by Osama bin Laden and are likely not to be undertaken by any others, or whether they sent out the message that they could be undertaken, albeit at a terrible cost. Many of the attacks on

American embassies and personnel, according to media reports, appear to be traceable to Osama bin Laden, which would suggest that most other Islamists restrict themselves to their local causes as far as militancy goes.

Third, with respect to anti-Western rhetoric, it is true that current ideological articulations of Islam necessarily look at the West through the remembered lens of colonization and the current lens of globalization as well as political interference of the West in local affairs, especially in the oil-bearing and strategically located nations. However, from an educated and larger historical perspective, the Islamic world has long been intertwined with the Western world in a manner that has been enriching for the latter, just as the former has been enriched by the latter. For instance, much of the greatness of Islamic civilization during its golden age, from about the ninth century to the fifteenth, can be attributed to Muslim developments of classical learning found in Greek texts pertaining to the sciences, music, medicine, astronomy, philosophy, and so forth, that were translated into Arabic in the eighth and ninth centuries. Muslim reflections upon these texts, and the subsequent developments contributed by Muslims as they read, studied, and worked on texts originating in Hellenistic, Persian, Hebraic, and Indic (South Asian) sources contributed to efflorescence in all the disciplines known in that day. Such knowledge was then retransmitted back to Europe via Spain through translations made into Latin, and although barely credited in our history books, Muslim thinkers and texts written by Muslims played a significant role in facilitating the European Renaissance through a revitalization of European academies of learning after the Dark Ages.

One cannot imagine the development in astronomy without the astrolabes of Nasir al-Din Tusi or his contributions to algebra (the term itself derives from the Arabic *al-jabr*), or architecture without the innovations of Rashid al-Din Sinan, or the ceramic techniques that went all along the Silk Road to China and beyond without the Persian tile makers and painters, or the intricate patterning and vegetable dye techniques of oriental fabrics and rugs without the tribal weavers spanning the Middle East and Central Asia, not to mention the many philosophical contributions to medieval philosophy, including the theology of St. Thomas Aquinas without an Ibn Rushd (Averroës). The medical canon of Ibn Sina (Avicenna) remained in European medical curricula up to the eighteenth century. All this is by way of noting that from a larger historical perspective, the Western world and the Islamic

world have not always been Crusader-like antagonists in their interactions, as has been touted by some academics in fashion today, but
rather that there have been periods of collaboration and, if not direct
collaboration, certainly mutual enrichment. Thus for those on either
side of the divide, whether Western or Islamist, to claim retrospec-
tively a conflictual relationship between the two does disservice to
the historical tradition and forgets that each is rooted in the other in
almost every discipline, if not culturally.

Fourth, the Islamist (and there are many varieties belonging to this
label) re-creation of all-encompassing shariah law as expressive of a
Muslim's piety is a move both to counter the privatization of religion
as well as to retroject a notion of a Golden Age of Islam that supposedly existed during the time of the Prophet and the first four
caliphs when the Muslim community is thought to have lived in perfect obedience to Muhammad's religious and political authority (contrary to the historical Golden Age, which, as mentioned earlier, came
later). At such a time, it is thought, the community was unified, all
the Muslims lived in harmony with no dissenting opinions, and shariah
law guided the actions of the community. As Nazih Ayubi has observed:

> Today, when most salafis and some fundamentalists call for the im-
> plementation of shari'a, what they really have in mind is the
> implementation of the jurisprudence formulated by the early ju-
> rists. This jurisprudence has now been extracted from its historical
> and political context, and endowed with essentialist, everlasting
> qualities. The point is thus overlooked that this jurisprudence was
> in the first place a human improvisation meant to address certain
> political and social issues in a certain historical, geographical and
> social context. What is also often overlooked is that the main body
> of the official jurisprudence fulfilled a certain political function by
> imparting religious legitimacy to the government of the day, which
> had usually come to rule by force or intrigue and which, in its daily
> conduct, was not generally living up to the Islamic ideal.[8]

THE CONSEQUENCES OF ISLAMIZATION

Now, it is true that in some cases the application of Islamic law is an
advance over tribal and feudally patriarchal forms of tribal council
(*panchayat* or *jirga*) law observed in many parts of the Islamic world
in which societies, especially rural societies, are still organized according to feudal structures that are inherently patriarchal. A recent
example of such tribal rulings is the notorious Pakistani case of a young

rural woman who was ordered to be raped by four men as a consequence of her brother's being seen walking with a woman from a higher caste. But in the main, shariah law has exacted its own price in allowing loopholes for men in cases of honor killings (Pakistan, Jordan, among others); blurring the line between adultery and rape (Pakistan); leveling charges of apostasy and consequent forcible divorce against those who wish to initiate discussions of the role of religion in civic life (Egypt); invoking charges of heresy and hence death against the same in the infamous case of the author Taslima Nasreen (Bangladesh); and so forth.

Two consequences of shariah law application can be identified. The first is that Muslim populations find themselves socially and sometimes physically terrorized by Islamists who seek to police not only the mode of dress worn by women and their comportment, but also attendance at the mosque for Muslim men, as well as the particular form of Islam espoused by the adherent. Thereby, Islamists attempt to remove all forms of Islam other than those promoted by their own ideology. In their attempts to enforce coercively their new orthodoxies, many historical variants of Islam find themselves under siege, whether they are the hybridized or syncretic Muslim mystically oriented traditions of South Asia, Indonesia/Malaysia, or Africa; discrete forms of Shiism (there are many forms of the latter in addition to the majority tradition found in Iran, commonly called Imami Shiism, Ithna Ashari Shiism, or Twelver Shiism); or Sufi (mystical) in their outlook and emphasis.

All of these run the risk of being supplanted either by a lately fashioned puritanical form of Islam popularly known as Wahhabism or by ideologies such as those constructed by Mawdudi and Sayyid Qutb at times when Islamic countries were seeking to escape the lingering yoke of colonization. Wahhabism itself, no more than three centuries old (its earlier antecedents exercised little influence among the majority of Muslims), had its genesis in Saudi Arabia and was granted politically expedient support by the contenders for power at the turn of the twentieth century, displacing the hereditary claims to the leadership of Saudi Arabia. The role of Western nations, interested in pliable Saudi leadership given their interests in recently discovered oil, in facilitating the transition of Wahhabi-sympathetic Saudi leadership at that critical juncture, is not the subject of this essay. What is germane, however is that oil funding makes it possible for Islamists, whether Wahhabi-, Mawdudi- or Sayyid Qutb-inspired, to establish or

take over Quranic schools or *madrasas* and disseminate their ideologies, all in the name of piety and in the interests of "education," a
deeply cherished Islamic principle. It is a short step thence for militants to find an ever-ready pool of men (and women) to coerce and
cajole surrounding populations, campaign against legal reforms, indeed, campaign for an Islamization of the law, not to mention an Islamization of all knowledge. Any opposition is effectively silenced by
charges of heresy (*kufr*), innovation (*bida'a*), or "Westernization"
(meaning "westoxification"), and governments find they have to barter
certain civic rights and especially women's rights to the Islamists in
order to gain legitimacy for their own often weak, embattled, and
sometimes undemocratic rule.

The second is that shariah law, which is not a singular phenomenon, comprises several discrete systems of jurisprudence that took at
least two centuries to develop in the Sunni cases and several centuries
to develop in the Shiite cases. These are, as pointed out by Ayubi and
others, specific to their historical, geographical, and political contexts.
Given the principle that the intent of any legal system must be to safeguard the good of the societies to which it is applicable, surely it would
make sense to construct legal systems, albeit in the spirit of cherished
Islamic principles, that would attend to the very real issues and challenges facing Muslim populations today. A blind adherence, even with
juristic intervention, to juridical systems developed a millennium ago
in most cases does disservice to the very populations it seeks to protect simply because the historical, cultural, social, and political conditions under which Muslims live today are very different from those
of the tenth-century Abbasid Empire under which several of the Sunni
and to some extent Shiah legal systems developed. Furthermore, under the various dynastic rulers (Abbasid, Fatimid, Buyid, Ottoman,
Mamluk, Mughal, to mention but a few), the administration of justice
was continually modernized as changing circumstances required in
contrast to the common misperception that "there is no separation
of church and state in Islam." The various caliphs took under their
control all aspects of law with the exception of law pertaining to pre-
scribed religious duties such as the paying of *zakat* (a form of tithing),
religious endowments, and family law. It is these latter that remained
the preserve of religious jurists, whereas every other aspect of the law
was overseen by the caliph's executives and given the stamp of religious legitimacy by dubbing the caliph both the religious leader of
prayer (*imam*), in whose name the Friday sermon was declared, and

the chief political authority (*malik* or sultan). Juridical writings also, over time, created theories of Islamic states, in which the jurists speculated what an Islamic state should look like, bearing very little resemblance to what actually occurred historically. Unfortunately, for moderns reading such texts, the fine distinction between an envisioned Islamic state and its historical nonreality has been blurred. So, indeed, has the fact that the Quran has very little to say about the state. Rather, later legal texts are used as evidence, as is the shariah itself, that a utopian Islamic state existed at the time of the Prophet, complete with shariah laws, and should now be resuscitated through a program of re-education of Muslims worldwide.

Thus we have a conundrum: On the one hand, it is assumed that shariah law is divinely revealed and hence immutable as well as nonnegotiable; on the other hand, the existence of several schools of shariah law, plus the fact that trained jurists declare in a *fatwa* (legal response) what is best suited to the particular case before the court, suggests that the jurist is, in fact, an interpreter of the vast resources he has before him (there are very few women jurists, hence the gendered pronoun), even though he claims to be upholding that which is divinely revealed. It is not difficult, then, to see that despite the fact that Islam claims to have no priestly class, a priestly caste has been created in the form of *fatwa*-issuing jurists who can block—or dictate—the administration of justice, using divinity as a shield to disengage from questions of whether their pronouncements are, in fact, in the best interests of society (*maslaha*). This is particularly germane with respect to gender issues but becomes even more critical with respect to structuring civil societies in modern-day conditions. Since the creation of a just society was Muhammad's divinely inspired aim, in the interests of which the Quran accorded rights and responsibilities to Muslims, surely, it is now more critical than ever in postcolonial Muslim societies to encourage debate and discussion regarding how these challenges can be met within the spirit and intent of Islam rather than adhering to the cultural forms in which that spirit was articulated in seventh-century Arabian terms. But to suggest so is immediately silenced as an attempt to deny the eternal validity of the Quran—which is not what is intended by this author—and dismissed in the name of "tradition," as though tradition somehow has value and the changing circumstances of people do not, since many "traditions" continue to perpetuate inequities that run contrary to the principles and ethos of Islam. Thus, in sum, the second consequence of the application of shariah law is that the linkage of Muslim piety with an adherence to shariah law has made it extremely risky for Muslims to engage in open discussion and reflection of what it might mean to construct a civil society, or to construct legal systems that would be fair and just to all citizens in the modern state. Nor can there be any open or critically informed discussion of the role that religious institutions—given that Islam is not a monolithic faith—ought to play in public life. Witness, for instance, the persecution and then execution of the Sudanese Muslim thinker and theologian Muhammad Husayn Taha. The difficulties attached to examining such questions are especially unnerving when one considers that the ideologies of a well-funded few, armed with morally and sometimes physically coercive tools, silence a larger majority of Muslims for whom the necessities of life, peace, safety, hospitality, and the exercise of their divinely endowed faculties, including the capacity to think within the boundaries of moral accountability, are what matters most.

CONCLUDING REMARKS

I want now to bring these reflections to a close with a few observations. From the foregoing, a case can be made that revivalist and reform movements such as the many forms of Islamist ideology and praxis found in the world today stem in response to several variegated but interconnected factors. First, they embody the search for an authentic identity as part of a resistance strategy to colonization and postcolonial Western hegemony. Second, they mount a platform of resistance in protest of governments that perpetuate Western hegemony and/or Western-mediated control over natural resources (especially when such governments do not act in the people's interest but in exchange for Western support will allow the establishment of military bases to protect access to oil, as an example), political stances (especially over Israel and the Occupied Territories), and economic policies in the name of globalization and the politics of aid (considered to be favorable for the West but not for much of the rest of the world). Third, they construct a desire in their recruits to return to a retrospective Golden Age utopia supposedly articulated and implemented by the community of the Prophet in which a total Islamic polity existed, pervading all areas of life. In so doing, they seek to overturn, infiltrate, or take over the government in order to provide such a society, and along the way, create civic conditions that are punitive toward Muslim minorities, members of other faiths, and women. Fourth, disappointed with the failure of their governments to provide the conditions necessary for healthy, vibrant societies, they provide social services unmet by the government in response to the poverty and material needs of the population.

If Islamist ideologies are to lose the moral and at times militant force they exercise over their recruits and over those they terrorize, then some of the very real concerns that feed and underlie such movements must be addressed by all those, Muslims and non-Muslims alike, who have a stake in civic societies, freedom of conscience, and democracy. Otherwise, as witnessed by the world on September 11, 2001, a Muslim, most likely an Islamist, can become a terrorist. Even though the Quran forbids it. There were Muslims killed in the Twin Towers, in direct violation of Quran 4:29, "and kill not one another." In a verse applicable to all Muslims as it remains unabrogated from a rule the Quran claims was laid down for the children of Israel, Quran 5:32 states, "whosoever kills a human being for other than manslaughter or corruption in the earth, it shall be as if he had killed all humankind, and who saves the life of one, it shall be as if he had saved the life of all humankind." Can the assertion of what constitutes "manslaughter" or "corruption" be left to the judgment of individuals not accountable to civic institutions? Surely not. This essay has sought to argue that violent, radically militant interpretations of Islam that consider jihad to be a religious duty, and that now seek to globalize jihad against those that do not, in their view, conform to their understanding of Islam, pose a significant threat to Muslims and non-Muslims alike. While such interpreters and interpretations of Islam run contrary to the largely peaceful and ethical stances taken by the majority of the world's diverse Muslims, nonetheless, their access to arms and networks makes their small number a sizeable source of risk. The colonial and postcolonial factors discussed here have fueled the albeit limited success such ideologies have had with most Muslims. To prevent such ideologies from gaining ground, a concerted effort must be made by liberal Muslims and non-Muslims alike to address the issues I have discussed, from which these ideologies draw support.

NOTES

1. That is, one who resorts to violent means toward attaining a political end.

2. Cheikh Hamidou Kane, *Ambiguous Adventure* (Portsmouth, NH: Heinemann, 1963), pp. 112–113.

3. Mehrzad Boroujerdi, *Iranian Intellectuals and the West: The Tormented Triumph of Nativism* (Syracuse, NY: Syracuse University Press, 1996).

4. John K. Cooley, *Unholy Wars: Afghanistan, America and International Terrorism*, 2d ed. (London, Sterling, VA: Pluto Press, 2000), p. 5.

5. *Guardian Weekly*, March 28–April 3, 2002, p. 32, reprint of *The Washington Post* article titled, "From U.S., the ABCs of Jihad," by Joe Stephens and David B. Ottaway.

6. Cooley, *Unholy Wars*, p. 1.

7. Aziz Al-Azmeh, *Islams and Modernities* (London, New York: Verso, 1993).

8. Nazih M. Ayubi, *Political Islam: Religion and Politics in the Arab World* (London and New York: Routledge, 1991), p. 2.

PART III

What Is a Morally Justified Response to Terrorism?

CHAPTER 7

The Moral Response to Terrorism and Cosmopolitanism

LOUIS P. POJMAN

On September 11 the worst terrorist attack on civilians in the history of the United States occurred. Four planes were hijacked by Arab Muslim terrorists, becoming in their hands massive murderous missiles. Two of them crashed into New York's World Trade Center, one into the Pentagon in Washington, DC, and a fourth, perhaps headed for the Capitol building, crashed into a Pennsylvania field. An estimated three thousand unsuspecting, innocent people were killed, besides the nineteen terrorists. The horrendous kamikaze attacks destroyed the symbols of global capitalism and dented the military headquarters of the most powerful military force on earth. Thus a new era in the history of warfare has been inaugurated, one that portends a new dimension of evil and a different type of war. The history of the United States will henceforth be divided into Before September 11 and After September 11.

Terrorism is not new, of course. In the 1980s 5,431 international terrorist incidents occurred in which 4,684 people died; and in the 1990s there were 3,824 incidents with 2,468 deaths. From 1970 to 1995 64,319 terrorist incidents were recorded, half of them attributed to religious extremists.[1] If one includes state-sponsored terrorism, the twentieth century will be hard to equal in terms of terrorist atrocities. It is estimated that governments killed 169 million of their own people between 1900 and 1987. Joseph Stalin, the all-time megamurderer, accounts for about 43 million deaths, Mao Tse Tung 38 million, and Adolf Hitler 21 million.[2] Northern Ireland and England have had to endure the terrorist threats of the Irish Republican Army (IRA) for decades, and Israel has had to live with suicide bombings for years.

135

Indeed, Israel, although the target of some of the worst terrorist attacks in history, shares the responsibility for the onset of modern terror. Seeking to drive the British from Palestine, the Zionist militant groups Irgun and the Stern Gang were early perpetrators of terrorist violence in the Middle East. On July 22, 1946, the Polish Jew Menachem Begin, later to become prime minister of Israel, led a group of Irgun saboteurs into the kitchen of the King David Hotel in Jerusalem, which served as the headquarters of British government offices. They deposited milk cans packed with gelignite in the hotel's lower floor, set the fuses, and fled. When the explosion occurred twenty-five minutes later, ninety-one British, Arabs, and Jews were killed and forty-five were injured. On April 9, 1948, the Stern Gang and Irgun invaded and captured the village of Deir Yassim, raping women and killing more than 230 Arab men, women, and children, mutilating their bodies.[3] Israel, it might be argued, was itself founded on terror and continues to vie with the Palestinians for that dishonorable label. Yet instead of calling Israel a terrorist state, we fund it to the tune of over $3 billion per year.

But Israel may simply be following a well-established practice of the Middle East, Hama Rules.

Hama Rules: The Background Metaphor for the Terrorism of September 11

In his book *From Beirut to Jerusalem*, Thomas Friedman describes atrocities that took place in Hama, Syria, in early February of 1982. After an assassination attempt on Syrian President Hafez Assad was traced to the Muslim Brotherhood, a group of Sunni Muslim militants in the town of Hama, Assad's forces, led by his brother Rifaat, launched an attack on the Brotherhood in Hama. A fierce civil war broke out between the Muslim guerrillas and the Syrian military. Prisoners were tortured and buildings, even mosques, were destroyed. In a few weeks much of Hama was in ruins. Assad brought in bulldozers to flatten rubble like parking lots. Between seven thousand and thirty-eight thousand people were killed. Normally, a politician would play down such a ghastly incident and dismiss the high casualty numbers as the enemy's propaganda, but Assad's forces claimed them as a badge of honor.

Friedman argues that the incident illustrates the rules of Arab warfare, Hama Rules, which come straight out of a Hobbesian state of nature, where life is "solitary, poor, nasty, brutish and short." Destroy or be destroyed. Warring tribes confront each other with no impartial arbiter to enforce mutually agreed-upon rules, so that the only relevant concern is survival, which entails that the enemy must be destroyed by whatever means necessary. Friedman describes the Middle Eastern states as brutal autocracies where leaders (despots) like Assad and Iraq's President Saddam Hussein have survived by oppressive tactics, including framing their enemies and the torture and execution of political rivals. "Restraint and magnanimity are luxuries of the self-confident, and the rulers of these countries are anything but secure on their thrones," writes Friedman.[4]

Friedman illustrates his theory with a Bedouin legend about an old man and his turkey. One day an elderly Bedouin discovered that by eating turkey he could restore his virility. He bought a small turkey and kept it around his tent, feeding it, so that it would provide a source of renewed strength. One day the turkey was stolen. So the Bedouin called his sons together and said, "Boys, my turkey has been stolen. We are in danger now." His sons laughed, replying, "Father, it's no big deal. What do you need a turkey for?" "Never mind," the father replied, "We must get the turkey back." But his sons didn't take this seriously and soon forgot about the turkey. A few weeks later the Bedouin's sons came to him and said, "Father, our camel has been stolen. What should we do?" "Find my turkey," the Bedouin replied. A few weeks later the sons came to him again, saying that the old man's horse was stolen. "Find my turkey," he responded. Finally, a few weeks after that, someone raped his daughter. The Bedouin gazed at his sons and said, "It's all because of the turkey. When they saw that they could take away my turkey, we lost everything."[5]

To let your enemy take an inch is to give him a mile, it is to lose your wealth, your status, your reputation, your integrity. In such a state the rule is not "an eye for an eye, a tooth for a tooth, a life for life," but "a life for an eye, two for a tooth, and the lives of your entire tribe for the life of my turkey." Friedman thinks that Hama Rules govern the Middle East conflict. They are the rules by which Israel has learned to play. Friedman notes that the prime minister of Israel, Ariel Sharon, is the one man Assad has feared and respects, because Sharon plays by those rules too. His support of the Lebanese Falangists in the mass killings at Sabra and Chatila and the recent Israeli reprisals against the Palestinian community are evidence of this.

If Friedman's thesis is correct, we in the West are dealing with warriors who are playing by a different set of rules than ourselves. Our notions of proportionate response and the distinction between combatants and noncombatants don't apply to Osama bin Laden, Iman al Zawahiri, and Al Qaeda. As bin Laden has announced, every American is an enemy and ought to be destroyed, whether he or she is a soldier or civilian:

> The ruling to kill the Americans and their allies—civilians and military—is an individual duty for every Muslim who can do it in any country in which it is possible to do it, in order to liberate the Al Asa Mosque and the holy mosque from their grip, and in order for their armies to move out of all the lands of Islam, defeated and unable to threaten any Muslim.[6]

During the terrible Cold War, at least we knew that our enemy loved life as much as we and would be motivated by secular self-interest, so that a policy of mutual assured destruction (MAD) was feasible. But now we are confronted by enemies who would just as soon cause a nuclear holocaust that would wipe us and them from the face of the earth, liberating them for heavenly bliss. They play by Hama Rules with a theocratic touch.

CLASH OF CULTURES

A second characteristic of the recent terrorist attacks is their religious underpinning. Unlike nationalistic terrorist attacks by the IRA, Tamil Tigers, or Palestine Liberation Organization (PLO), these are not done in the name of a nation. They are rooted in culture, namely a religious worldview and practice, and represent what Samuel Huntington refers to as a "clash of civilizations."[7] The terrorist attacks carried out against the Egyptian government and the Al Qaeda–sponsored attacks against the U.S. embassies in East Africa and on September 11 were religious in nature. Osama bin Laden, Iman al Zawahiri, and their cohorts have announced that this is a *jihad*, a holy war, against the *kafir*, the infidel, the Evil Empire of the West, and especially the United States. The Al Qaeda network sees itself as the vanguard of an Islamic movement, seeking to overthrow American and Western hegemony in the world and extirpate their influence in the Muslim world, removing American military bases and Western culture from countries like Saudi Arabia, Egypt, and Kuwait. The attack on America was intended to provoke a violent American reaction, which in turn would ignite a worldwide Islamic uprising against the West.

This clash of civilizations, pitting the culture of Islamic fundamentalism against Western culture, composed of modernity, secularity, and democracy, has become the new battleground for mankind. With the Cold War over, ideological differences between cultures reemerge as the source of conflict. Religion is surpassing nationalism as the foremost threat to world peace and stability. Although the majority of Muslims may eschew the terrorist's tactics, there is something in Islamic culture that predisposes it to violence, the idea of jihad, the holy war against the infidel. Saddam Hussein invoked the jihad, appealing to all Muslims to support Iraq against America in the Gulf War, and Iran's Ayatollah Khomeini has called for a holy war against the West, saying that "the struggle against American aggression, greed, plans and policies will be counted as a jihad and anybody who is killed on that path is a martyr." The Muslim schools, *madrasahs*, throughout the Muslim world teach children that the West is evil and that they have a duty to perpetuate the jihad against it. Although many Muslims reject Islamic fundamentalism, emphasizing peace, the idea of jihad is an essential part of Islam, and fundamentalist forms of Islam are embattled in war wherever it consists of a critical mass that confronts a different culture. In Lebanon, Islam battles Maronite Christians; in Israel, Jews; in Kashmir, Hindus; in Nigeria, Catholic and Protestant Christians; in Somalia and Sudan, evangelical Christians; in Ethiopia, Coptic Christians; in the Baltics and former Soviet Union, Orthodox Christians; in Pakistan, the small Christian minority; in Indonesia, Timorese Christians; in Europe and America, Christians, Jews, and secularists. Tolerance towards the "People of the Book" (Jews and Christians) may be officially advocated by the Quran, but fundamentalists, such as the Wahhabi sect in Saudi Arabia and Pakistan, seize upon the notion of the jihad against the kafir to override any tendency toward tolerance.

Religion can be a powerful motivating force. Invoking the authority of God and offering the rewards of eternal bliss, it can be an incentive to extreme acts of virtue and of vice. The religious picture of the universe is all-embracing and dominates the life of the true believer. It is hard to reason with religious fundamentalists, for they generally hold their faith or religious assumptions to trump what we in the West call *reason*. Reason, for them, always functions as a strategy within the "bounds of religion alone."

When Hama Rules are married to religious fundamentalism as clashing with a different religious or secular culture, we have the potential for violence, for terrorism. Let us now define *terrorism* before turning to the causes of and the moral response to that form of violence.

DEFINITION OF TERRORISM

Terrorism is a type of political violence that intentionally targets civilians (noncombatants) in a ruthlessly destructive, often unpredictable manner. Terrorism hardly constitutes mindless violence. Instead, it reflects a detailed strategy that uses horrific violence to make people feel weak and vulnerable, often disproportionate to either the terrorist act or to the terrorist's long-term power. This undermining fear is then utilized to promote concrete political objectives. While some of these objectives may be morally commendable, their moral quality tends to be annulled by the murderous means employed, so that terrorism must be discouraged by civilized governments. Essentially, terrorism employs *horrific violence against unsuspecting civilians, as well as combatants, in order to inspire fear and create panic, which in turn will advance the terrorists' political or religious agenda.* Although this definition can be qualified and refined, it will serve my purposes in this paper.

CAUSES OF TERRORISM

Although cultural attitudes, such as religious dogma, may be a significant cause of terrorism, despair or a sense of hopelessness rooted in oppression, ignorance, poverty, and perceived injustice may be the contributing causes, the soil in which fundamentalism can grow and flourish. Often it is those who have been frustrated by the powers that be who strike out against what they perceive as their enemy. Perceived oppression evokes sympathy in the hearts of many, even to the point of excusing or romanticizing violent responses against the "oppressor." Hence, French existentialist philosopher Jean Paul Sartre, writing in defense of the national Liberation Front in Algeria, wrote, "To shoot down a European is to kill two birds with one stone, to destroy an oppressor and the man he oppressed at the same time: there remains a dead man and a free man." Unfortunately for Sartre's analysis, most of the victims of terrorism are unsuspecting innocent civilians, no more engaged in oppression than a Bedouin sheep herder, a fireman trying to rescue people from a burning building, a passenger on United Airlines Flight 93, or a woman trying to run a business from the one-hundredth floor of the World Trade Center. But according to the logic of terror there is no difference between them and the commander at Auschwitz who is leading innocent people to the gas ovens. The attractiveness of terrorism is exacerbated by cultures that encourage violence as a response to perceived harms and wrongs. When a religious or political ideology is present, the tendency to resort to terror may be exponentially increased, so that otherwise normal people may resort to extreme measures in the name of religion, believing that by killing people they are serving God and, thereby, ensuring themselves eternal bliss.[8]

Peer pressure, religious sanctions, and a quasi-military scheme of hierarchical command-obedience, which causes the terrorist to focus on the importance of the action rather than his own self-interest, enables the terrorist to act in ways that we would normally consider irrational in the extreme. We are revulsed by terrorism, not because the terrorists are cowards, but because their misguided courage is directed at violating the rights of and even murdering unsuspecting innocents. In September 2001, shortly after the Day of Ignominy, CBS's *60 Minutes* produced a documentary direct by Bob Simon on the life of suicide bombers. Young Palestinian men were selected by radical Islamic leaders to be suicide bombers against Israelis. The youths, believing this call to jihad was a sacred honor, were indoctrinated to the point of believing that they would through the act of kamikaze missions become holy martyrs, and ascend straight to heaven. A video was made of their lives, recording their commitment to die for their cause, which was sent to their families, who were led to believe that their sons were dying a holy martyr's death. After such profound commitment, it would be hard for the youth to back out, return home, ring their doorbells, and announce, "Surprise, Mom, I decided that suicide bombing was not in my best interest." The comprehensive cultural reinforcement of the suicide bomber and terrorist marks this kind of fundamentalism off from our normal sense of prudent and moral behavior. Poverty and oppression are not sufficient (or even necessary) for terrorism, although they are contributing causes. The overriding impetus is a culture that endorses and reinforces violent responses against certain types of persons and property.

Terrorism has existed from time immemorial,[9] but now with the onset of modern technology, including rapid transport, the bomb, the airplane, and chemical, biological, radiological, and nuclear warfare, the threat to society has been exponentially increased. Furthermore, television and mass communication in general give terrorism widespread publicity. *Publicity is the oxygen of terrorism.* Terrorist acts displayed on worldwide networks like CNN compel our attention, and this point has not been lost on the terrorist leaders. It took just a couple of terrorists bombing the Marine barracks in Beirut in 1986, killing 241 servicemen, to cause the withdrawal of American and French forces from Lebanon.

A War on Terrorism

Although terrorism has been endemic to human history for a long time, there was something horrific about the suddenness and sheer magnitude of the events of September 11. In one fell swoop our illusion of invulnerability disintegrated: America's twin pillars of capitalism were struck down. Other nations like Israel had experienced terrorism for decades, but we naively thought ourselves safe. Now we know that no one is immune from unpredictable surprise violence. Our airlines are especially vulnerable, and the fear of chemical and biological attack is palpable.

A war on terrorism has been declared by President George W. Bush, and troops have been deployed to areas of the Middle East and Central Asia, where terrorist camps under the auspices of Al Qaeda prosper.[10] But it will be extremely difficult to defeat sophisticated modern terrorism, for these terrorists have neither a state nor identifiable public buildings or institutions. They operate in small semi-autonomous cells that are difficult to infiltrate. And if you attack one terrorist base camp, the terrorists move into the Afghanistan mountains or establish a new base in Iraq, Pakistan, or, possibly, Saudi Arabia.

Perhaps the answer is to alter the conditions in which terrorism thrives, such as poverty, ignorance, oppression, and injustice. While no doubt part of an enlightened strategy, this is extremely difficult to accomplish since in this case, the ignorance and oppression are associated with religion, namely, Muslim (Wahhabi) fanaticism, which opposes Western liberal values, including women's rights, tolerance of different lifestyles, and abortion. The same ideology that opposes secular liberal values gives deep meaning to the lives of the adherents of the terrorist groups. The religion of Allah gives purpose, hope, and a practical guide to action to millions of Muslims, who may live more virtuous, or at least more disciplined, lives than their secular counterparts. It is noteworthy that some of the terrorist leaders say the same thing about contemporary American decadence that American Christian fundamentalists leaders do, including Jerry Falwell and

Pat Robertson, who aver that God permitted this horror of the Day of Ignominy because of our drift into secularism and permissive liberalism. At bottom, this is a struggle of moral secularity against intolerant religious theocracy, of liberal open society versus the Hama Rules of the tribal closed society. And it represents a supreme challenge to civilization, not equaled since the rise of Hitler and Stalin.

TERRORISM AND JUST WAR THEORY

What strikes us as especially heinous about the Day of Ignominy was the callous disregard for innocent life, for the incredible imperviousness to destroying the lives of people who were not warriors. Osama bin Laden's announcement that there is no distinction between a soldier and an ordinary American civilian ("Whoever is a taxpayer in America is a legitimate target") strikes us as the epitome of immoral use of force, and its originator as a moral cretin. The terrorist fails to grasp the fundamental tenets of *jus in bello*, and so a strong moral presumption opposes it. But, even though normally unjustified, could there be extreme cases where terrorism is morally permitted?

Here is where just war theory becomes relevant. Our deepest ethical reflections do permit certain types of violent responses to evil under certain conditions. We are permitted (and even enjoined) to defend ourselves against harm by resorting to measured violence. The violence must not only be a last resort and aimed at restoring peace, but must also be proportionate to the morally endorsed goals, doing no more damage than necessary to accomplish our purposes. It must be delivered in careful ways so as to distinguish between legitimate targets—combatants and their instruments of destruction—and illegitimate targets—noncombatants, civilians not directly involved in the war effort. While there are hard cases for just war theory, including firing on innocent shields and struggles in situations of extreme emergency, the kind of horrific violence perpetrated by terrorists against innocent passengers in airplanes and the World Trade Center is beyond the pale of morally considerable action.

THE MORAL RESPONSE

In responding to the Day of Ignominy we have a number of converging goals. One salient goal is to honor the three thousand victims of the kamikaze attacks. It entails attacking the causes of terrorism, eradicating the moral swamp that breeds fanaticism, hatred, and indiscriminate violence. We can also honor the fallen more immediately by punishing those who perpetrated this deed, the terrorist leaders who trained, financed, and motivated the perpetrators to destroy innocent life and property on September 11. These two goals are conjoined. In the long term we must create a more just world, one conducive to peace, prosperity, and democracy. But in the short term we must end those regimes and organizations that sponsor and promote terrorism, such as the Taliban, Al Qaeda, and the Islamic Jihad. A measured, carefully executed military operation in Afghanistan, while not a substitute for long range and more comprehensive political strategy, can support, supplement, and augment the goal of global justice. Let me then outline some short-term and long-term goals in assessing the ethical response to the Day of Ignominy.

I have already mentioned the fact that just war theory would endorse a measured response to the terrorist attack of September 11, aiming to punish and deter terrorists and reduce their threat to our society. That we are building a broad coalition with other European, Asian, and Islamic nations, and even Russia in this pursuit is one of the good things resulting from wise handling of the disaster of September 11. Every civilized country has a stake in the battle against terrorism. We should also note, but not develop at length, the need for strategies for self-protection to include a homeland counterterrorist policy. Our present policy includes the following four principles:

1. Make no concessions to terrorists and strike no deals.
2. Bring terrorists to justice.
3. Isolate and apply pressure on states that sponsor terrorism, forcing them to change their behavior.
4. Bolster the counterterrorist capabilities of those countries that work with the United States and require assistance.[11]

All this seems responsible and worthy of our national support. In addition, counterterrorism must include cutting off the financial resources of terrorists. Terrorists need a support network, including financial support. By undermining a group's economic ability to wage war, as the United States has recently begun to do, we make terrorist attacks more difficult.[12]

An additional policy that seems entailed by these principles is a more scrutinizing immigration control policy. Several of the hijackers of September 11 were here legally, and background checks of others would have caused officials concern. Investigators reported that Mohammed Atta, a known Egyptian terrorist who is thought to be the mastermind behind the terrorist suicide bombings of September 11, originally entered the United States on a legal visa and, when it expired, was still able to use it to gain entry to the United States just before the events of September 11. No background check was ever done on him. The Immigration and Naturalization Act of 1990 (led by Senator Ted Kennedy of Massachusetts) forbids denying a visa to foreigners simply because they are members of terrorist organizations. Even though fifteen of the nineteen suicide hijackers were in the United States on legal visas, some of them on student visas, the immigration policy remains unchanged. In January 1999, the U.S. Commission on National Security cochaired by Colorado Senator Gary Hart warned that our immigration system was lax and warned of coming problems: "America will become increasingly vulnerable to hostile attack on our homeland, and our military superiority will not entirely protect us. Americans will likely die on American soil, possibly in large numbers."[13] The entire system for monitoring and managing foreign visitors is broken and needs reform.

A striking case that occurred in Canada is that of the Algerian terrorist Ahmed Rassem, who was apprehended before being able to complete his apparent plan to blow up the Los Angeles Airport in late 1999. Although Rassem had a forged French passport and a terrorist record, the Canadian immigration authorities (CSIC) allowed him into their country, where he soon obtained welfare benefits. This kind of immigration laxity violates the state's obligation to protect its citizens from attack by securing its borders from external threats. Granted, this is not easy, for we do not want to exclude visitors or immigrants altogether. Millions of foreigners enter our country each year, many of whom outstay their visas, but better monitoring of these people is necessary if we are to safeguard our freedom.

I now turn to long-term strategies.

National Service

Some good has already come out of the tragedy of September 11. Our country is united in an almost unprecedented way. Democrats and Republicans are bonding and cooperating to build a more vibrant and secure nation. Young people want to serve their country, and in the months succeeding the Day of Ignominy have been enlisting in the FBI, CIA, and the military services. We should take this opportunity to develop new opportunities for national and world service. A new model of national conscription seems a plausible option. Each able-bodied youth should be required to serve our nation or the world in some beneficial capacity, such as the military, AmeriCorps, Domestic Youth Corps, or Peace Corps. In a recent *New York Times* essay, "A New Start for National Service," Senators John McCain and Evan Bayh called for the government to institute new service programs to involve youth in civil defense, community service, and international service. In return the government would fund the college education of these young people.[14] Such programs have the virtue of helping young people internalize a moral patriotism and, at the same time, promote worthy goals, such as educating the poor, ministering to the sick and elderly, and serving one's nation and the world. If such programs are appropriately organized and administered, they will not hinder personal autonomy but will provide a channel for service. Serving one's country provides a mechanism for expressing one's gratitude for all the benefits membership provides us; creates a mechanism for identifying with the moral goals of the nation, thus internalizing a sense of citizenship; and enables us to help make this a better nation. Although the immediate sphere of service should be one's own country, eventually, the circle should be expanded to include the entire world. This leads to the next point, the recognition of a universal morality with universal human rights.

Spreading the Message of a Universal Morality with Universal Human Rights

The moral point of view, whether one takes a consequentialist or deontological perspective, is universalistic, based on rationally approved, impartial principles, recognizing a universal humanity rather than particular groups or persons as the bearers of moral consideration. When seeking to rescue a drowning man we do not ask him, "Are you an American or Arab?" before seeking to save him. We rescue him because he is a human being. We must come to see all humanity as tied together in a common moral network. If all do not hang together, each will *hang* alone. Since morality is universalistic, its primary focus must be on the individual, not the nation, race, or religious group. We are all human beings and are only accidentally citizens of the United States, Afghanistan, Germany, Japan, Brazil, or Nigeria. Many of us are grateful to be Americans, but we didn't earn this property, and we should recognize that our common humanity overrides specific racial, nationalistic identity. A global perspective must replace nationalism and tribalism as the leitmotif of ethical living. A nonreligious ethic, based on rational reflection and yielding universal human values, must become the underpinning of a renewed cosmopolitanism. The threats to morality today come from religious particularism, naive egoism, ethical relativism, and deconstructionism—a euphemism for moral nihilism. A defensible moral objectivism, the core of which is accepted by a consensus of moral philosophers, must permeate our society as well as every society under the sun. At present most people derive their moral principles either from religion or from narrow tribal ideology. An educational process inculcating universal norms in people everywhere is a crucial task for the leaders of the twenty-first century. Principles such as forbidding murder (the unjust killing of innocents), dishonesty, and exploitation and promoting reciprocal cooperation, freedom, and universal justice must be seen as the necessary conditions for the good life, civilization, and peace. This leads to the ultimate long-range goal, world government (the cosmopolitan moral imperative).

The Cosmopolitan Moral Imperative: The Possibility of World Government

Peace, justice, and the struggle against terrorism and violence may be attainable only by institutional cosmopolitanism, world government. There are two arguments for world government. The first one is the *Moral Point of View Argument*, which we have just adumbrated and which I will elaborate upon later. The second argument is from the *Trend Toward Globalism*, to which I now turn.

The geopolitics of the world has been transformed in the last decades, even before September 11. Instead of the Cold War threat of a global nuclear explosion, the trend in the past decades has been a geopolitical implosion of internecine atrocities, as the inhabitants of the former Yugoslavia revive the deadly ghosts of a former age; the Hutu engage in a genocidal slaughter of their neighbors, the Tutsi in Rwanda; Tamil rebels kill Sinhalese in the name of nationalism in Sri Lanka; Muslims battle non-Muslims in Kashmir, Lebanon, Israel, and the Baltics; and nationalist Catholic Irish engage in mutual murder with nationalist Protestants who are still fighting the Battle of the Boyne of 1690 in Northern Ireland, their nationalism trumping their common Christian heritage.

These atavistic exhibitions of violence, added to the kind of terrorism that occurred in the suicide bombings of September 11, raise the claim that a global organization creating institutions and enforcing laws is desirable to promote peace, assure compliance with contracts and treaties, and prevent international anarchy by promoting orderly processes, international morality, and reliable expectations. A universal set of laws with fixed penalties that is impartially enforced by a central policelike agency could be a catalyst for peace, the protection of human rights, and environmental wholeness. This last function is a modern one, having to do with the fact that air and water pollution tend to spread, impervious to political boundaries. For example, contaminated air from the nuclear explosion at Chernobyl wafted westward to Sweden and Switzerland. An increasingly depleted ozone layer over the Antarctic makes all people vulnerable to cancer-causing ultraviolet radiation. Greenhouse gases that originate in specific locales have global effects, changing climate patterns throughout the world. Recent international conferences on global warming and environmental policy, such as the Kyoto Accords in 1998, although they failed to reach universal agreements with strong sanctions, further demonstrate the need for an authoritative global body. As Hobbes wrote in 1651, "Covenants without swords are just words."

Add to these factors the modern development of an increasingly global economy, free trade, international transportation and communication systems (from the airplane to the Internet), the gradual spread of English as the lingua franca of trade and diplomacy, and the growing global consciousness (CNN and other news networks may now beam the latest Asian uprising or African coup into our living rooms before the government is even aware of it). We read of conflicts in the United States over free trade. Organized labor has shown resentment at what it perceives as conservative economic policies and corporate globalism, especially passage of the North American Free Trade Agreement between the United States, Canada, and Mexico. A coalition of anti-globalists has vigorously protested (and even rioted) during the World Trade Organization conferences in Seattle and Toronto in the last few years. The protests over the erosion of community and exploitation of the poor are valid concerns. But the wiser strategy seems to be to harness the powers of global capitalism and use the increased wealth for socially beneficial purposes. The ideal that world trade produces more wealth, and that "a rising tide lifts all boats," seems to have sufficient merit as to claim our cautious and critical commitment.

The fact is that the world is changing and large corporations are increasingly becoming as powerful as nation-states. Fifty-one of the world's top economies are multinational corporations. They have assets greater than the gross domestic product (GDP) of most nations. General Motors has revenues roughly the same size as Ireland, New Zealand, and Hungary combined, larger than Turkey or Denmark; Ford more than South Africa; Toyota and Exxon more than Norway or Poland. Microsoft's revenues are reported to exceed the GDP of France. The top five corporations double the GDP of all South Asia.[15] Global capitalism has one feature in common with moral cosmopolitanism. It is anti-nationalistic, recognizing not the nation-state but the free market as the operative arbiter of value. International economics is contributing to vast waves of migration, as workers from all over the globe, often at considerable risk, gravitate to where jobs are, resulting in new configurations of ethnic diversity and the alteration of centuries of stable cultural patterns, as is occurring in Scandinavia, France, Germany, and the Netherlands. At the same time progress has been made in joining the nations of Western Europe into a corporate European Union with a common currency. A similar movement is underway in Africa, the African Union. Combine these factors, and we get a picture of growing pressures for the eroding of national boundaries and national sovereignty and in favor of globalism, perhaps even some form of international government.

Thomas Friedman has argued that a globalized system of informal relations has replaced the Cold War as the dominant social-economic-political fact of our time. It consists of free market capitalism, through free trade and international competition, producing more efficient and private uses of wealth. Individuals, corporations, and nation-states are able "to reach around the world farther, faster, deeper and cheaper than ever before, and in a way that is also producing a powerful backlash from those brutalized or left behind by this new system."[16] Globalization is occurring in virtually every country in the world. Unlike the great nations and empires of the past, this supernational organization has no geographical capital, no center of power. No one nation or corporation can control it. Rapidly expanding, fluid, penetrating each segment of the globe, it is ushering in a new democratic revolution. The symbol of the Cold War system was the Wall, which divided everyone. The symbol of the global system is the World Wide Web, which unites everyone. Well, not quite everyone. The Indian peasant, the Bhutan nomad, and the poor of Afghanistan are as isolated and as badly off as ever. Rapid change, technological advances, and corporate tentacles spreading into every part of the world are also creating greater distances between the older, more atavistic or primitive cultures and the new ones budding in their midst. Friedman describes an automobile assembly plant outside of Tokyo where 310 robots, supervised by a few human beings, are building the "world's greatest luxury car, the Lexus." While witnessing this technological miracle, he received a report on his cell phone from Jerusalem, where Palestinians and Jews are fighting over who owns which olive tree. "It stuck me," he writes, "that the Lexus and the olive tree were actually pretty good symbols of this post–Cold War era: half the world seemed to be emerging from the cold War intent on building a better Lexus, dedicated to modernizing, streamlining, and privatizing their economies in order to thrive in the system of globalization, and half the world—sometimes half of the same country—was still caught up in the fight over who owns which olive tree."[17]

We are all intertwined in an interdependent global web in other ways as well. A German businessman, while making a deal in Pakistan, picks up a virus that originated somewhere in Africa. He gets on a plane for Frankfurt, infecting the entire planeload of passengers, who spread the disease throughout Europe. An infected American tourist brings the virus with her on a flight from Frankfurt to the United States, where the virus spreads over the country. For good and bad, and in-between, globalization is spreading, eroding prevailing national borders and creating a new informal network of relationships. It is the most significant political fact of our age. The world is becoming a global village. New worldwide regulations and behavior patterns are called for to deal with this new reality. A prima facie case may even exist for international government or, at least, for a sovereign body to enforce international laws, to safeguard the rights of individuals and individual nations against unjust incursions and exploitation. Perhaps the United Nations, which is really, as its name suggests, only a union of states, ineffectual as it is at present, is the precursor of a coming global governing body, and the World Court in the Hague is a precursor to an international system of law.

The main moral defenses of nationalism have been based on the need for primary particularist loyalties that give meaning to one's life. The question is whether these loyalties can be preserved within a cosmopolitan framework.

Consider two other salient reasons for supporting nationalism, the desire to own property and the claim to a common national territory. With regard to property rights, cosmopolitans criticize nationalists for their strong theory of property rights. Why should America or Saudi

Arabia get a sole monopoly on its resources, which are just part of the natural lottery? The United States and Saudi Arabia didn't do anything to deserve their superior natural resources. They were just more fortunate than poorer countries. As such, wouldn't it be fairer for the resources of these and all countries to be distributed more equitably? Shouldn't we use these resources for the good of humanity, rather than simply the good of a single nation? One might argue that although we do not deserve these resources, we deserve the benefits of what we have produced from these resources. But here, the Lockean Proviso seems relevant. We deserve the fruits of our labors with regard to resource consumption just as long as we leave "as much and as good left over for others." The world's resources should be used for the world's needs, not simply the needs of the fortunate. Being good stewards of our resources, including sharing them with the needy, may justify some ownership, but it is not the absolute, sovereign ownership that many of us have uncritically come to take for granted.

With regard to a national conjoined territory, the land over which nationalism claims complete jurisdiction, world government would only qualify that sovereignty, not abolish it. In a world government, nations might be made stewards of their land and resources, but not permitted complete sovereignty over their uses. Richer nations would have a duty to redistribute through taxation or aid some of their wealth to poorer nations in which not even people's basic needs were met. Peter Singer argues from a utilitarian perspective that, "If it is in our power to prevent something bad from happening, without thereby sacrificing something of comparable moral importance, we ought to do it."[18] What changes might we need to make in our lifestyles, if we attempted to live according to Singer's challenge? However, until such a Cosmopolitan regime is established, it's hard to see either nations or individuals giving up sovereignty to their territory and resources.

Some Objections to World Government

Cosmopolitanism appears to be a worthy ideal, embodying, as it does, the moral point of view in respecting individuals as the centers of meaning, rather than nations, races, or religious or ethnic groups, but the ideal is fraught with five seemingly *almost* insuperable problems. First, what kind of institution would be required to draw up and enforce the global scheme of taxation required for the kinds of wealth-redistribution schemes that might be warranted? Would its coercive powers be an unacceptable violation of individual and national liberties? Second, even if we could ensure a just world government to carry out a taxation scheme, how could it be certain that the funds distributed actually went to the poor and were not siphoned off by a corrupt elite and deposited into their Swiss bank accounts (as happens all too frequently with foreign aid to developing countries)? Third, how do we guarantee that, after the funds get to the poor, long-term good would result from the redistribution scheme? Fourth, it would also seem that population control should be a necessary condition for aid, for otherwise the ratchet effect would occur.

For example, Rwanda has been growing at a rate of as high as 8 percent per annum, resulting in a doubling of the population every 82 years or so. The Chinese policy of limiting families to one or two children appears harsh to many of us, but it may be seen as an emergency measure (to counteract the fanatical pronatalist policies of Mao Tse-Tung), and it is having a beneficial effect in slowing down population growth (compared to India, where rapid growth continues).

Fifth, how can one compare what constitutes a good life in different kinds of societies? The per capita gross national product (GNP) of many Western counties is around $25,000, whereas in the Third World it may be around $250, one hundred times less. Someone from a Third World country, say an Amazonian Indian in Brazil, may not value college education as much as Westerners and may live in a tribe that has a pattern of caring for the elderly, obviating the need for expensive retirement policies. In fact, the Amazonian Indian, upon being exposed to Western culture, may prefer to remain living in the rain forest.

These problems may not be insuperable, but they should give us pause. Until we understand the full implications of what we are doing, a move toward institutionalizing cosmopolitanism should proceed cautiously. Nonetheless, the principle of humanity embodied in the moral point of view, which focuses on the rights and duties of individuals, not groups, races, or nations, does point to a robust cosmopolitanism, which, it would seem, should be institutionalized into a democratic world government.

Another problem related to international relations concerns intervention in the internal affairs of a nation-state, such as what occurred in Afghanistan, where coalition forces led by the United States supported forces to bring down the Taliban regime and the Al Qaeda terrorist network, or in Serbia and Kosovo, when human rights violations, such as ethnic cleansing, became extreme. Even if we accept the principle of national sovereignty, intervention by other nations may be justified. The widespread ethnic cleansing that took place in the former Yugoslavia in the 1990s is a prime example of when the intervention of other nations might be warranted. Working out the criteria for when to intervene and when not to is one of the most urgent problems facing us. We want to be constructive rather than add to the destruction in these war-torn lands, but it is notoriously difficult to determine the likelihood of success. Such interventions are risky and should only be embarked upon when all attempts at peaceful solutions have been exhausted, when there is widespread international support, when there is willingness for a long-term occupancy, and when there is a reasonable chance of success.

Cosmopolitan institutions threaten the very existence of the traditional nation-state, so much a part of our world since the eighteenth century. If our ultimate allegiance is to a super global state, then what is the role of the nation? Does it have moral legitimacy?

Many philosophers would say no, the nation lacks any ultimate moral justification. It is, at best, a temporary and necessary evil, organizing people in restricted manners until the principle of universal humanity can take hold on our collective consciousness. Albert Einstein characterized nationalism as an infantile disease, "the measles of mankind" from which we must recover if we are to survive. But, as our analysis suggests, this may be a hard reaction. Certainly, there is a hard version of nationalism, epitomized in the slogan "My country, right or wrong, my country!"[19] which is not justified because it makes nationalism into an absolute principle. Such extreme nationalism is no more justified than giving special privilege to one's race or gender or ethnic group. We have an obligation to oppose our country when it violates human rights, even as some Germans, like the martyrs Dietrich Bonhoffer and Adam von Trapp, opposed Hitler's Nazism. We must transcend this kind of extreme, immoral *nationalism*, with its atavistic rituals, its narrow patriotism, and replace it with a universal loyalty. There is a prima facie duty to become *moral cosmopolitans*, committed to the well-being and rights of every person, regardless of country of origin. There are practical obstacles to overcome, as well as moral ones, so that we cannot immediately move into such an international allegiance, but this should be our goal. Moral cosmopolitanism, treating each person as a moral equal, is not equivalent to institutional cosmopolitanism, but it inclines in that direction. The benefits of world government are greater prospects of peace, enforcement of treaties and contracts, fluid trade and economic relations, and the allocation of resources according to need and desert, rather than according to purely the luck of being born in a resource-rich country or family.

Cosmopolitanism has had a checkered past. Marxist-Leninism purported to be the ultimate cosmopolitan philosophy, which gave rise to the Union of Soviet Socialist Republics, the completely "internationalist" society, and allowed Stalin's atrocities. Stalin shows that one doesn't have to be religious to be an evil fanatic: You can be an atheist and a socialist and perpetrate evil on a national or global scale. Cosmopolitanism can simply be a veneer for tyranny. Most of us have been immunized against the idea of world government through the inoculating effects of reading Huxley's *Brave New World* and Orwell's *1984*. Cosmopolitans can also propagate questionable moral advice on a more micro scale. The nineteenth-century cosmopolitan William Godwin held that "if two persons are drowning and one is a relative of yours, then it should make no difference in your decision as to whom to try to rescue first." Dickens satirizes this "telescopic philanthropy" in the person of Mrs. Jelleby, who could only recognize objects of benevolence at a very great distance.[20] It was said of President Woodrow Wilson that "He loved mankind but loathed individual men." Commonsense morality, as we noted earlier, informs us that this undermines the very substance of morality, those relationships that make life worth living. It is our basic communitarian values of family, friends, and community that constitute the bases of moral sentiments. To this extent, the particularists are correct. Our love and moral commitments must begin and always remain tied to particular people, not humanity in the abstract. Furthermore, some nationalists point out, we may take legitimate pride in our democratic institutions, our practices of equality before the law and moral traditions. These aspects of our culture are worth preserving and defending. From a moral point of view all cultures are not equal. Some instantiate the ideals better than others.

At this point, we might compromise and recognize the validity of both cosmopolitanism and nationalism. Nationalists may be divided into two groups: *soft* nationalists and *hard* nationalists. Hard nationalists hold that the nation is altogether justified as the ultimate locus of political obligation, so that internationalism is simply confused or immoral. Even as we have a natural duty to prefer our family to other people and strangers, we have a duty to prefer our nation, to be patriotic. Nationalistic concerns override all other loyalties or obligations. On the other hand, soft nationalists maintain that while we do have some obligations to people everywhere and that we need some adjudicating overseer to enforce treaties and prevent war, this doesn't completely override the need for nation-states. They agree with hard nationalists that we do have special obligations to our own country, but soft nationalists feel that the needs or rights of others may sometimes override our familial obligations and that our nationalistic obligations may be overridden at times by obligations to mankind at large or to people not citizens of our nation.

Soft nationalists are open to the possibility of world government, recognizing the ideals thereby attained, but they also are troubled by the problems of ensuring local autonomy and preventing unwieldy bureaucracy and tyranny. However, suppose we could attain an efficient world government, a sort of United Nations with *sovereignty*, that is, with authority and power. Then, the soft nationalists maintain, nations would still have local jurisdiction, much like the individual states do within the United States, only with greater autonomy (or *semi-sovereignty*). We would still have special obligations to people in our own states, relating to them in special moral ways, while at the same time sharing our resources with people throughout the world.[21]

CONCLUSION

September 11, the Day of Ignominy, has changed America and the world. We have been shocked out of our complacency, disabused of our illusion of invulnerability, and forced to face global terrorism. I have argued that the Day of Ignominy may become the Day of Opportunity, if we use it to take countermeasures to terrorism and the causes of terrorism and to begin to ameliorate the oppression and injustice in our nation and the world. I have outlined some short-term and long-term strategies, the most ambitious and controversial of which is a version of institutional cosmopolitanism–world government that would be based on secular rational morality. World Government may also be a fitting response to the growing pressures of globalism. I have also noted, but not developed as fully as I would like, the virtues of nationalism in its ability to develop the opportunities for close personal relationships and loyalties, so vital for personal identity. Some form of nationalism may always be part of the human psyche, although it may be a less all-encompassing variety than what we now experience, a soft nationalism. It will be balanced by a soft form of cosmopolitanism, either informally worked out between nations or by a formal world government that would still encourage and promote individual nation-state autonomy within its domain. One way or another, increased peace and international cooperation will be necessary as we become better educated people who live in a global village, where actions in Bosnia, South Africa, or the Island of Timor affect people in Siberia, Buenos Aires, and Los Angeles. However it happens and whatever the exact result in terms of formal structure or lack thereof, the process should encapsulate the vision of an expanding moral circle, wherein we begin with commitments to our family and friend, expand that to the community and nation, and expand that to the whole world.

NOTES

1. Quoted in Magnus Ranstorp, "Terrorism in the Name of Religion," *Journal of International Affairs* (1996).

2. R. J. Rummel, *Death by Government* (New Brunswick, NJ: Transaction Publishers, 1994). Long before Lord Acton, in the eighteenth century, Edmund Burke wrote, "Power gradually extirpates from the mind every humane and gentle virtue."

3. Howard Sachar, *A History of Israel: From the Rise of Zionism to Our Time* (New York: Knopf, 1996), pp. 267, 333. I do not mean to pick out Israel as worse than the Arab nations or Palestinian leaders. On the contrary, Israel at least approximates a democracy, whereas few of her Arab neighbors, including Saudi Arabia and Egypt, make the lightest pretensions thereof. While the Irgun and Stern Gang were carrying out terrorist acts on Palestinians, Palestinian groups led by such men as Fawzi el Kutub and Abdul Khader Husseini were blowing up Israelis. We should also include many incidents of America's treatment of the Native Americans as terrorist acts.

4. Thomas Friedman, *From Beirut to Jerusalem* (New York: Farrar, Giroux, Straus, 1989), p. 95.

5. Friedman, *From Beirut to Jerusalem*, p. 89.

6. Quoted in Jeffrey Goldberg, "The Education of a Holy Warrior," *New York Times Magazine*, June 25, 2000.

7. See Samuel Huntington's "The Clash of Civilizations?" *Foreign Affairs* (Summer 1993) for an analysis of this phenomenon.

8. See Salman Rushdie's "Yes, This Is About Islam," *New York Times*, November 2, 2001.

9. The idea of jihad or a holy war of terrorism occurs in the Jewish/Christian Bible. See for example the Old Testament book of Exodus (23:23), in which God commands Israel to blot out all of their neighbors, "the Amonites, and the Hivites, and the Hittites, and the Perizites, and the

Canaanaites, the Jebusites," and the book of Joshua, Chapter 8, in which in the battle for the city of Ai God commands Joshua to kill all of the people in the city.

10. A particular problem is that of finding and instituting a more progressive government in Afghanistan to replace the Taliban. As I write, a *loya jirga*, a Grand Council of Afghan leaders, has been convened by the former king, the eighty-seven-year-old King Zahir Shah, who has been living in Italy for several years. However, the ethnic, tribal, and political divisions in Afghanistan are so intense that providing a transition to enlightened democratic government will probably demand sustained U.S. and UN military, economic, and political support for a long time.

11. For a thorough discussion of these principles, see Paul R. Pillar, *Terrorism and U. S. Foreign Policy* (Brookings Institute Press, 2001).

12. For a cogent analysis of this thesis, see James Adams, *The Financing of Terror* (Simon & Schuster, 1986).

13. Quoted in "Immigration and Terror," *Middle American News* (November 2001).

14. John McCain and Evan Bayh, "A New Start for National Service" *New York Times*, November 6, 2001. The two senators plan to introduce legislation in the Senate to effect such a program.

15. *UN Human Development Report 1997*, p. 12, and CorpWatch: www.corpwatch.org/trac/glob101/background/2001/factsheet.html.

16. Thomas Friedman, *The Lexus and the Olive Tree* (Farrar, Straus, Giroux, 1999), p. 7. The backlash was in evidence in the Seattle riots against the World Trade Organization (WTO) in 2000 and the Toronto protests in 2001.

17. Friedman, *The Lexus and the Olive Tree*, pp. 26–27. But what happens when those fighting over the olive tree suddenly discover that the true enemy to their traditional ways of life is not their historic opponent but a vast impersonal, multinational complex? This is what the anti-technology movement is all about. See also Michael Hardt and Antonio Negri, *Empire* (Cambridge, MA: Harvard University Press, 2000).

18. Peter Singer, "Famine, Affluence and Morality," *Philosophy and Public Affairs*, 1.3 (1972).

19. This was uttered by the late Cardinal Spellman in the 1960s, signifying that he would support America's war in Vietnam even if it was morally wrong.

20. Charles Dickens, *Bleak House* (London: Bradbury and Evans, 1853). "Mrs Jelleby's eyes had the curious habit of looking a long way off. As if they could see nothing nearer than Africa." (p. 26).

21. For a good discussion of *extreme* versus *moderate* nationalism, see Stephen Nathanson, *Patriotism, Morality, and Peace* (Lanham, MD: Rowman & Littlefield, 1993). My views have profited by Nathanson's work.

CHAPTER 8

Envisioning a Global Rule of Law

DANIELE ARCHIBUGI AND IRIS MARION YOUNG

The attacks on the World Trade Center and the Pentagon in September 2001 can appear within two different frames of interpretation. The first sees them as attacks on the United States as a state and its people. The second views them as crimes against humanity. The difference in interpretation is not technical, but political, and each implies different strategies of reaction. Shortly after the attack some public leaders, such as Mary Robinson, director of the United Nations Commission on Human Rights, recommended that the United States and the rest of the world adopt the second interpretation. It seemed that there might be some open discussion of how to interpret the attacks as an event in international affairs, and what sort of response was called for. In a few weeks, however, the United States solidified its interpretation as an attack on a state for which the appropriate response would be war on another state or states.

In this essay we question this statist response to the terrorist attacks and offer some vision of how the United States and other global actors might have conceived and can still conceive of their possibilities for action under a cosmopolitan vision of political responsibility. We argue that a different response to these attacks, based on the rule of law and international cooperation, could have been equally effective to combat terrorism in the long run and, in our view, could have also opened the way to a more just and stable world order.

THE STATIST INTERPRETATION

The Bush administration framed the attacks as an act of war on America, for which military retaliation was judged to be the appropriate response. This frame meant finding a state or states to engage in war, and the United States chose Afghanistan on the grounds that the

Taliban government harbored and supported Al Qaeda. It has singled out Iraq, Syria, Somalia, and other countries as additional states toward which military action may be taken, although they have not been attacked so far. The construction of a response to the attacks as a state-to-state military conflict, however, has been difficult to sustain. Even within a traditional state-centered world politics, the fact that the government of Afghanistan allowed Al Qaeda leaders to run camps in its territory provides an uncertain justification for making war on the state. Aware of that shakiness, the United States shifted its reasons for the war against the Taliban from a rationale of self-defense to a humanitarian defense of freeing the Afghan people, especially its women, from oppression. We find this rationale cynical and opportunistic, since neither Bush nor the Clinton administration had previously articulated any concern with the plight of the Afghan people. Not surprisingly, this concern has almost disappeared from the agenda for reconstruction in Afghanistan. Responding to the terrorist attacks through the conduct of a war against a state neither fits the case nor is likely to be effective in making a safer world. Although the war has destroyed some Al Qaeda bases and the United States has captured some members of that group, there is no direct connection between the casualties and the nineteen suicidal attackers of September 11. Widely circulating estimates of civilian deaths in Afghanistan give a minimum of one thousand, some as many as thirty-seven hundred, and hundreds are likely to die from unexploded bombs.[1] It is still unknown the number of soldiers and armed men who have been killed, but some of the information, among it the massacre of hundreds of Taliban prisoners in the prison of Mazar-i-Sharif, has raised serious concerns about the legality in which the war operations have been conducted.[2] The number of refugees suffering hunger and frost because of the war is impossible to calculate, while civilian casualties attributed to military errors still continue despite the fact that the war formally ended many months ago.

There is no reason to think that the war has deterred other would-be terrorists around the world. After many months from the beginning of the war, there is little sign of political stability in Afghanistan or that the current government is genuinely respectful of human rights. The war may have contributed to destabilizing the region of central Asia with unforeseen consequences.

Although the United States did not act alone in prosecuting the war, it called the shots. The United States decided with whom to cooperate and assigned the role of other actors. It is difficult not to interpret U.S. policy in recent months as an effort to consolidate even more firmly its position as sovereign of the world. While many Americans no doubt think that this is a good thing, we believe that the existence of a single world military power that aims to enforce its will both is an anathema to democratic culture and impedes efforts to promote peace.[3]

In the last decade, the United States has used its military force in the Persian Gulf, Somalia, Panama, the Balkans, and many other places. In every case, the U.S. interventions have had victims, but few have been Americans. The magnitude of U.S. military and economic power and the willingness of the United States to wield it asymmetrically and with only the thinnest veneer of multilateralism elicit hostile reactions all over the world, even from people thought to be allies. A survey conducted by the Pew Research Center and the *International Herald Tribune* in December 2001 found that most of the non-Americans among the 275 political and business leaders polled believe that the United States wrongly uses its power and that some of its policies are responsible for growing global disparities in well-being.[4] In response to such hegemony, it seems to us imperative that leaders and citizens all over the world should envision a global rule of law and should try to shame and pressure the United States to act more in conformity with such a vision.

AN ALTERNATIVE VISION

Aspirations to a global society governed by fair rules should be counted among the casualties of September 11. The fall of the Berlin Wall brought with it hope of constituting a world order founded on international legality and with strengthened institutions of international cooperation. Recent debates and demonstrations about the policies and procedures of international trade and financial organizations have assumed the emergence of more global level governance. The question has been whether global regulatory regimes will represent solely the interests of the world's most powerful actors or can include the voices and interests of the global majority in transparent and accountable institutions.

We base a vision of an alternative response to terrorism on these aspirations for just and democratic global governance. Hitherto, discussions of an international rule of law and global regulatory systems have paid less attention to the prevention and investigation of crimes and their prosecution in an international system than to matters like international trade, investment, or environmental protection. We propose two premises for reasoning about what an alternative response to the terrorist attacks of September 11 might have been and still can be. First, the situation should be conceptualized in people-to-people, rather than state-to-state, terms.[5] The attackers were not representatives of a state, but members of private organizations, and those whom they killed were, for the most part, private individuals from at least seventy different countries. Thus, second, the events should be conceptualized as crimes, not acts of war, to which the proper response is criminal investigation and prosecution within a rule of law and legally mandated measures for preventing and deterring similar crimes. For this reason, we disagree with those who think that the concept of just war can be applied to the U.S. military reaction.[6]

Democratic states do not usually, and ought never, respond arbitrarily and with military power to terrorist attacks committed inside their borders. Spain in response to threats from the Basque separatist group ETA, Italy in dealing with the Red Brigades, the United States in response to the bombing in Oklahoma City—all mobilized the instruments of law and police power. Stepping out of legal bounds, as did the Spanish government for a while when it authorized some state agents to use extrajudicial methods to combat terrorism, seems to have the effect of increasing the risk of attack. The enemies of peace point to illegal actions by states to justify their own illegal actions.[7]

The world ought to respond to international terrorist organizations, we suggest, according to the same principles of the rule of law that these governments use in responding to domestic terrorist organizations. Responding to acts and threats of terrorism and to transnational terrorist networks under a global rule of law need not imply being "softer" on terrorists than using a state-to-state response led by a hegemonic state. On the contrary, a genuinely global cooperative law enforcement response would be more effective in identifying and apprehending culprits, as well as preventing future attacks, while at the same time harming fewer people and destroying fewer goods, than has the war against Afghanistan.

We offer five principles to guide international policy to respond to threats and problems of violence. They each point to ideals and institutions of global cooperation that do not now exist. In that sense we intend them as visionary. At the same time, we believe that all five principles can serve to guide action now in the following way. As they consider options for actions now to respond to threats of terrorism, political actors and citizens can and should ask which courses of action have the potential to help realize the ideals the principles express and which actions are more likely to move the world away from them.

LEGITIMIZE AND STRENGTHEN INTERNATIONAL INSTITUTIONS

Actions and policies that treat terrorism and threats of terrorism as involving all the world's peoples within a rule of law should utilize international organizations and legal instruments. The United Nations system is most important here. Although there are many flaws in its design and operations, which should be changed, the United Nations is the only transnational institution with representation of nearly all the world's peoples. Institutions, policies, and conventions of the United Nations, moreover, cover many of the most urgent world problems.

Currently the UN is in an impossible position. On the one hand, it is called on the scene to restore peace, build governments and infrastructure, aid refugees, conduct health campaigns, and pursue many other activities, in dozens of regions of the world simultaneously. On the other hand, member states routinely deny the UN the means for carrying out such missions, not only by failing to provide funds, but also by limiting its authority. When the UN's efforts prove inadequate to solve problems, as often happens, world leaders regularly heap abuse on the organization for being unresponsive and inept. The United States and other world powers cannot continue to dump the consequences of its wars and economic decisions on the United Nations while at the same time encouraging people to disdain the organization.

The present organization of the UN Security Council, with its five permanent members reflecting global politics in 1945, needs serious reform. That Security Council, however, passed three Resolutions after the attacks of September 11 (resolutions no. 1368, September 12, 2001; no. 1373, September 28, 2001; and no. 1377, November 12, 2001), which call for transnational cooperation among all member states to deter and investigate terrorist and other transnational criminal activity. If government leaders allied with social movements, the United States could be pressed to enter more genuinely multilateral efforts to transnational criminal networks, efforts that give more decision-making participation to the less developed world. The tragic paralysis of the international community in response to the worst killing in Palestine and Israel in two decades signals even more urgently the need to strengthen and reform the United Nations as a peacemaking institution.

Coordinate Law Enforcement and Intelligence-Gathering Institutions Across the World

The United States Congress apparently has little interest in investigating how two of the most sophisticated investigative and intelligence organizations in the world, the CIA and the FBI, could have been caught so unaware by a crime of such huge proportions. We suggest that one explanation is the state-centeredness of both agencies, along with the investigative and intelligence-gathering agencies of most states. Simultaneous with increased transnational organization and movement of capital, labor, technology, and culture is the transnational organization and movement of crime. Intelligence and law enforcement institutions, however, lag terribly behind this reality. Intelligence continues to be principally an instrument of individual states against their enemies; in a spy culture the agencies of one state engage in secret activities in relation to other states, explicitly not trusting one another. Domestic law enforcement agencies, furthermore, each have their own systems that make communication and cooperation across borders difficult. The September 11 attacks should serve as a siren call for reversing these structures of intelligence and law enforcement enable greater cooperation among agencies to protect *citizens* of the world, not states.

There are some international instruments on which to build for such a purpose. INTERPOL, the international police organization with 179 member nations, has worked against terrorism, drug trafficking, money laundering, white collar crime, computer crime, counterfeit money, organized crime, and traffic in women and children for decades. Even though its budget is minuscule compared to the task, it maintains extensive databases of known and suspected terrorists and criminals. It organizes data on counterfeit passports and stolen credit card accounts that can be useful to law enforcement agents in nearly any country. Yet state-based intelligence agencies infrequently work with the organization to access its data.[8]

At its millennium meeting in November 2000, the UN General Assembly adopted the Convention Against Transnational Organized Crime, which 140 countries, including the United States, have already signed. This convention requires states to strengthen domestic laws aimed to control organized crime and encourages states to enhance systems of transnational cooperation in legal expertise, extradition, and criminal investigation. It specifically calls for providing technical assistance to less developed countries to upgrade their capacities for dealing with organized crime. Although at the moment this Convention may be little more than a piece of paper, like some other UN negotiated treaties and conventions, it can be used by political leaders and social movements to demand institutions and resources that put its principles into action. The United States, along with any other states, can act to advance international cooperation in law enforcement, both domestic and transnational, as well as to create and strengthen global law enforcement agencies. A collective effort to combat terrorism with a greater involvement of the UN will certainly be beneficial to the United States, but this would imply that the United States commit itself to a greater loyalty toward the organization. As the president of the United Nations Association of the USA has rightly stressed, "to sustain the commitment of UN member states in this new war (against terrorism), and to dispel resistance stemming from resentment of American 'double standards,' Washington needs to affirm what the American public has long acknowledged—the rule of law applies to the great as well as the small."[9] A greater collaboration against organized political crime implies breaking down the statist distinction between domestic oriented police and internationally oriented spy agencies. Current policy in the United States and in many Western countries blurs this distinction, however, in just the wrong direction. By allowing the CIA and FBI to cooperate inside the United States, the government fosters a more repressive internal state at the same time that it becomes more defensive and suspicious externally. Increased transnational law enforcement cooperation should come with procedures of accountability and transparency in order to protect the rights of individuals.

Increase Financial Regulation

One of the most efficient ways to strike at terrorist networks, and organized crime more generally, is to hit their money. It is surprising that although Osama bin Laden has been known to head and fund terrorist operations for years, Al Qaeda has had the liberty to move the capital necessary. Why has no one until now succeeded at attacking the finances? We believe the answer lies partly in the fact that world business leaders resist financial regulation. Corporations regularly move their money around the world, for example, in order to avoid paying taxes. Tracking and regulating the movement of funds can dry up their flow to support criminal activities. A war on the free flow of money does not produce "collateral damage," create refugees, or pollute the air. The United States has indeed enhanced its capacity to investigate and regulate money flows. In this area it is obvious that even the most awesome military power of the world must depend on the cooperation of other governments, especially governments that dislike U.S. foreign policy. Such necessary cooperation is difficult to maintain when the same governments or their allies face military threats or covert intelligence operations from the United States.[10]

Use International Courts

The United States has put its response to attacks and threats of terrorism in a state-to-state frame only for as long as it suits its goals. By refusing to treat those captured in the war against Afghanistan as prisoners of war, the United States takes the picture out of the statist frame. The Bush administration argues that the prisoners are illegal combatants not covered by international law as stated in the Geneva Convention. At the same time, it has decreed that it will not apply its domestic principles of due process to noncitizen suspects apprehended in the United States or elsewhere. Thus the United States declares before the world that any non-Americans whom it apprehends and claims to connect with terrorism will not be given the protection of the law.[11] This stance is so outrageous that it has fomented dissent even within the Bush administration and from within its most loyal ally, Britain. In response the administration has slightly altered its stated position, but not its treatment of prisoners.

When the United States began putting into place its plan for military tribunals for those captured, Vice President Cheney said, "Terrorists don't deserve the same guarantees and safeguards that would be used for an American citizens going through the normal judicial process."[12] This statement reveals Cheney's scorn for the most elementary principles of due process: Presumably it is up to judicial procedure to determine who is and who is not a criminal.

If the September 11 attacks are seen as crimes against humanity rather than against only the United States, an international tribunal instituted by the United Nations, based on the model of those for the former Yugoslavia and Rwanda, with the processing judges coming from Western and Islamic countries, would be appropriate. This would also have the advantage of not appearing as a conflict between America and Islam, but rather between the entire international community and a limited group of criminals. In the end ad hoc tribunals should be handed over to a permanent International Criminal Court, which was approved by treaty in Rome in July 1998 and started to be implemented on April 12, 2002. (The United States has withdrawn its signature from this treaty, an unprecedented act.) "Had the International Criminal Court been in existence," noted international lawyer Christopher Greenwood, and had the relevant States been parties to its Statute, the perpetrators of the 11 September atrocities could have been tried by that Court for crimes against humanity."[13]

We have heard several arguments against using international courts to prosecute persons suspected of performing or materially contributing to terrorist acts. It's too slow, too expensive, and would wrongly give terrorists a forum in which to air their ideas. We find all these reasons disingenuous. It should not be any slower to pursue due process on an international level than at a state level; the speed the United States seeks seems to be at the expense of due process. Likewise, it should not be much more expensive to pay for an international trial than a state-level trial, if both are fair. Finally, any public court proceeding, at any level, offers opportunities for actors to express their point of view on the alleged crimes; that is what they are for, and that is, of course, why the military tribunals the Bush administration plans will not be open to public view.

Narrow Global Inequalities

Since September 2001 many commentators have suggested that the vast disparities in wealth and well-being between Northern Hemisphere societies such as the United States, the European Union, or Japan, on the one hand, and the Middle East and South Asia, on the other hand, be taken into account in understanding what causes and motivates individuals to join or form terrorist groups. We agree with those who respond that these structural injustices neither justify nor excuse criminal acts. Nor do these circumstances even explain terrorist acts, for there are many poor places that do not provide recruits for international terrorist organizations.

Still, a huge portion of the world's population lives in horrible poverty.[14] We believe, as do many others in both the less developed and more developed parts of the world, that this poverty persists at least partly because of policies of the rich states, private corporations based in those countries, and international organizations in which those states and corporations have disproportionate power. Even those skeptical of this claim, however, should condemn the apparent unwillingness of the people and government of the United States, Europe, and Japan to effect significant transfer of capital, technological capacity, and goods to raise the quality of life of the world's poorest people. There is no doubt that such indifference amidst affluence fosters resentment in many corners of the world and endangers peace and prosperity for many outside the shantytowns.

At another tragic moment of history, with the defeat of fascism at the end of World War II, the United States understood that its security and prosperity depended on the rebirth of Europe. To enable this rebirth, the United States dedicated a huge amount of resources to the Marshall Plan to rebuild the infrastructure of devastated European societies. No development aid program since that time has been as large in scale and as effective. That this was done once should give hope that having the will opens the way to invest in poor societies to enable them to flourish. For decades social movements and governments in the less developed world have demanded that the powerful economic actors of the world stop exploiting their resources and workers and start programs of real investment in the infrastructure and human beings of poor countries. The developed world remains largely unresponsive to this calamity. Official development assistance of the OECD countries in 1998 was 0.24 percent of their combined gross national products, and private funding is also paltry. The many attempts made by global civil society to increase the resources devoted to development have so far not been matched by concrete action.[15]

Even the Bush administration cannot avoid acknowledging this moral imperative. It could not stay away from the UN-sponsored conference on rebuilding Afghanistan in January 2002 as it walked out on the Conference on Racism in August 2001 and the Climate Change Conference in December. At the January 2002 conference the United States pledged a mere $300 million for the first year, and Japan and Europe each pledged $500 million for the first two and one-half years.[16] Before the earthquake of March 2002, the World Bank estimated that at least $4.9 *billion* was required for the two and one-half years to help rebuilt Afghanistan at the most minimal level.[17] What is certainly scandalous is that the majority of countries have not yet made available the resources promised in February 2002. Up to June 21, 2002, the United States has contributed to the Afghanistan Reconstruction Trust Fund $5 million only.[18] Even at this moment of crisis, the rich countries of the world remain unbelievably stingy, and the poor people of the world are watching.

The world will not be able to move toward fair, inclusive, and effective global governance without major reallocation of economic, technological, and organizational capacities to reduce existing global disparities in the quality of life and institutional order. For such ends we need new and strengthened international institutions that better represent the voices and perspectives of all the world's peoples moreso than existing international finance and development institutions such as the World Bank, with more ability to promote global redistribution. Without the global equivalent of the Marshall Plan, even the best designed cooperative efforts to respond to transnational organized crime can only be defensive and intermittent in their effectiveness.

Conclusion

The terrorist attacks of September 11, 2001, were a major challenge for the United States, its European allies, and the rest of the world. The Bush administration and its allies decided to retaliate against a country rather than individually punishing the culprits. Those who opposed to the recourse to war were often asked what the United States should have done. In this chapter we have addressed this question by arguing that there was an alternative way to combat terrorism. We do not argue that all culprits would have been taken and processed, and we do not believe that the implementation of the policies we have suggested would have been sufficient to destroy transnationally organized networks of killers. Certainly, the war undertaken has achieved neither of these goals. But we are sure that the number of "collateral casualties" would have been much lower if such an alternative strategy were followed. And, perhaps more importantly, the alternative reaction here recommended would have shown to the peoples of the world that the world's powerful leaders are able to support the rule of law and the instruments of justice also beyond its own borders.

Our suggestions should be conceived for the long term, and they have not lost their value after the bloodiest part of the military operations against Afghanistan has passed. They derive from a general perspective on world politics that dates much before the tragic events of September 11. The vision upon which we draw considers that it is both possible and necessary to develop global democratic institutions.[19] A major new global threat, such as terrorism on the scale of September 11, should provide the chance for democratic countries of the world to nurture a global rule of law rather than a clash of fundamentalisms.

NOTES

This is a revised version of "Toward a Global Rule of Law," *Dissent* (Spring 2002): pp. 27–32. We wish to thank Marc Herold, Mathias Koenig-Archibugi, Duncan Snidal, Michael Walzer, and Alexander Wendt for their criticism and suggestions. Thanks to Anne Harrington for research assistance.

1. The lower and upper estimations are reported from, respectively, the Project on Defense Alternatives and Marc Herold, University of New Hampshire. The latter report is available at http://www.cursor.org/stories/civilian_deaths.htm.

2. See Richard Falk, "In Defense of 'Just War' Thinking," *The Nation*, December 24, 2001, pp. 23–25.

3. See Robin Blackburn, "The Imperial Presidency, the War on Terrorism, and the Revolutions of Modernity," *Constellations*, 9.1 (2002): 3–33.

4. Brian Knowlton, "How the World Sees the U.S. and Sept. 11," *International Herald Tribune*, December 20, 2001.

5. See David Held, "Violence, Law and Justice, in a Global Age," *Debating Cosmopolitcs*, ed. Daniele Archibugi (London: Verso, 2002) Mary Kaldor, *Terror in the US: The Murky Road to War?* http://www.fathom.com/feature/122358.

6. It is not surprising that the petition supporting the conflict as a just war and signed by a number of important American intellectuals never mentions Afghanistan. Not even this document could establish a clear link between the action (the terrorist attacks) and the reaction (the war against Afghanistan). *What We're Fighting For*, Institute for American Values, released February 2002 and available at http://www.propositionsonline.com/Fighting_for.html. Signatories include Amitai Etzioni, Francis Fukuyama, Samuel Huntington, Robert Putnam and Michael Walzer.

7. See Montserrat Guibernau, *Nations Without States* Cambridge: Polity Press, 1999) especially pp. 145–148, "State Terrorism."

8. See David Zweshimo and Sbastian Rotella, "INTERPOL Hopes Terror Investigators Keep in Touch," *Los Angeles Times*, December 23, 2001.

9. In William H. Luers, ed., *Combating Terrorism: Does the U.N. Matter . . . and How* (New York: UNA-USA, 2002), p. 5.

10. See Phil Williams, "Crime, Illicit Markets, and Money Laundering," in *Managing Global Issues: Lessons Learned*, P. J. Simmons and Chantal de Jonge Oudraat, ed. (Washington, DC: Carnegie Endowment for International Peace, 2001), pp. 106–150.

11. The case is considered in Christopher Greenwood, "International Law and the 'War Against Terrorism,'" *International Affairs* 78.2 (2002): 301–317.

12. Reported in the *International Herald Tribune*, November 16, 2001, p. 5.

13. Greenwood, p. 317.

14. Data on world inequalities are scrutinized in the United Nations Development Program, *Human Development Report 2001* (New York: Oxford University Press, 2002). The ethical implications are addressed in an increasing vast literature, including Thomas Pogge, ed., *Global Justice* (Oxford: Blackwell, 2001).

15. Helmut Anheir, Marlies Glasius, and Mary Kaldor, eds., *Global Civil Society 2001* (Oxford: Oxford University Press, 2001).

16. The World Bank, *Afghanistan: Update on World Bank Activities*, note to update the Board of Executive Directors on a number of developments relating to World Bank activities in Afghanistan, Washington, DC, February 7, 2002.

17. World Bank, *Afghanistan*.

18. See The World Bank Group, *Afghanistan Reconstruction Fund. Contributions*, http://www.worldbank.org/artf. Figures reported are updated to June 21, 2002.

19. See, for example, David Held, *Democracy and the Global Order* (Cambridge: Polity Press, 1995); Richard Falk, *Law in an Emerging Global Village. A Post-Westphalian Perspective* (Ardsley: Transnational Publishers, 1998).

CHAPTER 9

Making War on Terrorism in Response to 9/11

CLAUDIA CARD

Insofar as terrorism does victims intolerable harm and (borrowing Immanuel Kant's language) treats them merely as means to ends they cannot rationally share, it is an evil.[1] But it is no ordinary evil, for it presents the challenge of how to respond effectively without doing further evil. Can war against terrorism, waged by the targets of that terrorism, meet that challenge? The question invites reflection on evil, terrorism, and war. Without fully answering the question, I raise issues that complicate an answer. Finally, by analogies with rape terrorism and terrorism in the home, I suggest a response preferable to that of victims declaring war.

EVIL

"Evil," like "terrorism," is a heavy, emotively laden term, liable to abuse in the interests of political manipulation. Some critics of responses to the attacks of September 11, 2001, elect not to use terms like "evil" and "terrorism" but prefer a more neutral vocabulary of "conflict," "opponent," "attacker," and "disaster." Political abuse is a real problem. I address it briefly in the section entitled "Justice in Responding and the Rules of War," in regard to representing a military opponent as an evil. Still, unlike critics who abandon such terms, I find the concepts of evil and terrorism philosophically too important to cede that vocabulary to political manipulators. I am not alone in this resistance. Despite Nietzsche's genealogy of evil, which refocused philosophers' and psychologists' attention for much of the twentieth century on people's (often unsavory) motives for judging in terms of evil, a growing number of philosophers of the past fifteen years are taking evils very seriously and doing so independently of religious ideas.[2]

171

On the view I have recently developed and defended, evils are reasonably foreseeable intolerable harms produced by culpable wrongdoing.[3] Evils are both suffered and perpetrated; they are experiences (with certain sources) and deeds (with certain consequences); they are not people or forces. Evils, on this definition, have two basic elements, harm and wrongdoing, neither reducible to the other. They are connected by causality and by reasonable foreseeability from the position of the perpetrator. By intolerable harms, I mean deprivations of the basics ordinarily required to make life tolerable and decent (or to make a death decent): nontoxic air, water, and food; sleep; freedom from severe and unremitting pain and humiliation; the ability to stretch (and contract) one's limbs and move about; affective ties with others; the ability to make choices and act on them; and a sense of one's worth as a person. It is not that those whose lives are already wretched cannot become victims of evil. For even they usually have some, although not enough, of the basics that make life tolerable and decent, and they can be deprived by evil doers of what little they have and robbed of hope.

In "culpable wrongdoing," I include not just overt acts but culpable omissions—negligence, carelessness, recklessness, the failure to attend. The content of even a culpable intention need not be "to do wrong." It might be, for example, "to kill." The doer might believe the killing justified. Ideological motivation does not excuse, as long as people can be held responsible for their ideologies. But evil doers need not be evil persons. An evil deed may not reflect deep-seated evil in the agent's character. My interest is more in evil deeds and doers than in evil people. What tends to distinguish evils from ordinary wrongs and ordinary bad things, on my view, are not so much the perpetrators' psychological states as the nature and severity of harms to victims, knowingly brought about or unreasonably risked. The 9/11 attacks are atrocities, paradigms of evil deeds. Regardless of the perpetrators' grievances and understandings of their religious commitments, mass killing of unarmed civilians targeted as such and without warning is evil. That judgment, I think, should not be controversial.

TERRORISM

A better candidate for controversy is whether those attacks were terrorist. The widespread assumption that they were is so far unsupported by public statements of purpose by the perpetrators or their

backers. Terrorism is not just any deed that terrifies, even intentionally (some films and carnival rides do that). The structure of terrorism's intent is critical and, apparently, complex. On Carl Wellman's
widely received view, articulated more than two decades ago, terrorism is coercive political violence characterized by two targets.[4] Harm
is aimed at the direct (but secondary) target. A message is sent to the
indirect (but primary) target by way of that harm, a message about
what the perpetrator wants the indirect target to do, in order that
more direct harm be avoided. Terrorism is manipulative and a form
of coercion. A bombing is terrorist, for example, when it is the vehicle of a message containing demands, such as to release prisoners.
Ordinarily, the direct and indirect targets are distinct individuals (or
groups). Often direct targets are "throw-away" victims (as in bombing). But the same people can be targeted both directly and indirectly.
Wellman notes that in armed hold-ups, for example, the people directly threatened are the same people to whom a message is being
given to hand over their money "or else."

By this complexity, Wellman distinguishes terrorism from torture.
Terrorism is an evil with ulterior motives. It threatens or inflicts reasonably foreseeable intolerable harm in order to motivate actions or
abstentions. Torture, in contrast, need not be intended to coerce. It
need have no ulterior motive but may be inflicted simply as sadism
or as punishment or revenge.

The 9/11 attacks were terrorist in Wellman's sense if their intent was
to manipulate the U.S. government (or people) politically. On this reading, workers directly targeted as they began their day were used merely
as a means to send a message to the U.S. government, or perhaps to
the people of the United States. Those killed were "throw-away" victims. The content of any intended message—at the time of this
writing—has not been spelled out, although there is speculations regarding implicit demands, especially in relation to the Israeli-Palestinian conflict.[5] No one has yet publicly claimed responsibility or offered
an official reason for the attacks. We are left to infer the larger intent.
Evidence, including tapes of Osama bin Laden, shows that the attacks,
including the surprise element, were planned.[6] But the evidence does
not unambiguously reveal an ulterior purpose.

If the attacks' intent was not coercive but was, say, punitive, or if
it was simply to show the world that the United States is not invulnerable, then the deed was not basically terrorist, in Wellman's sense,
regardless of how much terror it produced. The alternative readings

do not imply a lesser evil. If punitive, the attacks were administered without a shred of due process. If carried out simply to show the world it could be done, they did have an ulterior motive. People were treated merely as means to an end they could not rationally share. But the motive was not to coerce. Rather, it would seem to be to encourage others who might also want to attack the United States.

WAR

Philosophically still less clear than whether the attacks were terrorist is whether—supposing for argument's sake that the attacks *were* terrorist—the response of a war against terrorism waged by the victims of that terrorism is also an evil.

War is commonly understood as "a state of open and declared armed hostile conflict between states or nations."[7] Whether war can be a legitimate response to attacks carried out by persons unauthorized by any state raises philosophical issues about the meaning of war and the justice of a military force response, whatever we call it. What are the limits of a war on—or military force response to—terrorism? What less drastic measures must be exhausted first? How is the scope of the war's *opponents* limited?

Some may regard "war on terrorism" as metaphorical, like "war on drugs" and "war on crime." The expression is not a mere metaphor, however. "War" confers an appearance of legitimacy. Many believe war can be justified, but not terrorism, or that terrorism is harder to justify. On R. M. Hare's view, terrorism is the resort of people who lack the cooperation or resources to wage war in the conventional sense.[8] He notes that many people regard it as a live issue whether terrorism in Europe by the Resistance during World War II was justified. Activities of the Resistance, it might be replied, are better recognized as guerrilla warfare than described as terrorist because their aim was not to manipulate or coerce but to disable. Hare reminds us, however, that "to some extent terrorism is a substitute for conventional war" and that "it was an act of terrorism which sparked off the first World War."[9] Thus, the idea of a war on terrorism can have the effect of dignifying the original attack as an act of war (albeit unjustified), rather than simply a criminal act.

How metaphorical is "war on terrorism," one may ask, when military force is deployed to carry out the war? Despite drops of food and supplies by the United States for the Afghan people, U.S. armed forces have inflicted real intolerable harm, including death, on unarmed people there, including women and children. Were those harms evils? Since the drops of food and supplies is evidence that intolerable harms to unarmed people were reasonably foreseeable, the primary question appears to be that of culpable wrongdoing. Was the U.S. military response in Afghanistan morally justified? That question takes us naturally into just war theory.

JUSTICE IN RESPONDING AND THE RULES OF WAR

Appropriate responses to 9/11, on my view, would include global hunts(with international cooperation) for responsible survivors, those complicit in planning and supporting the attacks, including provision of training, financial backing, and safe harbors, and hunts for anyone taking criminal steps toward carrying out further such attacks. Ideally, persons apprehended under suspicion of complicity in the 9/11 attacks should then, if evidence warrants a trial, be duly charged and tried in international tribunals. Charges should depend on evidence regarding the attacks' intentions. So far, the evidence appears ambiguous between at least two interpretations.

It is commonplace to refer to the 9/11 attacks as both terrorist and hate crimes. Yet these two interpretations are distinct. Terrorism need not be motivated by bias. Hate crimes (also known as bias crimes) need not be terrorist in intent. The two interpretations can even compete with one another. If the deed was terrorist, there is some associated demand, its main objective. In that event, the direct target may have been as much the physical structures and the data and equipment therein as the human occupants. Was the attacks' timing determined by when workers would fill the World Trade Center offices? Or was it determined by the flight schedules of aircraft containing requisite amounts of fuel? On the terrorist interpretation, the timing might have been determined solely by the availability of suitably fueled aircraft. On the hate crimes interpretation, the presence of human occupants is more likely to have been a critical factor.[10]

Hate crimes target victims for their racial, religious, ethnic, national, or perhaps political identity.[11] If it was a hate crime, people in the World Trade Center and in the aircraft were targeted for their (perceived) identity, presumably as Americans, American sympathizers, or as capitalists. The structures and material contents were destroyed for their relationships to the human occupants (perhaps to others also).

There need be no demand. Hate crimes need not have a coercive intent, although, of course, they may. Cross-burnings and lynchings, for example, commonly do have associated threats and demands. So it is possible, finally, that the 9/11 attacks were both hate crimes directed against the American people in general, not just those killed, and also terrorist, intended to send a message (yet to be clearly deciphered) to survivors, sympathizers, and others.

On the hate crime interpretation, suspects might be charged with crimes against humanity for targeting victims by their perceived identity. Crimes against humanity, defined as acts of violence "against an identifiable group of persons, irrespective of the make-up of that group or the purpose of the persecution," are hate crimes.[12] Regarding it as a crime against humanity to kill individuals because they are (perceived as) capitalists does not presuppose commitment to the value of capitalism but only a commitment to protecting individuals from assault on the basis of their (perceived) membership in a larger group.

Universal jurisdiction applies to crimes against humanity.[13] Any nation can try the accused, regardless of where the alleged crimes were committed and regardless of the nationality of victims or the accused. Nevertheless, an international court would be especially appropriate for 9/11 suspects because victims represented many nations and because the deed threatens security globally. Suspects may try to avoid live capture, but pursuers can aim to take them alive and try them in court. But if war is declared, rather than a hunt for responsible individuals, who has the opportunity for a fair trial?

Internationally accepted rules of war evolved to regulate wars *with* or *between* opponents all of whom are agents (nations or states) and capable of making decisions.[14] But what guidelines regulate wars *on* or *against* such "opponents" as terrorism or drugs? Terrorism and drugs are not nations but are connected with agents in multiple ways. Which of these connections should make the associated agents themselves opponents can be far from clear.

The problem of agency applies to some extent even in the case of civil wars, which makes it unclear how the rules of war apply to them. Who, for example, has the authority to declare a civil war? Who justifiably speaks for the people against an existing government? Against whom does the government declare war when the opponent is internal? Somewhat analogous difficulties of agency arise for an international war against terrorism.

A first difficulty is this. By tradition, a just war must be declared by appropriate authorities. A major point of the declaration is to give fair notice to opponents. On whom is a war on terrorism declared? Who gets fair notice? When war is declared on terrorism globally, rather than on terrorists of a specified territory, it is unclear which individuals are targeted. This unclarity may even be intended, for wagers of such a war may not know who or where the terrorists are.

Unclarity of the enemy's identity has further ramifications with respect to rules of war. Heads of state can negotiate for peace. But who has the authority to negotiate for peace in a war on terrorism? If peace is not negotiable, how must such a war end? What is to prevent it from becoming a war of extermination?

Evils, intolerable harms produced by culpable wrongdoing, should not exist. Ideally, no one would wrongly inflict intolerable harm. Evils are deeds with certain consequences (intolerable harm) or experiences with certain sources (culpable wrongdoing). Evil doers may be evil, but they are not evils. They are people. Even people committed to evils are not evils. Representing as an evil the *enemy* at whom military force is directed—*human beings*, not harms or deeds—is abusive and politically opportunistic. It encourages the influence that the enemy should not exist and that its annihilation is justified.

According to just war theory, a principle of discrimination between combatants and noncombatants holds it unjust to target civilians directly. Civilians may not be killed to demoralize a military opponent, for example, or for revenge. By this principle, bombing civilians in retaliation for a like bombing of civilians by the enemy should be a war crime, as should bombing civilians to demoralize a military opponent, although such deeds by parties victorious in a war are not apt to be prosecuted by international military tribunals whose sponsors include those parties. Bombings so motivated violate Kant's principle that humanity in anyone's person must never be treated merely as a means but must be treated always at the same time as an end.[15]

It is often pointed out that weapons of mass destruction make it impossible to target combatants without risking the lives of large (often greater) numbers of noncombatants. Some appear to think this fact makes rules of war—at least, the discrimination principle—obsolete. One could as well draw the opposing conclusion, however, that wars conducted with such weapons cannot be just and therefore war should be obsolete. The principle of discrimination is not empty, as it implies that there are reasons for which civilians may not be targeted, such as revenge and demoralizing a military opponent. It rules out targeting civilians when risking their lives is not an unavoidable consequence of using weapons against combatants. Some might want to distinguish the Pentagon attack from the World Trade Center attack, arguing that the Pentagon was a military target and that killing civilians in the Pentagon was a necessary consequence of a legitimate military targeting, whereas no such argument is available regarding the World Trade Center killings. Even if it is valid to distinguish the Pentagon as a military target, however, it was hardly a *legitimated* military under just war theory, as no war had been declared, nor any warning issued.

But whom is it unjust for those defending themselves from terrorism to target directly in making war on terrorism? In war those who wear a military uniform are identifiable as combatants. Those who wear no uniform are presumed civilians. By tradition, medical personnel are exempt from combatant status. Producers of food and goods that people naturally consume during times of peace have also not been regarded as combatants (unlike producers of munitions). Guerrilla warfare complicates the distinction between combatants and noncombatants, as guerrilla fighters wear no uniform. Wars against opponents who are not nations raise more complications. What corresponds to civilians, or noncombatants, when one party to a war is not a nation or state?

How are nonterrorists identifiable? What must one's relationship to acts of terrorism be in order that one not count as a terrorist? It is easy to say that people are terrorists if they inflict the direct harm in a terrorist attack (hijack a plane used as a bomb), participate in its planning, knowingly supply money or materials, or knowingly shelter people who do. Less easily specified are what people are responsible to know, what counts as support, and how direct and specific the connections must be between individuals and terrorist acts.

OTHER TERRORISMS

The preceding concerns reveal that "terrorists" is not a well-defined group. "Terrorist" is not an identity. It is not a proper name, like British. To identify someone as a terrorist is to render a judgment on them, not simply to make a discovery. Not all terrorists have common goals, belong to a unified organization, or have the same opponents. There are terrorists within the United States who are citizens and were never immigrants. The Ku Klux Klan is an infamous terrorist organization, and the era of lynching is no doubt the most infamous episode of terrorism in U.S. history. Nor is home-grown terrorism in the United States a thing of the past. The National Coalition of Burned Churches is alive today, and its concerns are not lightning or faulty wiring.[16] The Southern Poverty Law Center has been vigilant against home-grown terrorism for decades.

Other domestic terrorists are less widely and publicly acknowledged as such. The reigning stereotype is of someone who carries out destructive acts against public institutions or in public places, seeking attention for national or international political causes. The stereotype ignores state terrorism (such as that of Hitler, Stalin, Idi Amin, and Pol Pot), which is often clandestine, as Emma Goldman, Jonathan Glover, and others have pointed out.[17] It also ignores terrorism in the home and the terrorism of rape, both stranger and acquaintance rape, with which women and girls are left to cope routinely, even in many states that are considered relatively secure from external attack. The poet Susan Griffin, for example, writes (in the United States):

> I have never been free of the fear of rape. From a very early age I, like most women, have thought of rape as part of my natural environment—something to be feared and prayed against like fire or lightning. I never asked why men raped; I simply thought it one of the many mysteries of human nature.[18]

Although she says she had never asked why men rape, she proposes an answer to that question:

> In the system of chivalry, men protect women against men. This is not unlike the protection relationship which the Mafia established with small businesses in the early part of this twentieth century. Indeed, chivalry is an age-old protection racket which depends for its existence on rape.[19]

Rape, she implies, is a terrorist practice, analogous to the terrorism of organized crime.[20]

Like much rape, much violence in the home serves the ulterior ends of creating and maintaining heterosexual male dominance and female dependence and service. Just as with punishment, so also with rape and domestic violence, it is the treat rather than the actual infliction of harm that does the work of intimidation.[21] In the institution of rape (as in punishment), not all whose conduct is guided by its widely known but generally unwritten rules need be motivated by the ends the institution services, although participants who have their own motives can often be held responsible for knowing what ends their conduct in fact serves. Individual rapists may assault women for fun or revenge, not to coerce service, but they can hardly be ignorant of the effects of fear of rape on women. Those motivated by the goal of domination are more likely to be men with power—men who do not investigate or prosecute when they could, judges who go easy on rapists—and those who blame women for "asking for it."

But assaults and threats of domestic violence often appear directly intended to coerce victims into providing perpetrators with services and into deference and permission-seeking for all sorts of mundane things. According to attorney Joyce McConnell, when a woman is held to the services of a wife by someone who batters her, she is the victim of involuntary servitude in the sense of the Thirteenth Amendment.[22] She is also the victim of terrorism, in Wellman's sense. As in armed hold-ups, direct and indirect targets in domestic violence are usually the same persons. But the structure of terrorism is there, although some batterers end by defeating their own ends with lethal violence (and some, apparently realizing this, turn lethal violence on themselves as well).

Rape is a terrorist institution that secures for men generally the willingness of women to serve them in everything from laundry and cooking to childcare and sexuality. A truly global war on terrorism would include among its targets rapists and their supporters as well as those who perpetrate domestic partner abuse, elder abuse, and child abuse. President Bush's war on terrorism does not yet recognize such perpetrators. They do not appear to be among his targets. But for those who would support a global war on terrorism, it should be an interesting question whether war would be an appropriate response to rapists and to terrorists in the home.

If the United States is justified in making war on international terrorists, should feminists make war on rapists and on terrorism in the home? Should battered women, battered children, battered elders, and rape survivors regard themselves as existing in a state of nature—as though governments, laws, and courts did not exist—with respect to batterers and rapists? The law has a poor track record of protecting victims. Let's see what we can learn from the histories of victims who finally did whatever seemed necessary to protect themselves.

In the famous Michigan case known as "the burning bed," Francine Hughes poured gasoline over her sleeping former husband and ignited it, one night in 1977, after years of having endured has battering and many times having appealed unsuccessfully to the law for protection for herself and her children.[23] She was tried for murder and finally acquitted, on a defense of insanity. But if killing without trial is an appropriate response to terrorists, should she even have been put on trial?

And what of the equally famous case, from the same era, of Inez García? In 1974, after receiving a phone call threatening her with murder, García pursued and shot at two men, one of whom had raped her minutes before, while the other, who weighed three hundred pounds, stood guard to prevent her escape. Her shots killed one man (the second), and she only regretted not having succeeded in killing the other as well (he was never charged with any crime).[24] She was tried for murder by the state of California. At first she was convicted and sentenced to five years to life. Later, on appeal. she was exonerated, defended by attorney Susan B. Jordan, who successfully argued self-defense. Should García not have been tried?

Perhaps it will be objected that feminists and victims of battery or rape lack authority to make war. Yet why is that important, if not as part of a broader understanding of rules defining conditions under which fighting is fair? Have not such rules been abandoned already if men can rape and batter women with legal impunity? Is the real objection that most rape victims and victims of terrorism in the home are female and war is not an appropriate response by females?

JUSTICE FOR THE UNJUST

When terrorists disregard fairness, victims face a hard question: To what extent ought one to be fair even to those who disregard fairness? Domestic criminals often disregard fairness. Still, the state offers them a trial. Trials reassure others who might one day be mistakenly identified as criminals, since a fair trial would give them an opportunity to rebut the charge and be exonerated. Striking back without trial, on the principle that those unfair to others do not deserve to be treated fairly, ignores the possibility that retaliators might often be mistaken about those they identify as criminal, mistaken about what was done, why it was done, the conditions under which it was done, or even who did it.

The same points apply to international terrorism. Without trials, what assurance have citizens of the world that they will not be mistakenly identified as terrorists or as supporters of terrorism and summarily dispatched? Such concerns support the creation of the International Military Tribunal (IMT) at Nuremberg at the end of World War II. The IMT was an alternative to the usual practice of victors in war, whose advocates proposed simply shooting Axis leaders from a select list decided on ("pricked") by the Allies. As Telford Taylor notes, in his memoir of the Nuremberg trials, "too many people believed that they had been *wrongfully* hurt by the leaders of the Third Reich and wanted a *judgment* to that effect," and "furthermore . . . the spectacle of Joseph Stalin, who had sent uncounted thousands of his own countrymen to their deaths by his 'political decisions,' sitting as one of a triumvirate to 'prick' a list of Germans, would have made their decisions a target of mockery as long as memory endured."[25]

Under the circumstances, given existing law, there was a good case for trying Francine Hughes and Inez García in court and making public, and as far as possible documenting, the facts that led them to their deeds.[26] A trial, inquest, or hearing is a formal and public way to determine whether those who kill are justified and to clear their names, if so. Trials assure others that they cannot be killed with impunity by just anyone who is afraid of them or who is apprehensive about what they might do. It would have been right, morally, to acquit Francine Hughes, even without the insanity defense, given her history of having exhausted less desperate methods of self-defense. What made self-defense in her case legally problematic was that the man she killed was asleep, not forewarned, unable at that moment to defend himself or try to escape, nor at that moment attacking her. Under Michigan law, there was no way to acquit Hughes of murder other than to use the insanity defense, although many would say her deed was one of the sanest of her life. She should never have been left in the position of having to defend herself by extreme means. The man she killed is the person who, ideally, should have had to stand trial, as should the men responsible for the rape of García.

When a nation makes war on terrorism, and not on another nation, it takes matters into its own hands in a manner that is in some respects analogous to what Hughes and García did. It steps somewhat outside the bounds and processes of law, instead of depending on them—in this case, the bounds and processes of international law. A state may "warn" terrorists by declaring war. But if "terrorist" is not well defined, who knows they are being warned? Of what values is a warning to everyone in a territory when many inhabitants who are not terrorists lack means of escape or self-defense?

If it was justifiable for Michigan to try Hughes and for California to try García, or if it would have been justifiable at least to hold an inquest or hearing regarding the killings, then perhaps it would also be justifiable, for similar reasons, for international tribunals to do likewise to the leaders of nations who make war on terrorists, when the wars kill masses of unarmed civilians who lack means of escape. A trial, inquest, or hearing should reassure others in the international community, who might one day wrongly be identified as terrorists, that no nation can assault them with impunity simply out of fear of what they might do. Such inquiries should also consider whether less drastic responses had been exhausted by wagers of war on terrorism.

Yet, would it not make better sense for an international team to capture and try, in an international court, those initially accused of international terrorism or of complicity in it, instead of leaving victim nations to take matters into their own hands, just as it would have made better sense to capture and try the man repeatedly accused of battering Hughes and the men accused of rapes such as that of García, rather than leaving women to defend themselves by whatever means necessary? An affirmative answer means nations of the world have serious work to do, collectively, regarding intervention policies where terrorism and fears of terrorism loom. The conclusion is not that nations defending themselves against terrorism militarily are necessarily wrong. Rather, they should not be left in the position of having to make the decision. Meanwhile, making war on terrorism may put leaders of nations doing so at risk of becoming justifiably liable to inquests or hearings, if not trials for war crimes, by international tribunals, just as Hughes and García became liable to trial by their states for murder.

NOTES

1. Immanuel Kant, "Groundwork of the Metaphysics of Morals," in Kant, *Practical Philosophy*, trans. and ed. Mary J. Gregor (Cambridge University Press, 1996), p. 80.

2. Friedrich Nietzsche, *On the Genealogy of Morality*, trans. Maudemarie Clark and Alan J. Swensen (Indianapolis: Hackett, 1998), pp. 9–33. Recent books taking seriously the concept of evil include Paul Woodruff and Harry

A. Wilmer, eds., *Facing Evil: Light at the Core of Darkness* (LaSalle, IL: Open Court, 1988); Nel Noddings, *Women and Evil* (Berkeley, CA: University of California Press, 1989); John Kekes, *Facing Evil* (Princeton, NJ: Princeton University Press, 1990); Mary Midgley, *Wickedness: A Philosophical Essay* (London, New York: Routledge, 1992); Jonathan Glover, *Humanity: A History of the Twentieth Century* (New Haven, CT: Yale University Press, 2000); Maria Pia Lara, ed., *Rethinking Evil: Contemporary Perspectives* (Berkeley, CA: University of California Press, 2001); Amelie Rorty, ed., *The Many Faces of Evil: Historical Perspectives* (New York: Routledge, 2001); Claudia Card, *the Atrocity Paradigm: A Theory of Evil* (New York: Oxford University Press, 2002); and Susan Nieman, *Evil in Modern Thought: An Alternative History of Philosophy* (Princeton, NJ: Princeton University Press, 2002). Among earlier works, outstanding contributions include Hannah Arendt, *Eichmann in Jerusalem: A Report on the Banality of Evil* (New York: Viking Press, 1963); Ronald D. Milo, *Immorality* (Princeton, NJ: Princeton University Press, 1984); and S. I. Benn, "Wickedness," *Ethics* (1985). 95: 795–810.

3. I develop this analysis of evil at length in Card, *The Atrocity Paradigm.*

4. Carl Wellman, "On Terrorism Itself," *Journal of Value Inquiry* 13 (1979): 250–258.

5. Failure to spell out the message should not be taken as good evidence that no message was intended. When I was a junior faculty member, senior faculty who voted on salary raises often meant to send a message by recommending no increase, a small increase, a large one, and so on. Since the message was almost never spelled out in those days, it was often not received. But many of the voters later said unequivocally that their intent was to send a message.

6. See Reporters, Writers, and Editors of [the German magazine] *Der Spiegel, Inside 9-11: What Really Happened* (New York: St. Martins, 2001) for discussion of many kinds of evidence.

7. *Merriam-Webster's Collegiate Dictionary*, 10th edition (Springfield, MA: Merriam-Webster, Inc., 1993).

8. R. M. Hare, "On Terrorism," *Journal of Value Inquiry* 13 (1979): 240–249.

9. Hare, p. 244.

10. I say "more likely" because hate crimes are sometimes directed against property, as in church burnings and cemetery desecrations.

11. A useful introductory pamphlet on hate crime legislation is David Rosenberg and Michael Lieberman, *Hate Crimes Laws* (n.p.: Anti-Defamation League, 1999). See also the special issue on hate crime legislation, ed. Christopher Wellman, of the journal *Law and Philosophy* 20.3 (March 2001), and Frederick M. Lawrence, *Punishing Hate: Bias Crimes Under American Law* (Cambridge, MA: Harvard University Press, 1999).

12. Roy Gutman and David Rieff, eds., *Crimes of War: What the Public Should Know* (New York: Norton, 1999), p. 107.

13. Gutman and Reiff, p. 108.

14. A useful brief overview of relatively recent elements of this evolution is offered by Telford Taylor in his memoir, *Anatomy of the Nuremberg Trials* (New York: Knopf, 1992), pp. 3–42.

15. Kant, *Groundwork*, p. 80.

16. News report on National Public Radio, June 21, 2002.

17. Jonathan Glover, "State Terrorism," in *Violence, Terrorism, and Justice*, ed. R. G. Frey and Christopher W. Morris (Cambridge: Cambridge University Press, 1991), pp. 256–75; Emma Goldman, "The Psychology of Political Violence," in *Anarchism and Other Essays* (New York: Dover, 1969), pp. 79–108; Claudia Card, "Rape as a Terrorist Institution," in Frey and Morris, pp. 296–319.

18. Susan Griffin, "Rape: The All-American Crime," in *Feminism and Philosophy*, ed. Mary Vetterling Braggin, Frederick A. Elliston, and Jane English (Totowa, NJ: Littlefield, Adams and Co., 1977), p. 313.

19. Griffin, "Rape," p. 320.

20. For extended development of this idea, see Claudia Card, *The Unnatural Lottery: Character and Moral Luck* (Philadelphia: Temple University Press, 1996), pp. 97–117.

21. See J. D. Mabbott, "Punishment," *Mind* n.s. 48 (1939): 152–167, for the argument, now classic, that it is the threat of punishment, rather than the infliction of punishment, that does the work of deterrence.

22. Joyce E. McConnell, "Beyond Metaphor: Battered Women, Involuntary Servitude and the Thirteenth Amendment," *Yale Journal of Law and Feminism* 4.2 (Spring 1992): 207–253.

23. Faith McNulty, *The Burning Bed* (New York: Harcourt Brace Jovanovich, 1980).

24. See Kenneth W. Salter, *The Trial of Inez García* (Berkeley, CA: Editorial Justa Publications, Inc., 1976), and Jim Wood, *The Rape of Inez García* (New York: G. P. Putnam's Sons, 1976).

25. Taylor, p. 33.

26. Elsewhere I have argued that the law ought to expand its understanding of battering to take account of patterns of behavior over time, and not just isolated acts viewed out of context, much as it did during the 1990s with regard to the crime of stalking. The current understanding of battering seems modeled on the idea of a barroom brawl, rather than on the idea of domestic violence. See Card, *Lesbian Choices* (New York: Columbia University Press, 1995), pp. 109–117.

CHAPTER 10

Terrorism, War, and Empire

RICHARD W. MILLER

In the war on terrorism, questions will often arise of the rightness and the further moral consequences of coercive intervention by the United States in other nations' affairs. I hope to show that moral scrutiny of the first wars launched or proposed in the war, against the Taliban and against Saddam Hussein's regime, has much to contribute to a moral framework for answering these questions. The framework that will emerge imposes such severe restrictions on war as a recourse of the war on terrorism that the Afghan war itself will probably present the last situation passing the test and connects coercive intrusions with such demanding responsibilities of aid that the war on terrorism can be expected vastly to expand the responsibility of the United States to enhance the well-being of people in poor countries.

AFGHANISTAN: THE BURDENS OF PROPORTIONALITY

The justification of the Afghan war, that is, the invasion of Afghanistan by the United States to overthrow the Taliban, could begin by appealing to a fundamental duty of any government to defend the residents of its territory from unjust violence. In light of the atrocities of September 11, it would have been profoundly wrong of the United States government not to aim at ending the conspiracy that had killed thousands on its soil and other ongoing conspiracies with similar goals. Al Qaeda's complicity was probable, and bin Laden had declared it a duty of every Muslim to kill Americans and Jews and was openly training and funding such missions of death.

Thus, traditional considerations of defense made Al Qaeda a legitimate target—say, for attack by guided missiles, bombs, and commandos. But what about the government of Afghanistan? Even though the Taliban were not engaged in foreign attacks, the legitimacy of an attack on this regime is grounded on a traditional distinction between alliance and neutrality, codified in one of the most elaborate parts of the international law of war, the determination of neutral status. According to traditional norms, the Taliban had forfeited its right to be left alone by, in effect, allying with Al Qaeda. "A neutral state," Westlake wrote, in 1913, "must not permit either its subjects or a belligerent to make any such use of its territory as amounts to taking part in an operation of war."[1] If the launching of a war in response to such conduct was always ruled out, governments could safely give vital sustenance to unjust and deadly attacks on foreign territory simply by avoiding an explicit declaration of participation in these projects. On the other hand, by creating an option of genuine neutrality and a duty to respect it, the traditional norms inhibit the spread of carnage, expressing a proper valuing of human life.

Admittedly, under pressure of imminent invasion, the Taliban described conditions under which they might expel bin Laden or even give him over to trial. But their long-standing, knowing provision of sanctuary for his unjust violent conspiracy made it permissible for the United States to assume a lack of good faith in the observance of duties of neutrality. As Westlake quaintly puts it, at the start of his long survey of the nuances of neutral status, "The duties which are incumbent on neutrals . . . are mainly founded on the importance, in international as in all other relations, of a frank sincerity."[2] The Taliban had no cause for complaint if their defeat was joined with the defeat of Al Qaeda as a goal of war.

Despite the positive bearing of well-established and plausible principles, the Afghan war is hard to justify because of the foreseeable effects of a war that would achieve the just goal of deposing the Taliban. The test that it passes with great difficulty, if at all, is often labeled "proportionality": War is wrong as a means of upholding goals that could rightly be pursued through war in other circumstances if it is an excessive response given its likely costs, its likely effectiveness in upholding these goals, and the likely effectiveness and likely costs of alternative responses that do not include war. Thus, most people would regard India's launching a war against Pakistan as an excessive response to Pakistan's harboring secessionists who engage in terrorism in Kashmir; in some circumstances, war might be a justifiable response to such sanctuary, but in the actual circumstances, the killing unleashed would make it grossly irresponsible.

Concern for proportionality directs us to a comparison of reasons pro and con, which must be carried out in the absence of a determinate general rule connecting available evidence with relevant moral conclusions. *Going to war is wrong when the likely costs of any war that might be launched sustain reasons to object to it that are, as a whole, more serious than reasons to object to some path of peace, given its alternative prospects.* In applying this precept, one will compare the prospects of the best sort of war under the circumstances— that is, the sort most strongly supported by considerations of aims and costs—with the prospects of the best response not including war.

In the war that was actually launched against the Taliban, the United States relied on overwhelming firepower and a small number of troops from the United States and Euro-American allies to facilitate the military triumph of a coalition of anti-Taliban factions whose previous history of atrocity, internecine strife, and crime signaled grave risks of consequent harms. In the wake of Soviet withdrawal, the future elements of the anti-Taliban alliance had figured prominently among the armed forces that, in the words of Amnesty International, plunged Afghanistan "into lawlessness and [made] much of the civilian population . . . [the] target of a reign of terror."[3] For example, in factional fighting over control of Kabul among future forces in the anti-Taliban alliance, twenty-five thousand died in 1994 alone, most of them civilians killed in indiscriminate rocket and artillery barrages.[4] In an ethnic reprisal in the previous year, the forces of Ahmed Shah Masoud, who was to become the leading figure of the coalition with whom the United States joined, rampaged through a Hazara neighborhood of Kabul, "killing—by local accounts—'up to 1000' civilians, beheading old men, women and even their dogs."[5] In the first of many large massacres by both sides in war with the Taliban, anti-Taliban forces massacred approximately three thousand prisoners, usually by sealing them in shipping containers, to suffocate and bake.[6] The Afghan war was launched in a country ravaged by twenty-two years of civil war and three years of drought, in which the Taliban had established basic stability and freedom from nonpolitical violence in areas they controlled; enjoyed much support, especially in the Pashtun countryside; engaged in stern repression in cities in the name of a specially severe reading of Islamic law; and imposed an alien and sometimes violent rule on ethnic minorities in some non-Pashtun regions.[7]

There was good reason to suppose that substantially less reliance on overwhelming firepower and on intelligence and combat provided by local allies would have led to a long, brutal war with dubious prospects of success, an appalling possibility foreshadowed by the Soviet intervention. So the kind of war that was chosen is the crucial kind to evaluate, a path of war threatening no greater harm than other kinds of war that would have a reasonable chance of achieving goals that might serve as just war aims.

The most troubling foreseeable consequence of this war was the killing of noncombatants through the use of bombs, helicopter gunships, artillery, and mines, often deployed in response to intelligence from those allies, in order to kill members of an armed force and a political movement diffused throughout much of a large and rugged country, without features clearly distinguishing them from the typical noncombatant (but frequently armed) Pashtun man. Although the Taliban were deposed much more quickly than expected, these deaths were numerous. Of the two extensive critical analyses of reports of civilian deaths from the first two months of U.S. bombing in Afghanistan, one estimates the toll at over three thousand,[8] the other at one thousand to thirteen hundred, a difference largely due to the severe numerical deflation of reported death tolls in the latter study.[9] Ian Traynor reports estimates of civilian deaths from the bombing campaign by Western medical and demining workers in post-Taliban Kabul that range from "between 2000 to 3000" to "up to 8000."[10]

The mayhem of war also foreseeably interfered with famine relief and unleashed a vast increase of criminal violence against noncombatants, often perpetrated by the allies whose triumph the United States assured. For example, "throughout northern Afghanistan, Pashtun communities [who share their ethnicity with most of the Taliban, 40 percent or more of Afghans and a large majority in the south and east] faced widespread looting, beatings, abductions, extortion, and incidents of killing and sexual violence."[11]

A war foreseeably generating such grave harms to noncombatants is wrong unless the imposition of its risks would be justifiable to the noncombatants in jeopardy. In addition, reasons of compassion dictate concern for consequent deaths of soldiers who are first made enemy combatants by the launching of a war, unless their prior goals and projects justify withholding compassion. This compassionate concern ought to extend to the vast majority of Taliban troops, who were conscripts, who sought to help restore peace based on rough but effective justice, who sought to uphold an interpretation of Islamic law that did not endorse murderous terrorist attacks and was not very different from interpretations current in the anti-Taliban alliance, or who participated in a local fighting force that protected their locale and family through traditional strategies of alliance that turned out to involve fealty to the Taliban.

Even though the overthrow of the Taliban was less prolonged and deadly than expected, "Taliban losses were considerable," as Michael O'Hanlon notes in his glowing assessment of the Afghan war ("for the most part, a masterpiece of military creativity and finesse") in *Foreign Affairs*. More specifically, he cites an estimate that "as many as 8,000 to 12,000 [Taliban combatants] were killed," and proposes that "another 7,000 or more were taken prisoner."[12] The captured included 2,000 held in Shebargan prison, 80–110 in cells meant for 10–15 men, "the water supply unclean, sanitation virtually absent, clothing meager, barred walls open to the elements in winter conditions," a place where, according to the commandant, "many, many, many prisoners" die.[13] Continuing a long-established pattern, the anti-Taliban coalition killed hundreds, perhaps thousands, of captives, often stuffing them by the dozens into sealed shipping containers.[14]

Foreseeable costs of these kinds constituted a serious reason not to launch a war. But the same kinds of risks have been generated by war efforts as just as U.S. participation (with a deeply immoral ally) in World War II. The Afghan war was not unjust if the distinctive foreseeable costs of taking the best feasible path of peace instead of launching the war generate reasons for war-launching that are at least as serious as those favoring that path of peace.

The central declared goal of U.S. responses to the September 11 atrocities is the protection of people in the United States. The most promising, otherwise acceptable path of peace in pursuit of this goal would include many of the police measures actually adopted in the United States and countries whose governments are sincerely and freely committed to track down terrorist groups threatening the United States. The usefulness of these measures is suggested by the September 11 attacks themselves, which took advantage of permission to carry knives on board aircraft if the blades were less than six inches long, flimsy cockpit doors, and the failure to investigate the flight training of people from countries supplying many recruits to groups such as Al Qaeda who made vigorously anti-American statements and showed notable disinterest in learning how to land. In addition, since "peace," here, means the absence of war against another country, the most promising path of peace can be assumed to include specifically targetted attacks on Al Qaeda, for example, the destruction of Al Qaeda bases, forces, and arsenals from the air and by airborne special forces.

The most promising path of peace would also include measures in foreign policy reducing the strength of recruitment for Islamic terrorist groups threatening U.S. security and making it less likely that they would be harbored by a friendly populace or a government fearing this populace or reflecting its convictions. Al Qaeda's own recruiting videos made the importance of such measures clear by emphasizing the coercive humiliation of Palestinians by Israeli soldiers, whose arming absorbs 51 percent of all U.S. military aid;[15] the injuries to civilians of U.S.-initiated measures against Iraq; and the stationing of American troops, whose conduct violates traditional Islamic prescriptions, in the holy land of Islam.[16] Relevant shifts in foreign policy might include a sincere threat to withdraw the U.S. aid that makes it possible for Israel to occupy the West Bank and Gaza Strip unless Israel withdraws both forces and settlements to create an intact and viable Palestinian state, the ending of the embargo on Iraq (perhaps after extracting concessions in weapons monitoring), and the ending of the U.S. military presence in Saudi Arabia. Such changes would make some difference to the current state of opinion in the Muslim world, in which respondents to a Gallup poll in early 2002 "overwhelmingly described the United States as 'ruthless, aggressive, conceited, arrogant, easily provoked, biased.'"[17]

I will call this path of nonwar the "protective response" (a term that I will also use for analogous strategies of policing, foreign policy, and specifically targeted attacks in other contexts). The crucial question of proportionality is whether the foreseeable lesser effectiveness of the protective response in pursuing just war aims such as homeland security, together with other distinctive costs of this path of peace, provided reasons, at least as morally serious, to engage, instead, in the best war response, the Afghan war.

That the Afghan war significantly added to the homeland security that the protective response would have provided is one plausible hypothesis. But it is no more than that. The Afghan war led to the death or imprisonment of many Al Qaeda fighters and some leaders, and turned the rest of the leadership into fugitives. But many cells and leaders of this international and diffuse organization survive. In any case, the essential lethal work of Al Qaeda was the funding and coordination of deadly projects outside of Afghanistan, a process best attacked by the police work of the protective response. In the first six months after the fall of the Taliban (this essay was written in July 2002), the coerced confessions, boasts, or disinformation of Al Qaeda captured within Afghanistan seem to have generated a series of false alarms and have led to no arrests. The armed overthrow of the Taliban discourages support for terrorism by other governments. But the previous expulsion of bin Laden from Sudan indicates that measures short of war that are part of the protective response also discourage such support.

On the other hand, the war response makes it harder to engage in the reconciliation with Muslim political sentiments that is part of the protective response. The immediate, foreseeable additional costs of the Afghan war were many Muslim deaths, giving further force to doubts about the worth of Muslim lives in U.S. foreign policy.[18] Less directly, the resort to war and the justifications for the Afghan war make it more difficult to restrain countries with which the United States seeks to ally against terrorism from pursuing policies that appall the world Muslim community—a difficulty resourcefully exploited by the prime ministers of Israel and India.

Of course, plausible goals of the Afghan war and costs of the protective response are not limited to matters of security in the United States. The doubts that I have raised often extend to these further justifications, such as the reduction of terrorism worldwide or the goal of punishment (which hardly seems to justify launching a war that foreseeably visits death, injury, and dispossession on thousands of innocents). But one further goal demands separate assessment: the ending of the Taliban's grave injustice.

This appeal to political remedy must be judged in light of the foreseeable political consequences of the war that was in question, not some ideal consequences that the war-maker might proclaim as best. Because of a prior history in which the United States played a crucial role, the likely outcome of the war in question was dominance of the countryside by an unstable network of regional warlords, sometimes viciously repressive. Foreseeably, in the countryside, women's rights are not much more advanced than before, and an upsurge of violence against women has been the predictable consequence of the disorder of war. Even in Kabul, women still wear the burqa for fear of sexual violence or harassment.[19] Although non-Pashtun minorities hostile to the Taliban no longer fear vicious reprisals, Pashtun communities have been subjected to vicious reprisals. From the perspective of most

Afghans whose legitimate interests were jeopardized by the Afghan war, the gain in political good order seems to have been small, large though it is for many in the urban centers whose culture the Taliban hated and repressed.

In the face of likely gains on this scale, Afghans could justly fight against the Taliban, hoping for larger gains in justice and imposing grave risks on compatriots whom they ask to join their struggle. They could reasonably take the offense to their own dignity of submission to Taliban rule to be unacceptable. But whether outsiders, not suffering the injustice of the Taliban, may rightly impose such dangers is another matter. Given the limited likely political gains for most Afghans, the likely harms, and the absence of evidence of informed consent among the vast majority of those to whom a justification was owed, a military intervention in the cause of Afghan justice seems too risky a cure to be imposed from outside. If so, it remains to be seen how this cause could justify a war whose advancement of other goals is just one speculative hypothesis among others.

If the judgment of the Afghan war is seen as continuous with efforts to judge the imposition of risks by one person on another in order to reduce future threats, then the limited, conjectural gains seem inadequate justification. I oughtn't set fire to my neighbor's field on the basis of a mere plausible hypothesis that the firebreak will protect us from worse devastation by future forest fires. Still, there is, I think, an effective defense of the Afghan war because of its specific nature, as a response to unjust attack and alliance.

In applying the precept of proportionality, costs and benefits of the alternative courses of conduct in the circumstances at hand are not to be assigned individual weights and then added up, on each side. In the case of the diverse costs and benefits that are sometimes relevant, for example, the end of communal autonomy and the saving of lives if an invader is not resisted, it is not even clear what the weighing and adding procedure would be. Rather, one has to consider the consequences of adopting general precepts that rule out war in certain kinds of circumstances. Suppose that all morally responsible people shared a commitment to oppose the launching of a war jeopardizing many innocent lives in response to a foreign government's facilitating an unjust deadly attack unless there is warranted confidence that security from unjust deadly attacks will be significantly increased by this response, compared to the best path of nonwar. Because this epistemic warrant is usually so hard to acquire, such a general prohibition observed by morally responsible people would give a substantial advantage to those who resort to unjust violence. Concern for the dangers of social life in which aggressors can count on such security might lead someone reasonably to reject a system of principles including the prohibition.

It is at least (if no more than) a plausible hypothesis that confinement to the protective response would have significantly increased risks of large-scale terrorism in the United States and elsewhere. The harms that war would prevent on this plausible hypothesis seem to constitute concerns as morally serious as the harms that war would impose. So, on the epistemically permissive standard, the Afghan war was not a disproportionate response.

WAR AND AID

Even if the Afghan war was not unjust, the difficulty of establishing this legitimacy is important—among other reasons, because what makes justification difficult creates a responsibility of the United States to enhance Afghan well-being. For many Afghans whose interests deserve to be taken into account, the Afghan war violently imposed grave losses and risks, imposing them in other people's interests. Americans, whose interests are central to the war's justification and whose government was the vehicle of the burdens, owe them a debt, to be discharged by government means.

Other features of the Afghan war both broaden and deepen the responsibility to aid. For one thing, the United States did not simply mount the most intensive possible attack on Al Qaeda, defeat the Taliban in the field, and then leave Afghans to their own devices. Rather, the United States deployed pressure rooted in its military victory and continuing military presence to install its preferred interim government. The U.S. military continued to pursue those who played a role in the deposed indigenous government. The United States steers the Afghan project of reconstituting political community in the wake of a long civil war, tightly restricting reconciliation with those who supported the Taliban or who endorse religious, social, or political doctrines at odds with American interests. Even apart from the terms of Afghan political unity, the outcome of American suzerainty will not be neutral when Afghan interests conflict with American interests in such matters as the transport of Central Asian gas or the sphere of influence of Iran.[20]

With this suzerainty comes a special duty of concern. It is a familiar premise of decent government within borders that the just exercise of coercive influence over the enduring terms of social life is a trusteeship, which must be directed at the common good of all. There is no nonarbitrary basis for restricting the connection between power, trusteeship, and justice to those within the official borders of a political authority, denying a special duty of concern for foreigners subject to its power. If the human dignity of a citizen is violated when she is forced to conform to measures framed by a government of which she is a citizen that shows no concern for her nonvicious interests, so, too, is the human dignity of a foreigner who is politically subordinated but neglected. In both the domestic exercise of political power and the imposition of terms of political life abroad, a just regime tries to base stability on justified loyalty, rather than fear. Nineteenth-century fantasy paintings of dark-skinned subjects bringing tokens of loyalty to Victoria, as empress, may have appallingly misrepresented her subjects' attitudes, but they were at least an emblem of the attitude that had to be merited if the British Empire was to be just. And merited loyalty requires responsiveness to serious needs.

In addition to its current political domination, the prior history of U.S. activity affecting Afghanistan creates a further reason to enhance Afghan well-being. The attacks and continuing risks that motivated the Afghan war were due, in significant part, to prior U.S. activities in which the United States gambled with Afghan live in pursuit of goals that many Afghans did not share, producing devastating losses for them, but gains in geopolitical power for the United States.

In an interview with *Le Nouvel Observateur*, Zbigniew Brzezinski has said that "secret aid to the opponents of the pro-Soviet regime in Kabul" was approved in light of his opinion that "this aid was going to induce a Soviet military intervention." In response to the question, "You don't regret anything today?", he answers, "That secret operation was an excellent idea. It had the effect of drawing the Russians into the Afghan trap and you want me to regret it?"[21] The death toll from that trap is generally estimated at over a million, most of them Afghan civilians.

From the Soviet invasion to the Soviet withdrawal, the United States provided about $2.8 billion in military aid to anti-Soviet forces (i.e., about $3.7 billion in 2000 producer prices), including $630 million ($825 million in 2000 prices) in 1987.[22] Supervised by the CIA, this aid was channeled through Pakistan's Interservices Intelligence to conceal the extent of U.S. involvement and strengthen Pakistan's regional counterweight to Iran. Although spontaneous, village-based resistance to the Soviet invaders soon became widespread, Pakistan sought to arm an opposition more easily controlled and more apt to serve its interests, certifying seven groups headquartered in Pakistan as the exclusive recipents of aid and giving most to the party of Gulbuddin Hekmatyar, a fundamentalist Islamist group strongly departing from the tolerant pluralism of traditional Afghan culture.[23] After the Soviet withdrawal, Hekmatyar, who continued to receive aid originating from the United States, played the leading role in the indiscriminate rocket assaults that reduced much of Kabul to rubble.[24]

In guiding armed resistance to the Soviet presence, the United States also relied on a further resource, the cultivation of violently anti-communist fundamentalist groups in the Muslim world. In collaboration with Pakistan, Saudi Arabia, and Egypt, it financed and transported foreign fighters recruited by these groups to take part in the anti-Soviet jihad.[25] In this process, bin Laden came to Afghanistan. "To counter these atheist Russians," he recalled in a 1998 interview with Agence France Presse, "the Saudis chose me as their representative in Afghanistan. . . . I set up my first camp where these volunteers were trained by Pakistani and American officers. The weapons were supplied by the Americans, the money by the Saudis."[26] Eventually, this process generated Al Qaeda, providing shock troops for the Taliban, whose rise to power depended on violent strife among the anti-Soviet warlords created by U.S. aid. Thus, the obligation of the United States to compensate for the damage of manipulation of Afghans' fates in pursuit of U.S. interests is more, not less, demanding because of the injustice of the regime that the United States overthrew.

Six months after the triumph of the United States in the Afghan war, a United States Agency for International Development survey of Afghanistan found that "diet security," its measure of safety from famine, had fallen from nearly 60 percent in 2000 to 9 percent.[27] In Kabul, many loving parents try to give to orphanages children whom they cannot feed, and often fail because enrollment has nearly doubled since before the Afghan war, with economic "orphans" who have a parent accounting for half the increase.[28] In the first six months after the defeat of the Taliban, the United States had spent $230 million on assistance to Afghanistan. This is about 0.5 percent of the first annual appropriation for the war on terrorism,[29] amounting to the production cost of two and a half F-22 fighter planes.[30] It provides less than $9 per Afghan. In contrast, half of the annual economic assistance to the foremost U.S. recipient, Israel, is $87 per capita.[31] This is not a promising start in discharging duties of concern that are generated by present and past enmeshment of Afghan fates in U.S. interests and power.

BEYOND COUNTERATTACK?

Once the Taliban had been defeated, controversy over war shifted to Iraq, where, the Bush administration argued, an invasion to overthrow the Hussein regime would be a legitimate part of the war on terrorism. The justification of this war soon focused on an innovative just cause. First sketched in broad outline in the State of the Union address in which President Bush located Iraq in an "axis of evil," it seems to have evolved (as I write this in July 2002) into the following characterization of what can make a regime an appropriate target for war by the United States: the regime is hostile to the United States; past dealings with terrorist organizations together with grave injustices indicate that moral scruples would not prevent it from implementing this hostility by support for massive terrorist atrocities; and there is reason to believe that it has or is developing a capacity to produce weapons of mass destruction.

The alleged just cause for war radically extends traditional appeals to actual attack and current active alliance, on which the justification of the Afghan war relied. The rationale for this radical extension is the radical nature of dangers illuminated by the atrocities of September 11, namely, the vast scale of the disaster should a malevolent dictator succeed in conveying means of mass destruction to a terrorist group that uses them successfully. For example, a relatively crude, one-kiloton atomic bomb concealed in a truck in midtown Manhattan exploding on a workday afternoon might kill twenty thousand people in a matter of seconds, and hundreds of thousands all told.[32]

Given its ultimate rationale, one test of the proportionality of a war launched on the proposed new basis is clear: There must be reason on balance to suppose that it does not increase the probability of massive terroristic attacks. War against Iraq fails this test.

For proportionality, the baseline for risk assessment is the protective response, the most effective way short of war of coping with the relevant threats, involving strategies of policing, strictly targeted strikes, and foreign policy such as I have described. In connection with Iraq, the most salient foreign policy shift would be the lifting of economic sanctions. The current barriers to trade are too porous to prevent the introduction of all dual-purpose material that could, in principle, be converted to ghastly uses. But the impediments to trade, constraints on currency reserves, and discouragement of investment have claimed the lives of many innocents by crippling an economy that once thrived and public health measures that were once effective. Since sanctions were imposed, the mortality rate among children under five, which had been approximately halved under Hussein's regime,[33] has more than doubled outside of the UN protectorate in the Kurdish north,[34] implying hundreds of thousands of excess deaths.[35] Quite apart from humanitarian gains, the ending of the sanctions would reduce the incidence, among Muslims worldwide, of the hatred of the United States that provides recruits for the widespread, complex, well-hidden cooperation in barbarity needed to convert materials for mass destruction into an actual terrorist atrocity. Moreover, the end of the sanctions might help to convert the frenzy of victimhood that is the basic stance of the Iraqi regime now into the combination of social and economic development with political repression that had been characteristic of Hussein's Iraq before the Gulf War.

In the policing that is part of the protective response, the efforts most relevant to dangers posed by the Hussein regime concern Iraqi weapons of mass destruction. In December 1998, Iraq refused further entry to inspectors from United Nations Special Commission (UNSCOM), the UN agency charged with discovering weapons of mass destruction in Iraq, in response to a three-day missile attack that the United States had launched, unilaterally, on the basis of an UNSCOM report of incomplete compliance. Since then, policing of Iraqi weapons and capabilities has been based on intensive surveillance by the United States and its allies combined with import control. Writing in June 2000, Scott Ritter, who had been famously resourceful and aggressive as head of the UNSCOM Concealment Investigation Unit, assessed the Iraqi threat in these terms: "[I]t was possible as early as 1997 to determine that, from a qualitative standpoint, Iraq had been disarmed. Iraq no longer possessed any meaningful quantities of chemical or biological agents, if it possessed any at all, and the industrial means to produce these agents had either been eliminated or were subject to stringent monitoring. The same was true of Iraq's nuclear and ballistic missile capabilities. . . . Conjecture aside, . . . there is absolutely no reason to believe that Iraq could have meaningfully reconstituted any element of its WMD [weapons of mass destruction] capabilities [from the end of UNSCOM to the time when the article appeared.]"[36] Here and elsewhere, Ritter has noted that a moderate regime of monitoring within Iraq, dispensing with "aggressive inspections of Iraqi presidential and security sites," would be a significant addition to current surveillance.[37] The likely means of achieving Iraqi acceptance of such a regime would be an exchange for the lifting of economic sanctions.

Despite the importance of policing as part of the protective response, the most important safety measure is, probably, an underlying threat of retaliation. Hussein may currently possess sufficient chemical, biological, or nuclear materials to fuel catastrophe if put to successful terrorist use. The protective response does not rely on moral scruples on the part of Hussein and his regime to contain this threat. Rather, this response relies on a difference between Hussein and his regime and bin Laden and his followers. The former, unlike the latter, strongly prefers continued survival and control over their country to death in a conflagration, even if the conflagration is part of a disaster for the United States. If Iraqi participation in a project of mass destruction aimed at the United States were discovered, Hussein and his regime would be the target of the full armed wrath of the United States. They know this, and, hence, have nonscrupulous reasons not to set such projects in motion.

The crucial flaw in the war response is its disabling of this safety mechanism. The intended uses of capacities for mass destruction that Ritter infers from Iraqi documents are means of fending off imminent defeat.[38] No scenario for the conveyance of a canister of weapons-grade anthrax or radioactive waste from hidden places under Hussein's control to terrorist hands is more probable than an act of vengeance by Hussein and his henchmen when they face imminent death or degradation as a U.S.-led invasion triumphs.

In addition, long-term risk would be increased by the specific war response that has been portrayed as the best means of reducing risk: a massive invasion by U.S. troops of a Muslim country with a hostile attitude toward the United States that is not complicit in an attack on the United States. This would further inflame for many years the sentiments of Muslims who suspect the United States of hostility toward Islam and contempt for Muslim lives. Because the disintegration of the Soviet Union has created risks of access to resources for mass destruction that can be expected to endure for some time, whatever heightens the pervasiveness of the desire to put these resources to terrorist use is a significant source of danger.

Finally, apart from its impact on the risk of terrorist mass destruction, an invasion in response to hostile attitudes and potential dangers creates a dangerous precedent. For the removal of the stigma of war that is not counterattack encourages premature recourse to violence and an international milieu of suspicion and militarization.

Not just as compared with the protective response with its shifts in foreign policy, but also as compared with the apparatus of surveillance and background retaliatory threat that was already in place, an invasion to overthrow the Hussein regime increases deadly perils. Might it be justified, in any case, as a means of removing an unjust regime, albeit one that is not engaged in large-scale massacres? The gain in justice from such an invasion would have to be very great and of worldwide significance to justify imposing its grave risks, that is, the jeopardizing of U.S. and world security already described as well as risks imposed on Iraqis, including conscripted cannon fodder deserving moral concern. A sufficient gain is not likely as a consequence of an invasion by the United States. In the wake of this invasion, as in the wake of the Gulf War, the United States will have reason to prevent too much democracy in Iraq, since its secessionist consequences in the Kurdish north would appall Turkey and Syria while its consequences in the Shiite south would threaten to shift the balance of power in the Persian Gulf in favor of Iran. The likely outcome, a new strongman or repressive clique in Baghdad friendly to U.S. interests, might control Iraq less viciously than Hussein. But this hardly seems a prospect that would justify undermining traditional norms of nonintervention, at such grave risk to human life.

LARGER LESSONS

These arguments concerning the first questions of war raised by the war on terrorism support some larger morals. First, the major proposed addition to the traditional just causes for war would seem to be misguided in general, not just in the case of Iraq. The overriding interest in continued political control on the part of suspect regimes and the danger of rage and humiliation in the world Muslim community, which favored the protective response to Iraq, are general features of the current threat of terrorism.

Second, although war can be a legitimate response to the provision of sanctuary for a group mounting foreign terrorist operations, the demands of proportionality are hard to meet, and not just in Afghanistan. The violent deposing of a sovereign government is almost always a deadly process for many people meriting concern. If losses from a prior or imminent attack and plausible gains in security are not on the same scale of moral seriousness as the likely costs imposed by war, war in a just cause of deposing an ally of terrorism is unjust. For this reason, an Indian war on Pakistan would be wrong, and so would an American war on Iran, even if the dominant part of the political congeries that is the government of Iran supports groups who commit terrorist acts in Israel and is not energetic and sincere in closing the border with Afghanistan to Al Qaeda fugitives. The Taliban's active alliance with a terrorist group organizing operations of war on a large scale in its territory reflected a very special combination of power and vulnerability. Groups with the territorial strength to constitute a government rarely permit, much less welcome, another organization on their territory that develops and coordinates its own large-scale lethal apparatus. It is unlikely that harboring will ever again be a basis for a proportionate response of war.

Finally, if the war on terrorism takes a likely course, the rationale for a strong duty of aid that emerged in Afghanistan will take hold on a worldwide scale. The coercive resources of the United States are not limited to war. They include threats of war, embargos and severe trade discrimination and the threat of their imposition, aid to repressive regimes favoring U.S. interests, military support for a favored side in a civil war or secession struggle, and the arming or the threat to arm regional rivals of disfavored governments. Within the first few months of the war on terrorism, the United States embarked on the use of diverse coercive resources to set the terms for accommodation with Islamic political groups within Muslim countries and the terms for responding to armed secessionist movements and other insurgencies, whose weaker weaponry and need for disorder almost always lead to some terrorism (as happened, for example, in the African National Congress's fight against apartheid). In this sort of war on terrorism, American policies exploiting coercive advantages will strongly influence the terms of political life in countries with Muslim majorities, countries whose Muslim minority includes actually or potentially militant elements, relatively weak countries in which terrorist organizations strive for political power or secure regional bases, and unstable or militarily weak neighbors of such countries. This is a very large part of the world's population and territory.

I have already argued in the case of Afghanistan that such coercive influence on the terms of political life entails responsibilities of trusteeship. And in this larger sphere, as in Afghanistan, the responsibilities are deepened by the consideration that the United States contributed to the deadly disorder by which it justifies its pursuit of suzerainty, by prior manipulation of fates in countries in which it now seeks enhanced control. The United States played an active role for decades in contributing to fanaticism in Muslim countries through support of fundamentalist groups reliably and ferociously opposed to the secular left, including the group that became Al Qaeda.

The vast power that the United States seeks in the war on terrorism is, at best, justifiable if joined with profound concern for the well-being of people in the vast territories that the United States seeks to supervise and a concern to help them ultimately to reclaim full sovereignty.[39] Such a political duty of concern would not be discharged even if the current level of U.S. development aid ($35 per U.S. resident)[40] were multiplied severalfold and even if there were a considerable change in policies in international commerce and finance that presently disadvantage poor countries yet benefit the United States. Thus, the war on terrorism lends urgency to a single task in the economic, the political, and the military realms: making the United States a responsible hegemon.

This essay has been confined to a moral perspective in which duties to avoid the direct, foreseeable causing of harm, obligations of trusteeship, and responsibilities to compensate play an independent role and are not just devices for pursuing one authoritative goal of maximum welfare over the long run. Too little space remains, to put it mildly, to engage with rival perspectives on international relations. But a consequentialist moral perspective, based on that one maximizing goal, would not seem to yield different conclusions. Indeed, on the question of foreign aid, it would support demands for increased U.S. aid to poor countries more directly and on an even broader scale. Perhaps, in contrast, those who favor an amoral perspective on international relations in which a goal of increased geopolitical power for the United States provides the only justification needed for U.S. conduct would reach very different conclusions. Lacking the space to criticize this perspective, I can only express the hope that anyone drawn to this basis for a more aggressive, less supportive policy than I have recommended will spare us talk of evil and good.

NOTES

1. John Westlake, *International Law, Part II: War*, 2d ed. (Cambridge: Cambridge University Press, 1913), p. 193; his emphasis.

2. Westlake, p. 191.

3. Amnesty International, "Afghanistan: Political Crisis and the Refugees," January 9, 1993, www.amnesty.org, p. 2.

4. See Human Rights Watch, "Military Assistance to the Afghan Opposition," October 2001, www.hrw.org/backgrounder/asia/afghan-bck1005.htm, p. 4.

5. Michael Griffin, *Reaping the Whirlwind* (London: Pluto Press, 2001), p. 31.

6. See Human Rights Watch, *Fueling Afghanistan's War*, December 15, 2000, www.hrw.org/backgrounder/asia/afghanistan/afghbk.html, p. 4; Ahmed Rashid, *Taliban* (New York: Yale University Press, 2001), p. 63.

7. See Rashid, especially Chapters 1–5; William T. Vollmann, "Letter from Afghanistan: Across the Divide," *New Yorker*, May 15, 2000, www.newyorker.com/archive/content/?010924fr_archive05.

8. Marc Herold, "A Dossier on Civilian Victims of United States' Aerial Bombing of Afghanistan," www.zmag.org/herold.htm, largely relying on news dispatches from reporters in Afghanistan to British, French, Canadian, and American newspapers.

9. See Carl Conetta, "Operation Enduring Fredom: Why a Higher Rate of Civilian Bombing Casualties," Project on Defense Alternatives, www.comw.org/pda/021oef.html. By his severer standard, refugees' reports of "some deaths" are treated as indicating one, "a dozen or more," three or four, "dozens," eight to ten, "hundreds," forty to sixty.

10. Ian Traynor, "Afghans Still Dying," *Guardian* (London), February 12, 20002, www.guardian.co.uk/archive. The Associated Press Kabul bureau announced an estimate based on their "examining hospital records, visiting bomb sites and interviewing eyewitnesses and officials" of "500 to 600"—although their own tabulation of "confirmed deaths" in sixteen cities and villages came to over seven hundred. See "Afghan Civilian Deaths Lower," February 11, 2002, www.rr.com/v5/my/news/story/0,1800,120928,00.html.

11. Human Rights Watch, "Paying for the Taliban's Crimes," www.hrw.org/reports/2002/afghan2/afghan0402-03.htm.

12. Michael O'Hanlon, "A Flawed Masterpiece," *Foreign Affairs* 81.3 (March/April 2002): pp. 47, 55. The death toll derives from Nicholas Kristof, "A Merciful War," *New York Times*, February 1, 2002, op-ed page.

13. Physicians for Human Rights, *A Report on Conditions at Ghebargan Prison*, January 28, 2002, www.phrusa.org/research/afghanistan/report/html.

14. See Carlotta Gall, "Prisoners: Witnesses Say Many Taliban Died in Custody," *New York Times*, December 11, 2001; Gall, "Prison Packed with Taliban Raises Concern," January 5, 2002, www.nytimes.com/archives; "Ce documentaire qui accuse les vainqueurs de crimes de guerre en Afghanistan," *Le Monde*, June 13, 2002, www.lemonde.fr/article/o,5987,3208—28239—,00.html.

15. Statistical Abstract of the United States: 2001 (Washington: U.S. Census Bureau, 2001), Table 1294.

16. See Columbia International Affairs Online, "A Recruiting Tape of Osama bin Laden," www.ciaonet.org/cbr/cbr00/video/cbr_v/cbr_v.html.

17. According to Frank Newport, Gallup editor in chief. "Poll Says Muslims Angry at US," *BBC News*, February 27, 2002, news.bbc.co.uk.

18. In the Gallup poll, only 9 percent regard U.S. military action in Afghanistan as justified.

19. See Human Rights Watch, "Taking Cover: Women in Post-Taliban Afghanistan," May 8, 2002, www.hrw.org/backgrounder/wrd/afghan-women-2k2.htm, especially pp. 5f.

20. In a characteristically deft discussion, Brierly describes suzerainty as a relationship of partial dependence in which one state is controlled by another to some degree, but maintains its own relations with states other than the one that controls it. His remark in 1963, "[T]he growth of national sentiment in all parts of the world makes any extension of the status unlikely," may come to sound archaic as the war on terrorism progresses. See J. L. Brierly, *The Law of Nations* (New York: Oxford University Press, 1963), p. 136.

21. For the whole interview, see "How Jimmy Carter and I Started the Mujahideen," *Counterpunch*, October 8, 2001, www.counterpunch.org/brzezinski/html. This interview originally appeared in *Le Nouvel Observateur*, January 15–21, 1998, p. 76, but not in the shorter edition sent to the United States. John Cooley presents some excerpts in *Unholy Wars* (London: Pluto, 2000), pp. 19f.

22. Human Rights Watch, *The Forgotten War* (1991), www.hrw.org/reports/1991/afghanistan/1AFGHAN.htm, chapter VI, p. 4; *Statistical Abstract of the United States: 2001*, Table 691.

23. On the history and nature of the channelling of aid, see Cooley, Chapter 3; Rashid, pp. 83–85 and Chapter 10; Human Rights Watch, Chapter 6.

24. See Human Rights Watch, Chapter 6; Griffin, Chapter 2.

25. See Rashid, Chapter 10; Cooley, Chapter 5.

26. See Rashid, p. 132.

27. Philip Smucker, "A Fight to Feed Hungry Afghanistan," *Christian Science Monitor*, June 3, 2002, www.reliefweb.int/w/rwb.nsf/668.

28. Scott Baldauf, "Poverty Forces Kabul Parents to Send Kids to Orphanages," *Christian Science Monitor*, June 3, 2002, www.reliefweb.int/w/rwb.nsf/668.

29. Smucker.

30. See www.fighter-planes.com/info/f22.htm.

31. *Statistical Abstract of the United States: 2001*, Table 1295; World Bank, *World Development Indicators: 2002* (Washington: World Bank, 2002), Table 2.1.

32. An estimate by the Natural Resources Defense Council cited in Bill Keller, "Nuclear Nightmares," *New York Times Magazine*, May 26, 2002, p. 57.

33. See UNICEF, "Iraq—Under-Five Mortality" (1999), www.unicef.org/reseval/pdfs/irqu5est/pdf, Chart 1; Mohamed Ali and Iqbal Shah, "Sanctions and Childhood Mortality in Iraq," *The Lancet* 355 (2000): 1851.

34. Shah and Iqbal, p. 1854.

35. UNICEF, p. 1.

36. Scott Ritter, "The Case for Iraq's Qualitative Disarmament," *Arms Control Today*, June 2000, www.armscontrol.org/act/2000_06/iraqjun.asp, pp. 1ff., 8.

37. Ritter, "The Case for Iraq's Qualitative Dissonament," p. 9. See also Ritter, *Endgame* (New York: Simon and Schuster, 1999), pp. 211ff.

38. Ritter, *Endgame*, pp. 218–221.

39. Given its intrusions on communal autonomy and its increase of the humiliated, impotent rage that breeds terrorism, the expansion of power might not be justifiable, even then.

40. World Bank, Table 6.9.

CHAPTER 11

Terrorism and International Justice

JAMES P. STERBA

INTRODUCTION

How should we think about terrorism within a context of international justice? To answer this question it is helpful to start with a definition of terrorism. Since 1983, the U.S. State Department has defined terrorism as follows:

> Terrorism is premeditated, politically motivated violence perpetrated against noncombatant targets by subnational groups or clandestine agents, usually intended to influence an audience.[1]

In a recent U.S. State Department document in which this definition is endorsed, there is also a section that discusses state-sponsored terrorism.[2] It is clear then that the U.S. State Department does not hold that only subnational groups or individuals can commit terrorist acts; it further recognizes that states can commit terrorist acts as well. So let me offer the following definition of terrorism, which is essentially the same as the U.S. State Department's definition once it is allowed that states too can commit terrorist acts, and once it is recognized that it is through attempting to elicit terror (that is, intense fear, fright or intimidation) that terrorists try to achieve their goals. The definition is:

> Terrorism is the use or threat of violence against innocent people to elicit terror in them, or in some other group of people, in order to further a political objective.[3]

Using this definition, there is no problem seeing the attacks on New York City and Washington, DC, particularly the attacks on the World Trade Center, as terrorist acts.[4] Likewise, the bombing of the U.S. embassies in Kenya and Tanzania in 1998 as well as the suicide bombings directed at Israeli civilians are terrorist acts.[5]

But what about the U.S. bombing of a pharmaceutical plant in Sudan with respect to which the United States blocked a UN inquiry and later compensated the owner, but not the thousands of victims who were deprived of drugs;[6] or the U.S.-sponsored sanctions against Iraq that kill an estimated three thousand to five thousand children in Iraq each month;[7] or the United States's $4 billion a year support for Israel's occupation of Palestinian lands, now in its thirty-fifth year, which is illegal, that is, in violation of UN resolutions the same sort of resolutions over which the Bush administration now wants to go to war with Iraq that specifically forbid in the case of Israel "the acquisition of territory by force," and which has resulted in many thousands of deaths? If we want to go back further, what about the U.S. support for the Contras in Nicaragua and the death squads in El Salvador, especially during the Reagan years, and the United States's use of terrorist contra-*city* threats of nuclear retaliation during the Cold War and its actual use of nuclear weapons against Hiroshima and Nagasaki at the end of World War II, resulting in over one hundred thousand deaths?[8] Surely, all of these U.S. actions also turn out to be either terrorist acts or support for terrorist acts, according to our definition. How can we tell then, which, if any, of these terrorist acts, or support for terrorist acts, are morally justified?

THE PERSPECTIVE OF JUST WAR THEORY AND PACIFISM

My preferred approach to addressing this question is provided by pacifism and just war theory. This is because I think that pacifism and just war theory provide a very useful way to think morally about terrorism. Thinking morally about terrorism involves trying to think about it from the perspectives of all those involved, which is something we almost never fully manage to pull off, particularly when we are dealing with perspectives that are alien to our own. But the degree to which we fail to reach out and take into account the perspectives of all those involved is the degree to which we fail to reach a morally correct approach to the practical problems we face. That is why pacifism and just war theory are particularly helpful in this context; they tend to keep us focused on what we need to take into account if we are to achieve a morally correct response to terrorism. So this is the approach that I will adopt here.

Most people identify pacifism with a theory of nonviolence. We can call this view "nonviolent pacifism." It maintains that *any use of violence against other human beings is morally prohibited.* Nonviolent pacifism has been defended on both religious and philosophical grounds. New Testament admonitions to turn the other cheek and to love one's enemies have been taken to support this form of pacifism. The Jains of India endorse this form of pacifism and extend it to include a prohibition of violence against all living beings. Philosophically, nonviolent pacifism has also seemed attractive because it is similar to the basic principle of "Do no evil" that is found in most ethical perspectives.

It has been argued, however, that nonviolent pacifism is incoherent. In a well-known article, Jan Narveson rejects nonviolent pacifism as incoherent because it recognizes a right to life yet rules out any use of force in defense of that right.[9] A strict nonviolence principle is incoherent, Narveson argues, because having a right entails the legitimacy of using force in defense of that right at least on some occasions. But nonviolent pacifism does not prohibit all force or resistance in defense of one's rights but only that which is violent.[10] Thus, Rosa Parks was nonviolently defending her rights when she refused to give up her seat in a bus to a white person in Montgomery, Alabama, in 1955.

Some pacifists have thought that the best way to respond to objections like Narveson's is to endorse a form of pacifism that clearly does not rule out all force but only lethal force. We can call this view "nonlethal pacifism." It maintains that *any lethal use of force against other human beings is morally prohibited.* This may have been the form of pacifism endorsed by Christians in the early church before the time of Constantine. Mahatma Gandhi is also often interpreted to be defending just this form of pacifism, as rooted in both Christianity and Hinduism. Cheyney Ryan, attempting to defend this form of pacifism, has argued that a difference between the pacifist and the nonpacifist is whether we can or should create the necessary distance between ourselves and other human beings in order to make the act of killing possible.[11] To illustrate, Ryan cites George Orwell's reluctance to shoot at an enemy soldier who jumped out of a trench and ran along the top of a parapet half-dressed and holding up his trousers with both hands. Ryan contends that what kept Orwell from shooting was that he couldn't think of the soldier as a thing rather than a fellow human being.

However, I do not believe that Ryan's example is compelling as a support for nonlethal pacifism. It is not clear that Orwell's inability to shoot the enemy soldier was because he could not think of the soldier as a thing rather than a fellow human being. Perhaps it was because he could not think of the soldier who was holding up his trousers with both hands as a threat or a combatant.

It also appears that Gandhi himself did not endorse this form of pacifism. In his essay "The Doctrine of the Sword," Gandhi wrote,

> I do believe that where there is only a choice between cowardice and violence, I would advise violence. Thus, when my eldest son asked me what he should have done, had he been present when I was almost fatally assaulted in 1908, whether he should have run away and seen me killed or whether he should have used his physical force which he could and wanted to use, and defended me, I told him that it was his duty to defend me even by using violence.[12]

There is, however, a form of pacifism that remains relatively untouched by the criticisms that have been raised against both nonviolent pacifism and nonlethal pacifism. This form of pacifism neither prohibits all uses of force nor even all uses of lethal force. We can call the view "anti-war pacifism" because it holds that *any massive use of lethal force, as in warfare, is morally prohibited.* Some historians claim that this is the form of pacifism endorsed by the early Christian church because, after 180 C.E., but not before, there is evidence of Christians being permitted to serve in the military, doing basically police work, during times of peace. Anti-war pacifism is also the form of pacifism most widely defended by philosophers today, at least in the English-speaking world. Two excellent defenses are Duane L. Cady, *From Warism to Pacifism*, and Robert L. Holmes, *On War and Morality*. Among the members of the primarily U.S. Canadian Concerned Philosophers for Peace, anti-war pacifism seems to be the most widely endorsed pacifist view.

In defense of anti-war pacifism, it is undeniable that wars have brought much death and destruction in their wake and that many of those who have perished in them are noncombatants or innocents. In fact, the tendency of modern wars has been to produce higher and higher proportions of noncombatant casualties, making it more and more difficult to justify participation in such wars.[13] At the same time, strategies for nonbelligerent conflict resolution are rarely intensively developed and explored before nations choose to go to war, making it all but impossible to justify participation in such wars.

In my previous work, I attempted to further defend this form of pacifism by developing it along side of just war theory. I argue that when just war theory is given its most morally defensible interpretation then it too can be reconciled with the practical requirements of anti-war pacifism.[14]

In traditional just war theory, there are two basic elements: an account of just cause and an account of just means. Just cause is usually specified as follows:

1. There must be substantial aggression.
2. Nonbelligerent correctives must be either hopeless or too costly.
3. Belligerent correctives must be neither hopeless nor too costly.

Needless to say, the notion of substantial aggression is a bit fuzzy, but it is generally understood to be the type of aggression that violates people's most fundamental rights. To suggest some specific examples of what is and is not substantial aggression, usually the taking of hostages is regarded as substantial aggression while the nationalization of particular firms owned by foreigners is not so regarded. But even when substantial aggression occurs, frequently nonbelligerent correctives are neither hopeless nor too costly to pursue. And even when nonbelligerent correctives are either hopeless or too costly, in order for there to be a just cause, belligerent correctives must be neither hopeless nor too costly.[15]

Traditional just war theory assumes, however, that there are just causes and goes on to specify just means as imposing two requirements:

1. Harm to innocents should not be directly intended as an end or a means.
2. The harm resulting from the belligerent means should not be disproportionate to the particular defensive objective to be attained.

While the just means conditions apply to each defensive action, the just cause conditions must be met by the conflict as a whole.

Now, in previous work, I have argued that when just war theory is given its most morally defensible interpretation, it

1. Allows the use of belligerent means against unjust aggressors only when such means minimize the loss and injury to innocent lives overall.

2. Allows the use of belligerent means against unjust aggressors to indirectly threaten innocent lives only to prevent the loss of innocent lives, not simply to prevent injury to innocents.

3. Allows the use of belligerent means to directly or indirectly threaten, or even take the lives of, unjust aggressors when it is the only way to prevent serious injury to innocents.[16]

Obviously, just war theory, so understood, is going to place severe restrictions on the use of belligerent means in warfare. In fact, most wars throughout history have been unjustified either in whole or in part. For example, the U.S. involvement in Nicaragua, El Salvador, and Panama; the Soviet Union's involvement in Afghanistan; and Israeli involvement in the West Bank and the Gaza Strip all violate the just cause and just means provisions of just war theory as I defend them. Even the U.S.-led Gulf War against Iraq seems to have violated both the just cause and just means provisions of just war theory.[17] In fact, one strains to find examples of justified applications of just war theory in recent history.[18] Two examples that come to mind are India's military action against Pakistan in Bangladesh and the Tanzanian incursion into Uganda during the rule of Idi Amin. But, after mentioning these two examples, it is difficult to go on. What this shows, I have argued, is that when just war theory and anti-war pacifism are given their most morally defensible interpretations, both views can be reconciled. In this reconciliation, the few wars and large-scale conflicts that meet the stringent requirements of just war theory are the only wars and large-scale conflicts to which anti-war pacifists cannot justifiably object. We can call the view that emerges from this reconciliation "just war pacifism."[19] It is the view that claims that because of the stringent requirements of just war theory, only very rarely will participation in a massive use of lethal force in warfare be morally justified.

Now one might think that from the perspective of just war pacifism acts of terrorism could never be morally justified. But this would require an absolute prohibition on intentionally harming innocents, and such a prohibition would not seem to be justified, even from the perspective of just war pacifism.[20] Specifically, it would seem that harm to innocents can be justified for the sake of achieving a greater good when the harm is

1. Trivial (e.g., as in the case of stepping on someone's foot to get out of a crowded subway)

2. Easily reparable (e.g., as in the case of lying to a temporarily depressed friend to keep her from committing suicide)
3. Nonreparable but greatly outweighed by the consequences of the action.

Obviously, it is this third category of harm that is relevant to the possible justification of terrorism. But when is intentional harm to innocents nonreparable yet greatly outweighed by the consequences?

Consider the following example often discussed by moral philosophers.[21] A large person who is leading a party of spelunkers gets himself stuck in the mouth of a cave in which flood waters are rising. The trapped party of spelunkers just happens to have a stick of dynamite with which they can blast the large person out of the mouth of the cave; either they use the dynamite or they all drown, the large person with them. Now it is usually assumed in this case that it is morally permissible to dynamite the large person out of the mouth of the cave. After all, if that is not done, the whole party of spelunkers will die, the large person with them. So the sacrifice imposed on the large person in this case would not be that great.

But what if the large person's head is outside rather than inside the cave, as it must have been in the previous interpretation of the case? Under those circumstances, the large person would not die when the other spelunkers drown. Presumably after slimming down a bit, he would eventually just squeeze his way out of the mouth of the cave. In this case, could the party of spelunkers trapped in the cave still legitimately use the stick of dynamite they have to save themselves rather than the large person?

Suppose there were ten, twenty, one hundred, or whatever number you want of splunkers trapped in the cave. At some point, won't the number be sufficiently great that it would be morally acceptable for those in the cave to use the stick of dynamite to save themselves rather than the large person, even if this meant that the large person would be morally required to sacrifice his life? The answer has to be yes, even if you think it has to be a very unusual case when we can reasonably demand that people thus sacrifice their lives in this way.

Is it possible that some acts of terrorism are morally justified in this way? It is often argued that our dropping of atomic bombs on Hiroshima and Nagasaki was so justified. President Truman, who ordered the bombing, justified it on the grounds that it was used to shorten the war. In 1945, the United States demanded the unconditional surrender of Japan. The Japanese had by that time lost the war, but the leaders of their armed forces were by no means ready to accept unconditional surrender.[22] While the Japanese leaders expected an invasion of their mainland islands, they believed that they could make that invasion so costly that the United States would accept a conditional surrender. Truman's military advisors also believed the costs would be high. The capture of Okinawa had cost almost 80,000 American casualties, while almost the entire Japanese garrison of 120,000 men died in battle. If the mainland islands were defended in a similar manner, hundreds of thousands of Japanese would surely die. During that time, the bombing of Japan would continue, and perhaps intensify, resulting in casualty rates that were no different from those that were expected from the atomic attack. A massive incendiary raid on Tokyo early in March 1945 had set off a firestorm and killed an estimated 100,000 people. Accordingly, Truman's Secretary of State James Byrnes admitted that the two atomic bombs did cause "many casualties, but not nearly so many as there would have been had our air force continued to drop incendiary bombs on Japan's cities."[23] Similarly, Winston Churchill wrote in support of Truman's decision "To avert a vast, indefinite butchery . . . at the cost of a few explosions seemed, after all our toils and perils, a miracle of deliverance."[24]

Yet the "vast, indefinite butchery" that the United States sought to avert by dropping atomic bombs on Hiroshima and Nagasaki was one that the United States itself was threatening and had already started to carry out with its incendiary attack on Tokyo. And the United States itself could have easily avoided this butchery by dropping its demand for unconditional Japanese surrender. Moreover, a demand of unconditional surrender can almost never be morally justified since defeated aggressors almost always have certain rights that they never are required to surrender.[25] Hence, the United States's terrorist acts of dropping of atomic bombs on Hiroshima and Nagasaki cannot be justified on the grounds of shortening the war and avoiding a vast, indefinite butchery because the United States could have secured those results simply by giving up its unreasonable demand for unconditional surrender.

A more promising case for justified terrorism is the counter-city bombing by the British during the early stages of World War II. Early in the war, it became clear that British bombers could fly effectively only at night because too many of them were being shot down during day raids by German anti-aircraft fire. In addition, a study done in

1941 showed that of those planes flying at night recorded as having actually succeeded in attacking their targets, only one-third managed to drop their bombs within five miles of their intended target.[26] This meant that British bombers flying at night could reasonably aim at no target smaller than a fairly large city.[27]

Michael Walzer argues that under these conditions, the British terror bombing was morally justified because at this early stage of the war, it was the only way the British had left to them to try to avert a Nazi victory.[28] Walzer further argues that the time period when such terror bombing was justified was relatively brief. Once the Russians began to inflict enormous casualties on the German army and the United States made available its manpower and resources, other alternatives opened up. Unfortunately, the British continued to rely heavily on terror bombing right up until the end of the war, culminating in the fire-bombing of Dresden in which something like one hundred thousand people were killed. However, for that relatively brief period of time when Britain had no other way to try to avert a Nazi victory, Walzer argues, its reliance on terror bombing was morally justified.

Suppose then we accept this moral justification for British terror bombing during World War II. Doesn't this suggest a comparable moral justification for Palestinian suicide bombings against Israeli civilians? Israel has been illegally occupying Palestinian land for thirty-five years now in violation of UN resolutions following the 1967 Arab-Israeli War. Even a return to those 1967 borders, which the UN resolutions require, still permits a considerable expansion of Israel's original borders as specified in the mandate of 1947.[29] Moreover, since the Oslo Peace Accords in 1993, Israeli settlements have doubled in the Occupied Territories. In the year that Sharon has been prime minister, some thirty-five new settlements have been established in the Occupied Territories.[30] In Gaza, there are 1.2 million Palestinians and four thousand Israelis, but the Israelis control 40 percent of the land and 70 percent of the water. In the West Bank, there are 1.9 million Palestinians and 280,000 Israelis, but the Israelis control 40 percent of the land and 37 percent of the water.[31] In addition, Israel failed to abide by its commitments under the Oslo Peace Accords to release prisoners, to complete a third redeployment of its military forces, and to transfer three Jerusalem villages to Palestinian control.[32] Moreover, at the recent Camp David meeting, Israeli's proposals did not provide for Palestinian control over East Jerusalem, upon which 40 percent of the Palestinian economy depends.[33] Nor did Israeli's proposals provide for a right of return or compensation for the half of the Palestinian population that lives in exile (President Clinton proposed that Chariman Arafat should just forget about them), most of them having been driven off their land by Israeli expansion. So the Palestinian cause is clearly a just one, but just as clearly the Palestinians lack the military resources to effectively resist Israeli occupation and aggression by simply directly attacking Israeli military forces. The Israelis have access to the most advanced U.S. weapons and $4 billion a year from the United States to buy whatever weapons they want. The Palestinians have no comparable support from anyone. It is under these conditions that a moral justification for Palestinian suicide bombers against Israeli civilians emerges.[34] Given that the Palestinians lack any effective means to try to end the Israeli occupation or to stop Israel's further expansion into Palestinian territories other than by using suicide bombers against Israeli civilians, why would this use of suicide bombers not be justified in much the same way that Walzer justifies the British terror bombing in the early stages of World War II?[35] If the Israelis have the ultimate goal of confining most Palestinians to a number of economically nonviable and disconnected reservations, similar to those on which the United States confines Native American Indian nations, then surely the Palestinians have a right to resist that conquest as best they can.[36]

Beginning with just war pacifism, I have argued that there are morally defensible exceptions to the just means prohibition against directly killing innocents. The cave analogy argument aims to establish that conclusion. British terror bombing at the beginning of World War II, but not the American dropping of atomic bombs on Hiroshima and Nagasaki at the end of that war, is offered as a real-life instantiation of that argument. The Palestinian use of suicide bombers against Israeli civilians is then presented as a contemporary instantiation of that very same argument.

Yet even if there is a moral justification for the Palestinian use of suicide bombers against Israeli civilians under present conditions, clearly most acts of terrorism cannot be justified, and clearly there was no moral justification for the terrorist attacks on New York City and Washington, DC, particularly the attacks on the World Trade Center.[37]

Even so, the question remains as to whether the United States was morally justified in going to war against Afghanastan in response to these unjustified terrorist acts. According to just war pacifism, before using belligerent correctives, we must be sure that nonbelligerent correctives are neither hopeless nor too costly. The three weeks of diplomatic activity that the United States engaged in did not appear to be sufficient to determine whether it was hopeless or too costly to continue to attempt to bring Osama bin Laden before a U.S. court or, better, before an international court of law, without military action. We demanded that the Taliban government immediately hand over bin Laden and "all the leaders of Al Qaeda who hide in your land." But how could we have reasonably expected this of the Taliban, given that months after we have overthrown the Taliban government and installed a friendly one, we still have not been able to turn up bin Laden and most of his key associates? How could we have expected that the Taliban government, with its limited resources and loose control over the country, to do in three weeks what we still have not been able to accomplish in over a year?

It is conceivable that our leaders never really expected that the Taliban government would be able to meet our demands even if they had wanted to do so. After we began our military offensive, the Taliban government expressed a willingness to hand over bin Laden and his associates at least for trial in an international court if we would stop our military offensive. But we never took them up on their offer.[38] Perhaps we knew that the Taliban government really lacked the resources to hand over bin Laden and his key associates, even while we used their failure to do so as the justification for our waging a war against them.[39]

Something similar may now be happening in the Israeli-Palestinian conflict. The Israeli government has demanded that Yasir Arafat put a stop to the suicide bombings, and arrest those who are behind them. But it is far from clear that Arafat has the power to do so. The Israeli government, with many more military resources than Arafat has at his disposal, has been unable to put a stop to the suicide bombings; in fact, the number of such bombings has escalated as Israel has escalated its military responses. The Israeli government repeated its demand that Arafat stop the suicide bombings at the same time that it held Arafat under virtual house arrest in Ramallah and attacked members of his Palestinian Authority throughout the Occupied Territories. Clearly, the Israelis must know that Arafat lacks the power to put an end to the suicide bombings in the absence of a political settlement guaranteeing the Palestinians virtually everything they have a right to under the relevant UN resolutions.[40] Moreover, if Arafat is foolish enough to speak out against the suicide bombings, as he has in the past, in the absence of the political guarantees that he needs, the bombings will just continue, and Arafat will be branded as ineffectual. So, either the failure of Arafat to speak out against the suicide bombings or his ineffectiveness at stopping them when he does speak out is used by the Israeli government as a justification for reoccupying the Palestinian territories and expanding Israeli settlements in them. But neither the actions taken by the Israeli government with respect to the Palestinians nor the actions undertaken by the U.S. government with respect to the Al Qaeda network are morally justified because neither government exhausted its nonbelligerent correctives before engaging in a military response.[41]

In the United States, public opinion rather than the exhaustion of nonbelligerent options has served to motivate our military response to 9/11. The military response has been well received by at least a majority of American people, who want to see their government "doing something" to get bin Laden and fight terrorism. But satisfying public opinion polls is not the same as satisfying the requirements of just war pacifism. The United States first called its military action Infinite Justice and then later, in view of the religious connotations of that term, began calling it Enduring Freedom, but our military action is neither just nor does it acceptably promote freedom unless nonbelligerent correctives are first exhausted, and they were not exhausted in this case. Nor has our military response yet delivered up for trial bin Laden or any of his top associates or even any of the top Taliban leaders, although some were killed by our military action, and some good detective and police work, not military action, has recently led to the capture in Pakistan of Abu Zubaydah, who is thought to be bin Laden's second or third lieutenant.[42]

So, even if the United States itself had not engaged in any related terrorist acts or supported any related terrorist acts, there would still be a strong objection to its relatively quick resort to military force as a response to the terrorist attacks of 9/11. Given that the United States itself arguably has engaged in terrorist acts in Sudan, and through the UN against Iraqi children, as well as has supported terrorist acts through its political and financial support of Israel's illegal occupation of Palestinian lands, and given that these acts of terrorism, and support for terrorism, have served at least partially to motivate terrorist attacks on the United States itself, the United States surely needs to take steps to radically correct its own wrongdoing if it is to respond justly to the related wrongdoing of bin Laden and his followers. Unfortunately this is also something we have not yet done.[43]

What then should we be doing if we are to respect the requirements of just war pacifism in our response to the terrorist attacks of September 11?

1. We should let Israel know in no uncertain terms that our continuing political and financial support depends upon its reaching an agreement with the Palestinians on the establishment of a Palestinian state in accordance with the relevant UN resolutions relatively quickly, within, say, three to six months. So many plans for a Palestinian state have been discussed over the years that it should not be that difficult to settle on one of them that accords with the relevant UN resolutions, once Israel knows that it can no longer draw on the political and financial support of the United States to resist a settlement. The evidence of serious negotiations between Israel and the Palestinians will be welcomed by people around the world.

2. The sanctions against Iraq imposed since 1991 must be radically modified to permit sufficient humanitarian assistance to the Iraqi people, particularly the children.[44] (Obviously, I am opposed to a pre-emptive military strike against Iraq—one that does not exhaust nonbelligerent correctives.) According to a UNICEF study done in 1999, if the substantial reduction in child mortality throughout Iraq during the 1980s had continued through the 1990s, there would have been half a million fewer deaths of children under five in the country as a whole during the eight year the period of 1991 to 1998.[45] Moreover, the current oil-for-food program, which was only introduced in 1997 (six years into the sanctions), does not, by the UN's own estimate, provide sufficient food and medicine to prevent conditions in Iraq from getting even worse.[46] This all has to change. The oil-for-food program must immediately be expanded to arrest and reverse the deteriorating humanitarian conditions in Iraq.

3. There should have been three to six months of serious diplomatic negotiations to bring Osama bin Laden and the leaders of his Al Qaeda network either before a U.S. court or, preferably, before an international court of law. Substantial economic and political incentives should have been offered to

the relevant individuals and nations to help bring this about. Now that we have overthrown the Taliban in Afghanistan and helped establish a friendly government, we should end our military campaign immediately and return to nonbelligerent correctives, which can include the same sort of good detective and police work that has made possible the capture of Abu Zubaydah, the highest-ranking Al Qaeda member captured to date. This will even give us the unintended benefit of conveying to our enemies and to others that we are serious about engaging in belligerent correctives should the nonbelligerent ones prove ineffective.

One of the main lessons we should have drawn from the 9/11 terrorist attacks on the World Trade Center and the Pentagon is how vulnerable our costly high-tech military defenses are to smart, determined enemies using even the simplest of weapons imaginable—knives and boxcutters. And as bad as 9/11 was, it could have been far worse. There is little doubt that the terrorists who hijacked the airplanes and flew them into the World Trade Center and the Pentagon would not have hesitated to detonate a nuclear explosive, maybe one they would have hidden in the World Trade Center, if they could have done so.

It would also not be that difficult for terrorists to target chemical plants or, more easily, shipments of industrial chemicals such as chlorine that are transported in tank cars and trucks. Before 9/11, only about 2 percent of all the containers that move though U.S. ports were actually inspected. Currently, that number has been doubled, but that still means that 96 percent of such containers that are shipped from all over the world are not inspected when they enter the United States.[47] Detonating thousands of tons of ammonium nitrate loaded on a ship in a harbor would have the impact of a small nuclear explosion. Just last year, three hundred tons of ammonium nitrate apparently exploded in France, killing twenty-nine people and injuring more than twenty-five hundred.[48]

Building another layer of high-tech military defense, like the $238 billion George W. Bush proposes to spend on a missile defense system, does little to decrease our vulnerability to such terrorist attacks.[49] In fact, because such high-tech military expenditures divert money from projects that would significantly decrease our vulnerability to terrorist attacks, they actually have an overall negative impact on our national security.

What then should we do to prevent future terrorist attacks from being directed at the United States or U.S. citizens? In addition to the changes of policy I mentioned earlier with respect to Israel, Iraq, and Osama bin Laden's Al Qaeda network, there are many other things that the United States could do to project a more just foreign policy. For starters, there are a number of international treaties and conventions, for example, the Kyoto Climate Change Treaty, the Treaty Banning Land Mines, and the Rome Treaty for the establishment of an International Criminal Court, that the United States has failed to sign for reasons that seem to simply favor U.S. special interests at the expense of international justice or what would be of benefit to the world community as a whole.

Furthermore, looking at things from an international justice perspective can require a considerable modification of our usual ways of thinking about the relationships between nations and peoples. From an international justice perspective or, more generally, from a moral perspective, actions and policies must be such that they are acceptable by all those affected by those actions and policies (that is, the actions and policies must be such that they ought to be accepted, not necessarily that they are accepted by all those affected by those actions and policies). Thus, the fact that the United States, which constitutes 4 percent of the world's population while using 25 percent of its energy resources, refuses to sign the Kyoto Climate Change Treaty and make the cuts in its energy consumption that virtually all other nations of the world judge to be fair makes the United States, in this regard, something like an outlaw nation from the perspective of international justice.[50]

Yet the failure of the United States to accord with international justice cuts even deeper. According to the World Food Program, three-quarters of a billion people are desperately hungry around the world. According to that same program, even Afghanistan, the subject of so much of our recent attention, has received only 5 percent of the $285 million in emergency aid it needs to feed its people for the rest of the year.[51] One of two women ministers in the provisional Afghan government, Sima Samar, who is in charge of women's affairs, has an unheated office and no phone or money to effect policies in Afghanistan that would improve the situation for women,[52] There is no way that we can achieve international justice without a radical redistribution of goods and resources from rich to poor to eliminate hunger and desperation around the world.[53] The United States needs to be a champion of this redistribution if it is to be perceived correctly as measuring up to the standard of international justice, and thus to be a just nation, whose resources and people should be respected. But the United States has not done this. In fact, its contribution to alleviate world hunger is (in proportion to its size) one of the smallest among the industrized nations of the world—roughly .11 percent, which President Bush proposes to increase to .13 percent; Britain's contribution is about three times as much, and Sweden, the Netherlands, and Norway proportionately give about eight times as much.[54]

Clearly, then, there is much that the United States can do if it wants to respond to the terrorist attacks of 9/11 in a way that accords with international justice. I have argued that the best account of pacifism and the best account of just war theory combined in just war pacifism requires that, as soon as possible, the United States put an end to its military response; that the U.S. make it clear that it is taking radical steps to correct for related terrorist acts of its own or of those countries it supports; and that it give nonbelligerent correctives a reasonable chance to work. I have further argued that the United States has to do more to be a good world citizen. It must stop being a conspicuous holdout with respect to international treaties, and it must do its fair share to redistribute resources from the rich to the poor as international justice requires. Only then would the United States be living up to the moral ideals that could make it what it claims to be. In turn, living up to those ideals may prove to be the best defense the United States has against terrorism directed against its own people.

NOTES

Earlier versions of this paper were presented to the Philosophy Department at the University of Illinois at Chicago, the Philosophy Department at the University of North Carolina at Charlotte, an Amnesty International Forum at the University of California at Irvine, and the University of Notre Dame. I wish to thank Thomas Bushnell, Bill Gay, Bernard Gert, Gary Gutting, Vittorio Hosle, Robert Johanson, Matthew Kennedy, Anthony Laden, Mark Levine, Deborah Marble, Charles Mills, Paul Quirk, James Rakowski, Kristin Shrader-Frechette, David Solomon, Rosemarie Tong, and Paul Weithman for their helpful comments.

1. *Patterns of Global Terrorism—2000*. Released by the Office of the Coordinator for Counterterrorism, April 2001.

2. *Patterns of Global Terrorism—2000*.

3. This definition is not subject to objections that have been raised by Tony Dardis and Walter Sinnott-Armstrong to a somewhat similar definition defended by Igor Primoratz. Dardis objects that terrorist attacks do not always give rise to terror or fear but rather sometimes "to defiance and the strengthening of resolve" or "anger and disgust." But my definition defines terrorism in terms of the intentions of the terrorists not in terms of what they are successful in bringing about. Sinnott-Armstrong takes the fact that many countries threaten to impose harsh penalties, including death, on anyone who commits certain actions, such as murder to be an objection to any definition such as mine. But those threatened by the criminal law, even in unjust countries are would-be violators of that law, and these individuals are not innocent in the appropriate sense because they have a status similar to combatants who are understood to be either threatening or inflicting on us a military attack. See Tony Dardis, "Primoratz on Terrorism," *Journal of Applied Philosophy* 9 (1992): 93–97 and Walter Sinnott-Armstrong, "On Primoratz's Definition of Terrorism," *Journal of Applied Philosophy* 8 (1991): 115–120.

4. If we use the just war distinction between combatants and noncombatants, those killed at the Pentagon might be viewed as combatants in some undeclared war.

5. Since the bombings in Kenya and Tanzania were of U.S. government installations, they are only classified as terrorist acts by virtue of the fact that they were intended to maximize civilian casualties.

6. From an interview with Phyllis Bennis, *Z magazine*, September 12, 2001. While the bombing of the pharmaceutical plant may have involved unintentional harm to innocents, refusing to compensate the thousands of victims who were deprived of the drugs they needed is to intentionally harm innocents.

7. "Life and Death in Iraq," *Seattle-Post-Intelligencer*, May 11, 1999. See also Jeff Indemyer, "Iraqi Sanctions: Myth and Fact," *Swans Commentary*, September 3, 2002.

8. During the Reagan years and after, there was also support for Jonas Savimbi—Reagan referred to Savimbi as Angola's Abraham Lincoln. Savimbi personally beat to death a rival's wife and children. He also shelled civilians and bombed a Red Cross factory. From 1975 until his recent death, he refused to give up a struggle for power in a civil war that resulted in more than five hundred thousand deaths. See Nicholas Kristof, "Our Own Terrorist," *New York Times*, March 5, 2002.

9. Jan Narveson, "Pacifism: A Philosophical Analysis," *Ethics* 75 (1965): 259–271.

10. We can understand "violence" here and throughout the paper as "the prima facie unjustified use of force."

11. Cheyney Ryan, "Self-Defense, Pacifism and the Possibility of Killing," in *The Ethics of War and Nuclear Deterrence*, ed. James P. Sterba (Belmont, CA: Wadsworth Publishing Co., 1985), pp. 45–49.

12. M. K. Gandhi, "The Doctrine of the Sword," in *Nonviolent Resistance* (New York: Schocken Books, 1961) p. 132.

13. Paradoxically, this has been true even as weapons have become more and more precise because now that weapons are more precise, even more targets are selected, and the increased destruction therefrom leads to more civilian deaths, sometimes after open hostilities have ceased. For example, if you knock out a country's water purification facilities, as in Iraq, and then don't let the people in that country import the purification chemicals (or the materials to produce such chemicals) to restore its water purification facilities (because of the possibility of dual use), you can kill lots of noncombatants without directly targeting them with your precision weapons. For a general discussion of this issue, see George Lopez, "The Death Knell of the Just War Tradition," *Commonweal* 129 (2002): 14.

14. James P. Sterba, *Justice for Here and Now* (Cambridge: Cambridge University Press, 1998), Chapter 7.

15. Built into the "too costly" requirement is the traditional proportionality requirement of just war theory. Clearly various nonbelligerent and belligerent measures can be either too costly to ourselves, to the other side, or to both sides together. When belligerent measures are too costly either to ourselves or to the other side or to both sides together, they are rightly judged disproportionate.

16. Sterba, Chapter 7.

17. The just cause provision appears to have been violated because the extremely effective economic sanctions were not given enough time to work. It was estimated at the time that when compared to past economic blockades, the blockade against Iraq had a near 100 percent chance of success if given about a year to work. (See *New York Times*, January 14, 1991, p. 9). The just means provision was violated because the number of combatant and noncombatant deaths was disproportionate. As many as 120,000 Iraqi soldiers were killed according to U.S. intelligence sources. Moreover, what we have learned about Iraq's resistance to the less stringent economic blockade that followed the war does not undercut the reasonableness of pursuing a more stringent economic blockade on the basis of the available information we had before the war. Moreover, the humiliating defeat of Iraqi forces in the Gulf War may have contributed to the hardened Iraqi resistance to the less stringent postwar economic blockade.

18. This view is not so unusual once you grant that there are justified and unjustified parts of even the so-called best wars (e.g., the firebombing of Dresden and Hamburg is generally thought to be an unjustified part of World War II), and further that the unjustified parts are not necessary for, and even work against, the success of the justified parts. If this is granted, then rather than make an overall judgement about a war, it would seem more appropriate to say that parts of wars have been justified and other parts unjustified.

However, if you still want to force an overall judgment, then I think you would have to say that any war with a significant number of unjustified parts cannot be regarded as justified overall.

19. For another use of this term, see Kenneth H. Wenker, "Just War Pacifism," *Proceedings of the American Catholic Philosophical Association* 57 (1983): 135–141. For a defense of a similar view to my own, which is considered by the author to be a defense of pacifism, see Richard Norman, 'The Case for Pacifism," *Journal of Applied Philosophy* 2 (1988): 197–210.

20. This is because the requirements of just war pacifism, as I stated them earlier in this article, do not directly address the question of whether there are exceptions to the prohibition on intentionally harming innocents. Moreover, once that question is taken up by means of the same case-by-case analysis with which I defended the earlier stated requirements of just war pacifism (for the defense of these requirements, see my *Justice for Here and Now*, Chapter 7), certain exceptions to the prohibition on intentionally harming innocents turn out to be morally justified, as I go on to show.

21. See Philippa Foot, "The Problem of Abortion and the Doctrine of Double Effect," *Oxford Review* 5 (1967): 5–15.

22. See Michael Walzer, *Just and Unjust Wars*, 2d ed. (New York: Basic Books, 1992), 263–268.

23. James Byrnes, *Speaking Frankly* (New York: Harper Row, 1947), p. 264.

24. Winston Churchill, *Triumph and Tragedy* (New York: Houghton Mifflin, 1962), p. 639.

25. Another way to put this is to claim that a right not to have to unconditionally surrender is one of our basic universal human rights.

26. Noble Frankland, *Bomber Offensive* (New York: Ballantine Books, 1970), pp. 38–39.

27. As examples of how inaccurate night bombing was at the time, one oil installation was attacked by 162 aircraft carrying 159 tons of bombs, another by 134 aircraft carrying 103 tons of bombs, but neither suffered any major damage. See Charles Webster and Noble Frankland, *The Strategic Air Offensive Against Germany 1939–45*, Vol. I (London: HMSO, 1961) p. 164.

28. Walzer, pp. 255–262.

29. The Palestinians made a big concession to Israel in the Olso Peace Accords by accepting this expansion (23 percent more than Israel was granted according to the 1947 UN partition plan), hoping thereby to gain Palestinian control of the remaining 23 percent of historic Palestine.

30. Editorial, *New York Times*, April 26, 2002, p. 26.

31. Avishai Margalit, "Settling Scores," *New York Review*, August 22, 2001, pp. 20–24.

32. See Robert Malley and Hussein, "Camp David: The Tragedy of Errors, *New York Review*, August 9, 2001, pp. 59–65; "A Reply to Ehud Barak," *New York Review*, June 11, 2002, pp. 46–49; "A Reply," *New York Review*, June 27, 2002, p. 48. See also Benny Morris and Ehud Barak, "Camp David and After:

An Exchange," *New York Review*, June 13, 2002, pp. 42–45; "Camp David and After—Continued," *New York Review*, June 27, 2002, pp. 47–48.

33. Jeff Halper, The Israeli Committee Against House Demolitions, www. icahd.org.

34. There is a further requirement that must be met here. It is that the Palestinians must have exhausted nonbelligerent correctives. The evidence that this is the case can, I believe, be found in the numerous Palestinian peace initiatives, especially from the early 1970s on when the Palestinians had acquired political standing in the international community. In 1976 the United States vetoed a UN Security Council Resolution calling for a settlement on the 1967 borders, with "appropriate arrangements . . . to guarantee . . . the sovereignty, territorial integrity and political independence of all states in the area and their right to live in peace within secure and recognized boundaries," including Israel and a new Palestinian state in the occupied territories. The resolution was backed by Egypt, Syria, Jordan, the PLO, and the USSR. See Noam Chomsky, *The Fateful Triangle* (Cambridge: South End Press, 1999), pp. 64ff. Israel has rejected every peace plan put forward by the Arabs and the United States except for the bilateral treaty with Egypt and the Olso Peace Accords, and these Accords have now been, in effect, abandoned by the current Israeli government. See Paul Finlay, *Deliberate Deceptions* (Brooklyn, NY: Lawrence Hill Books, 1993), pp. 201ff.

35. Nor will it do to distinguish British terror bombing from Palestinian suicide bombing on the grounds that the Nazis represented an unprecedented evil in human history because at the early stage of World War II, the British could not have known the full character of the Nazi regime.

36. Some will contest whether this correctly represents Israeli intentions. But even in its best offer at Camp David, Israel proposed dividing Palestine into four separate cantons: the Northern West Bank, the Central West Bank, the Southern West Bank, and Gaza. Going from any one area to another would require crossing Israeli sovereign territory and consequently subject movements of Palestinians within their own country to Israeli control. Restrictions would also apply to the movements of goods, thus subjecting the Palestinian economy to Israeli control. In addition, the Camp David proposal would have left Israel in control of all Palestinian borders, thereby giving Israel control not only of the internal movement of people and goods but international movement as well. Such a Palestinian state would have had less sovereignty and viability than the Bantustans created by the South African apartheid government, which both Israel and the United States once supported. The Camp David proposal also required Palestinians to give up any claim to the occupied portion of Jerusalem. The proposal would have forced recognition of Israel's annexation of all of Arab East Jerusalem. Talks after Camp David in Egypt suggested that Israel was prepared to allow Palestinian sovereignty over isolated Palestinian neighborhoods in the heart of East Jerusalem. However, these neighborhoods would have remained surrounded by Israeli colonies

and separated not only from each other but also from the rest of the Palestinian State. See www.nad-plo-org. For a map of the Camp David proposal with its partition of Palestine into four cantons see www.nad-plo-org/maps/map13.html. Although Yassir Arafat and the Palestinians were roundly condemned in the U.S. media for rejecting the Camp David offer, to my knowledge no maps of the U.S.-Israeli proposal, which would have undercut the claim that it was a reasonable offer, were published in the United States, although they were widely published elsewhere. For the closest U.S. media source that I found to come to acknowledging these facts, see Anthony Lewis, "Waiting for America," *New York Times*, November 17, 2001, p. 23.

37. Al Qaeda have shown themselves capable of inflicting significant damage on both military (the *U.S.S. Cole*) and diplomatic targets (the U.S. embassies in Kenya and Tanzania). So their opposition to the United States could have continued in just this fashion. Moreover, the attack on the Pentagon differs morally from the attack on the World Trade Center, although the deaths of innocent airline hostages is objectionable in both cases. So Al Qaeda could still have effectively waged its war against the United States without attacking the World Trade Center. With respect to the possibility of effectively attacking military or government targets, Al Qaeda is much better situated vis-à-vis the United States and its allies than the Palestinians are vis-à-vis Israel. This is because Al Qaeda can target the far-flung military and government outposts of the United States all around the world, and through such attacks it has effectively brought the United States and its allies to withdraw their military forces from such places as Somalia, Yemen, and even, in terms of effective use, from Saudi Arabia.

38. Of course, it might be questioned whether Al Qaeda effectively exhausted nonbelligerent corrections before it resorted to belligerent ones. If we take Al Qaeda's grounds for just cause to be U.S. support for the Israeli occupation, the U.S. stance against Iraq, U.S. bases in Saudi Arabia, and U.S. support for repressive governments in the Middle East, then I think we can say that in each case Al Qaeda gave nonbelligerent correctives some chance to work. Genaro Armas, "Bush Rebuffs Taliban Offer," *Associated Press*, October 15, 2001. See also Elizabeth Bumiller, "President Rejects Offer by Taliban for Negotiations," *New York Times*, October 15, 2002, p. 1.

39. It is worth noting that the U.S. State Department had been negotiating with the Taliban for handing over bin Laden before 9/11. One Taliban proposal suggested that bin Laden be turned over to a panel of three Islamic jurists, one chosen by Afghanistan, Saudi Arabia, and the United States. When the United States rejected that proposal, the Taliban countered that it would settle for only one Islamic jurist on such a panel. Although the negotiations went on for some time, the United States rigidly held to the position that bin Laden had to be turned over for trial in the United States, and some say the United States thereby missed a chance before 9/11 to get bin Laden before an international court of law. Possibly the United States never believed that

the Taliban could deliver on their promises, but why then did it keep negotiating with them for so long? See David Ottaway and Jeo Stephens, "Diplomats Met with Taliban on bin Laden: Some Contend U.S. Missed Its Chance,"
Washington Post, October 29, 2001, p. A01.

40. See James Bennet, "Israeli Analysis Raises New Doubt About Arafat's
Power," *New York Times*, November 27, 2001, p. 43.

41. Of course, in theory, one could know or reasonably believe that nonbelligerent correctives are ineffectual or too costly without actually having exhausted them. But, in the cases under discussion, there is no way that one
could do this with respect to the particular nonbelligerent correctives under
consideration without actually having exhausted them. In addition, making
impossible demands in response to an attack and using military means when
those demands are not met is just another way not to exhaust nonbelligerent correctives.

42. Ann Scott Tyson, "US Task: Get Inside the Head of Captured bin Laden
Aide," *Christian Science Monitor*, April 4, 2002, p. 1.

43. The reason why the United States must do all these things if it is to
justly respond to the related wrongdoing of bin Laden and his followers is
that these actions are part of the nonbelligerent correctives that must be employed before the use of belligerent correctives can be justified.

44. Here I am arguing against the current form of the economic sanctions
against Iraq; I also see no merit at all in President Bush's plan to preemp-
tively attack Iraq. If there was any merit to such a plan, it should be able to
get the approval of the UN Security Council.

45. "Life and Death in Iraq." See also Jeff Indemyer, "Iraqi Sanctions: Myth
and Fact."

46. On May 15, 2002, the United Nations Security Council passed a resolution that tries to cut through the bureaucracy on the flow of civilian
goods to Iraq. Military items continue to be barred outright. New is a list
of thousands of "dual use" goods that could have military applications, rang-
ing from trucks to telecommunications. These would need review, but items
not on the list can move to Iraq more quickly. What sort of effect this change
in the sanctions will have on humanitarian conditions in Iraq remains to be
seen.

47. David Carr, "The Futility of Homeland Defense," *The Atlantic Monthly*,
January 2002, pp. 53–55.

48. Richard Garwin, "The Many Threats of "Terror," *The New York Review*,
October 2, 2001, pp. 17–19; Bruce Hoffman, *Terrorism and Weapons of Mass
Destruction* (Santa Monica, CA: Rand, 1999). For numerous senerios by which
terrorists could fairly easily create massive destruction, see Stephen Bowman,
When the Eagle Screams: America's Vulnerability to Terrorism (New York:
Birch Lane Press, 1994), especially Chapters 8–14.

49. James O. Goldsborough, "The Real Costs of Missile Defense," *San Diego
Union-Tribune*, April 1, 2002.

50. Thomas Friedman, "Better Late Than Never," *New York Times*, March 17, 2002, p. 51. The reason that this conclusion follows from an international justice perspective is that it is impossible to imagine how it could be the case that all other nations of the world ought to regard as morally acceptable the self-serving U.S. stance on the Kyoto climate-change treaty.

51. Barbara Crossette, "Food Aid for Afghans Way Short of Need, U.N. Agency Says," *New York Times*, April 26, 2002, p. 12. According to a more recent assessment, foreign governments have pledged more than $4.5 billion in aid over five years, but little of that money has arrived. See Eric Schmitt, "Rumsfeld Says Lag in Aid Has Stymied Afghans," *New York Times*, August 16, 2002. According to an even more recent assessment, progress in reducing hunger in Afghanistan has ground to a halt and failure to provide immediate food and agricultural aid will lead to famine. Elizabeth Becker, "U.N. Sounds Famine Alarm for Africa, Afghanistan," *The Miami Herald*, October 22, 2002.

52. Ales Spillius, " 'People, Say I Make Too Much Noise,' Dr. Sima Samar, Afghanistan's First Minister for Women's Affairs, Talks to Alex Spillus," *The Daily Telegraph* (London), February 22, 2002, p. 23.

53. It is sometimes argued that addressing the unjust distribution of resources and meeting the basic needs of people around the world will do little to eliminate terrorism because those who engage in terror are not usually poor people (see Alan Krueger and Jitka Maleckova, "Does Poverty Cause Terrorism? *The New Republic*, June 24, 2002), pp. 27–33. But while it is probably true that most terrorists are not themselves poor, many of them appear to be motivated by the plight of the poor or by what they perceive to be other gross injustices, even when they themselves have the means of escaping the harmful effects of those injustices (e.g., Osama bin Laden). So if we intend to rid the world of terrorism in a morally justifiably way, we definitely need to address these questions of international justice. They are part of a nonbelligerent way of ridding ourselves of the threat of terrorism.

54. Jon Sawyer, "U.S. Wrestles with Notions That Massive Aid Can Stop Terrorism: Nation Pledges More to Front-Line States, but Little Change for Others," *St. Louis Post-Dispatch*, December 3, 2001, p. 1 and Paul Krugman, "The Heart of Cheapness," *New York Times*, May 31, 2002, p. 23 It might be objected that while Americans are relatively stingy in the foreign aid provided by their government they make up for it with private and corporate largess. See Carol Adelman, "America's Helping Hand," *Wall Street Journal*, August 21, 2002, p. 12. But even when U.S. private and corporate giving is taken into account, the United States still gives privately and publicly only half as much as Sweden, Netherlands, and Norway give publicly. The percentage shrinks to only one-quarter as much if we remove the $18 billion that immigrants in the U.S. send to relatives back home, which probably shouldn't be counted as it is not that similar to giving foreign aid to needy people around the world.

CHAPTER 12

Compassion and Terror

MARTHA C. NUSSBAUM

The name of our land has been wiped out.
—Hecuba, in Euripides, *Trojan Women*

Not to be a fan of the Greens or Blues at the races, or the light-armed or heavy-armed gladiators at the Circus.
—Marcus Aurelius, *Meditations*

I

The towers of Troy are burning. All that is left of the once-proud city is a group of ragged women, bound for slavery, their husbands dead in battle, their sons murdered by the conquering Greeks, their daughters raped. Hecuba their queen invokes the king of the gods, using, remarkably, the language of democratic citizenship: "Son of Kronus, Council-President of Troy, father who gave us birth, do you see these undeserved sufferings that your Trojan people bear?" The Chorus answers grimly, "He sees, and yet the great city is no city. It has perished, and Troy exists no longer." A little later, Hecuba herself concludes that the gods are not worth calling on, and that the very name of her land has been wiped out.

In one way, the ending of this drama is as bleak as any in the history of tragic drama. Death, rape, slavery, fire destroying the towers, the city's very name effaced from the record of history by the acts of rapacious and murderous Greeks. And yet, of course, it did not happen that way, not exactly. For the story of Troy's fall is being enacted, some six hundred years after the event, by a company of Greek actors, in the Greek language of a Greek poet, in the presence of all the adult citizens of Athens, most powerful of Greek cities. Hecuba's cry to the gods even imagines him as a peculiarly Athenian type of civic official, president of the city council. So the name of the land didn't get wiped out after all. The imaginations of the conquerors were haunted by it, transmitted it, and mourn it. Obsessively their arts repeat the events of long-ago destruction, typically inviting, as here, the audience's compassion for the women of Troy and blame for their assailants. In its very structure the play makes a claim for the moral value of compassionate imagining, as it asks its audience to partake in the terror of a burning city, of murder and rape and slavery. Insofar as members of the audience are engaged by this drama, feeling fear and grief for the conquered city, they demonstrate the ability of compassion to cross lines of time, place, and nation—and also, in the case of many audience members, the line of sex, perhaps more difficult yet to cross.

Nor was the play an aesthetic event cut off from political reality. The dramatic festivals of Athens were sacred festivals strongly connected to the idea of democratic deliberation, and the plays of Euripides were particularly well known for their engagement with contemporary events. In this case, the audience that watched *The Trojan Women* had recently voted to put to death the men of the rebellious colony of Melos and to enslave the women and children. Euripides invites them to contemplate the real human meaning of their actions. Compassion for the women of Troy should at least cause moral unease, reminding Athenians of the full and equal humanity of people who live in distant places, their fully human capacity for suffering.

But did those imaginations really cross those lines? Think again of that invocation of Zeus. Trojans, if they worshiped Zeus as king of gods at all, surely did not refer to him as the president of the city council. The term *prytanis* is an Athenian legal term, completely unknown elsewhere. So it would appear that Hecuba is not a Trojan but a Greek. Her imagination is a Greek democratic (and, we might add, mostly male) imagination. Maybe that's a good thing, in the sense that the audience is surely invited to view her as their fellow and equal. But it still should give us pause. Did compassion really enable those Greeks to reach out and think about the real humanity of others, or did it stop short, allowing them to reaffirm the essential Greekness of everything that's human? Of course compassion required making the Trojans somehow familiar, so that Greeks could see their own vulnerability in them and feel terror and compassion as for people related to themselves. But it's so easy for the familiarization to go too far: They are just us, and we are the ones who suffer humanly. Not those other ones, over there in Melos.

America's towers, too, have burned. Compassion and terror are in the fabric of our lives. And in those lives we have seen evidence of the good work of compassion, as Americans made real to themselves the sufferings of so many different people whom they never would otherwise have thought about: New York firefighters, that gay rugby player who helped bring down the fourth plane, bereaved families of so many national and ethnic origins. We even sometimes noticed with a new attention the lives of Arab Americans among us or felt a sympathy with our Sikh taxi driver when he tells us how often he is told to go home to "his own country"—even though he came to the United States as a political refugee from the miseries of police repression in the Punjab. Sometimes our compassion even crossed that biggest line of all, the national boundary. Tragedy surely led many people to sympathize with the women of Afghanistan in a way that feminists tried to get people to do for ages, without success. And other civilian victims of the violence, or people threatened by the violence, sometimes caused imaginations to stop, briefly, before they rushed back home to see what latest threat the evening news has brought our way.

The events of September 11 make vivid a philosophical problem that has been debated from the time of Euripides straight on through much of the history of the Western philosophical tradition. This is the question of what do to about compassion, given its obvious importance in shaping the civic imagination, but given, too, its obvious propensity for self-serving narrowness. Is compassion, with all its faults, our best hope as we try to educate citizens to think well about human relations both inside the nation and across national boundaries? So some thinkers have suggested. I count Euripides among them, and I would also include in this category Aristotle, and Rousseau, and Hume, and Adam Smith. Or is compassion a threat to good political thinking and to the foundations of a truly just world community? So the Greek and Roman Stoics thought, and before them Plato, and after them Spinoza, and Adam Smith. The enemies of compassion hold that we cannot build a truly wise concern for humanity on the basis of such a slippery and uneven motive; impartial motives based on ideas of dignity and respect should take its place. The friends of compassion reply that without building political morality on what we know and on what has deep roots in our childhood attachments, we will be left with a morality that will be empty of urgency—as Aristotle puts it, a "watery" concern all around.

I shall not trace the history of the debate in this essay. Instead, I shall focus on its central philosophical ideas and try to sort them out, offering a limited defense of compassion and the tragic imagination, and then making some suggestions about how its pernicious tendencies can best be countered—with particular reference, throughout, to our own political situation and to the role of the terrorist attacks in engendering emotions, good and bad. Let me set the stage for the analysis to follow by turning to Smith, who, as you will have noticed, turns up in my taxonomy on both sides of the debate. Smith offered one of the best accounts we have of sympathy and compassion, and of the ethical achievements of which this moral sentiment is capable. But later, in a section of the work entitled "Of the Sense of Duty," he offers a very solemn warning against trusting this imperfect sentiment too far when duty is what we are trying to get clear about. His concern, like mine, is with our difficulty keeping our minds fixed on the sufferings of people who live on the other side of the world.

> Let us suppose that the great empire of China, with all its myriads of inhabitants, was suddenly swallowed up by an earthquake, and let us consider how a man of humanity in Europe, who had no sort of connexion with that part of the world, would be affected upon receiving intelligence of this dreadful calamity. He would, I imagine, first of all, express very strongly his sorrow for the misfortune of that unhappy people, he would make many melancholy reflections upon the precariousness of human life, and the vanity of all the labours of man, which could thus be annihilated in a moment. And when all this fine philosophy was over, when all these humane sentiments had been once fairly expressed, he would pursue his business or his pleasure, take his repose or his diversion, with the same ease and tranquillity, as if no such accident had happened. The most frivolous disaster which could befall himself would occasion a more real disturbance. If he was to lose his little finger tomorrow, he would not sleep to-night; but, provided he never saw them, he will snore with the more profound security over the ruin of a hundred millions of his brethren, and the destruction of that immense multitude seems plainly an object less interesting to him, than this paltry misfortune of his own.

That is just the issue that should trouble us, as we think about American reactions to September 11. We see a lot of "humane sentiments" around us, and extensions of sympathy beyond people's usual sphere of concern. But how often, both now and at other times, those sentiments stop short at the national boundary. Americans thought the events of September 11 were bad because they involved *us* and *our* nation. Not just human lives, but American lives. The world came to a stop—in a way that it never has for Americans when disaster befalls human beings in other places. The genocide in Rwanda didn't even work up enough emotion in us to prompt humanitarian intervention. The plight of innocent civilians in Iraq never made it onto our national radar screen. Floods, earthquakes, cyclones—and the daily deaths of thousands from preventable malnutrition and disease—none of these makes the American world come to a standstill, none elicits a tremendous outpouring of grief and compassion. At most we get what Smith so trenchantly described: a momentary flicker of feeling, quickly dissipated by more pressing concerns close to home.

Frequently, however, we get a compassion that is not only narrow, failing to include the distant, but also polarizing, dividing the world into an "us" and a "them." Compassion for our own children can so easily slip over into a desire to promote the well-being of our children at the expense of other people's children. Similarly, compassion for our fellow Americans can all too easily slip over into a desire to make America come out *on top*, defeating or subordinating other nations. One vivid example of this slip took place at a baseball game I went to at Comiskey Park, the first game played in Chicago after September 11—and a game against the Yankees, so there was heightened awareness of the situation of New York and its people. Things began well, with a moving ceremony commemorating the firefighters who had lost their lives, and honoring local firefighters who had gone to New York afterwards to help out. There was even a lot of cheering when the Yankees took the field, a highly unusual transcendence of local attachments. But as the game went on and the beer began flowing, one heard, increasingly, the chant, "U-S-A. U-S-A," a chant left over from the Olympic hockey match in which the United States defeated Russia, expressing the wish for America to defeat, abase, humiliate, its enemies. Indeed, the chant USA soon became a general way of expressing the desire to crush one's enemies, whoever they were. When the umpire made a bad call against the Sox, the same group in the bleachers turned to him, chanting "U-S-A." Anyone who crosses us is an evil terrorist, deserving of extinction. From "humane sentiments" we had turned back to the pain in our little finger.

With these Smithean examples before us, how can we trust compassion, and the imagination of the other that it contains? But if we don't trust that, what else can we plausibly rely on to get ethical responsibility out of horror?

I shall proceed as follows. First, I offer an analysis of the emotion of compassion, focusing on the thoughts and imaginings on which it is based. This gives us a clearer perspective on how and where it is likely to go wrong. Second, I examine the countertradition's proposal that we can base political morality on respect for dignity, doing away with appeals to compassion. This proposal, at first attractive, contains, on closer inspection, some deep difficulties. Third, I return to compassion, asking how, if we feel we need it as a public motive, we might educate it so as to overcome, as far as we can, the problem that Smith identified. This will lead me to a sketch of some educational reforms that may possibly extend compassion in a more reliable way than the contemplation of terrorist threats.

II

Compassion is not just a warm feeling in the gut, if it is that at all. It involves a set of thoughts, quite complex. We need to dissect them, if we are to make progress in understanding how it goes wrong and how it may be steered aright. There is a good deal of agreement about this, among philosophers as otherwise diverse as Aristotle and Rousseau, and also among contemporary psychologists and sociologists who have done empirical work on the emotion.[1]

Compassion is an emotion directed at another person's suffering or lack of well-being. It requires the thought that the other person is in a bad way, and a pretty seriously bad way. (Thus we don't feel compassion for people who lose trivial items like a toothbrush or a paper clip.) It thus contains within itself an appraisal of the seriousness of various predicaments. Let us call this the *judgment of seriousness*.

Notice that this assessment is made from the point of view of the person who has the emotion. It does not neglect the actual suffering of the other, which certainly should be estimated in taking the measure of the person's predicament. And yet it does not necessarily take at face value the estimate of the predicament this person will be able to form. As Smith emphasized, we frequently have great compassion for people whose predicament is that they have lost their powers of thought; even if they seem like happy children, we regard this as a terrible catastrophe. On the other side, when people moan and groan about something, we don't necessarily have compassion for them, for we may think that they are not really in a bad predicament. Thus when very rich people grumble about taxes, many of us don't have the slightest compassion for them: We judge that it is only right and proper that they should pay what they are paying—and probably a lot more than that! The suffering of Hecuba and the Trojan women becomes the object of the audience's compassion directly, because it is understood that their predicament is really grave: Slavery, loss of children, loss of city, are among the calamities all human beings typically fear.

So the judgment of seriousness already involves quite a complex feat of imagination: It involves both trying to look out at the situation from the suffering person's own viewpoint and then assessing the person's own assessment. Complex though the feat is, young children easily learn it, feeling sympathy with the suffering of animals and other children, but soon learning, as well, to withhold sympathy if they judge that the person is just a crybaby, or spoiled.

Next comes the *judgment of non-desert*. Hecuba asked Zeus to witness the "undeserved sufferings" of the Trojan women, using a Greek word, *anaxia*, that appears in Aristotle's definition of tragic compassion. The tradition claims that we will not have compassion if we believe that the person fully deserves the suffering, just brought it on herself. There may be a measure of blame, but then, in our compassion we typically register the thought that the suffering exceeds the measure of the fault. The Trojan women are an unusually clear case, because, more than most tragic figures, they are hit by events in which they have no active share at all, being women. But we can see that non-desert is a salient part of our compassion even when we do also blame the person: Typically we feel compassion at the punishment of a criminal offender, say, only to the extent that we think circumstances beyond his control are at least in good measure responsible for his becoming the bad person he is. People who have the idea that the poor brought their poverty upon themselves by shiftlessness and laziness fail, for that reason, to have compassion for them.

Next there is a thought much stressed in the tradition, which I shall call the *judgment of similar possibilities*: Aristotle, Rousseau, and others suggest that we have compassion only insofar as we believe that the suffering person shares vulnerabilities and possibilities with us. I think we can clearly see that this judgment is not strictly necessary for the emotion, as the other two seem to be. We have compassion for nonhuman animals without basing it on any imagined similarity—although, of course, we need somehow to make sense of their predicament as serious and bad. We also imagine that an invulnerable god can have compassion for mortals, and it doesn't seem that this idea is conceptually confused. For the finite imaginations of human beings, however, the thought of similar possibilities is a very important psychological mechanism through which we get clear about the seriousness of another person's plight. This thought is often accompanied by empathetic imagining, in which we put ourselves in the suffering person's place, imagine the predicament as our own.

Finally, however, there is one thing more, not mentioned in the tradition, which I believe must be added in order to make the account complete. This is what, in writing on the emotions, I have called the *eudaimonistic judgment*, namely, a judgment that places the suffering person or persons among the important parts of the life of the person who feels the emotion. In my more general analysis of emotions, I argue that they are always eudaimonistic, meaning focused on the agent's most important goals and project. Thus we feel fear about damages that we see as significant for our own well-being and our other goals; we feel grief at the loss of someone who is already invested with a certain importance in our scheme of things. Eudaimonism is not egoism. I am not claiming that emotions always view events and people as mere means to the agent's own satisfaction or happiness. But I do mean that the things that occasion a strong emotion in us are things that correspond to what we have invested with importance in our account to ourselves of what is worth pursuing in life.

Compassion can evidently go wrong in several different ways. It can get the judgment of non-desert wrong, sympathizing with people who actually don't deserve sympathy and withholding sympathy from those who do. Even more frequently, it can get the judgment of seriousness wrong, ascribing too much importance to the wrong things or too little to things that have great weight. Notice that this problem is closely connected to obtuseness about social justice, in the sense that if we do not think a social order unjust for denying women the vote, or subordinating African Americans, then we will not see the predicament of women and African Americans as bad, and we won't have compassion for them. We will think that things are just as they ought to be. Again, if we think it's unjust to require rich people to pay capital gains tax, we will have a misplaced compassion toward them. But finally, and obviously, compassion can get the eudaimonistic judgment wrong, putting too few people into the circle of concern. On my account, then, we will not have compassion without a moral achievement that is at least coeval with it.

My account, I think, is able to explain the unevenness of compassion better than other more standard accounts. Compassion begins from where we are, from the circle of our cares and concerns. It will be felt only toward those things and persons that we see as important, and of course most of us most of the time ascribe importance in a very uneven and inconstant way. Empathetic imagining can sometimes extend the circle of concern. Thus psychologist Daniel Batson has shown experimentally that when the story of another person's plight is vividly told subjects will tend to experience compassion toward the person and form projects of helping. This is why I say that the moral achievement of extending concern to others need not antedate compassion, but can be coeval with it. Still, there is a recalcitrance in our emotions, given their link to our daily scheme of goals and ends. Smith is right: Thinking that the poor victims of the disaster in China are important is easy to do for a short time, hard to sustain in the fabric of our daily life, where there are so many things closer to home to distract us, and these things are likely to be so much more thoroughly woven into our scheme of goals.

Let us return to September 11, armed with this analysis. The astonishing events made many Americans recognize the nation itself as part of their circle of concern with a new vividness. Most Americans rely on the safety of our institutions and our cities and don't really notice how much they value them until they prove vulnerable—in just the way that a lover often doesn't see how much he loves until the loved one is ill or threatened. So our antecedent concern emerged with a new clarity in the emotions we experienced. At the same time, we actually extended concern, in many cases, to people in America who had not previously been part of our circle of concern at all: the New York firefighters, the victims of the disasters. We extended concern to them both because we heard their stories, like a tragic drama being played out before us, and also, especially, because we were encouraged to see them as one part of the America we already loved and for which we intensely feared. When disaster struck in Rwanda, we did not in a similar way extend concern, or not stably, because there was no antecedent basis for it: Suffering Rwandans could not be seen as part of a larger "us" for whose fate we trembled. Vivid stories can create a temporary sense of community, but they are unlikely to sustain concern for long, if there is no pattern of interaction that would make the sense of an "us" an ongoing part of our daily lives.

Things are of course still worse with any group that figures in our imaginations as a "them" over against the "us." Such people are not only by definition non-us, they are also, by threatening the safety of the us, implicitly bad, deserving of any misfortune that might strike them. This is the sports-fan mentality so neatly depicted in my baseball story. Compassion for a member of the opposing team? You've got to be kidding. "U-S-A" just *means* kill the ump.

III

In the light of these difficulties, it is easy to see why much of the philosophical tradition has wanted to do away with compassion as a basis for public choice and to turn, instead, to detached moral principles whose evenhandness can be relied on. The main candidate for a central moral notion has been the idea of human worth or dignity, and the principle that has been put to work, from the Stoics and Cicero on through Kant and beyond, is the idea of acting, always, in such a way as to show respect for the dignity of humanity. We are to recognize that all humans have dignity, and that this dignity is both inalienable and equal, not affected by differences of class, caste, wealth, honor, status, or even sex. The recognition of human dignity is supposed to impose obligations on all moral agents, whether the humans in question are conationals or foreigners. In general, it enjoins us to refrain from all aggression and from fraud, since both are seen as violations of human dignity, ways of using a human being as merely a tool of one's own ends. Out of this basic idea Cicero developed much of the basis for modern international law in the areas of war, punishment, and hospitality.[2] Other Stoics used it to criticize conventional norms of patriarchal marriage, the physical abuse of servants, and many other aspects of Roman social life.

This Stoic tradition was quite clear that respect for human dignity could move us to appropriate action, both personal and social, without our having to rely at all on the messier and more inconstant motive of compassion. Indeed, for separate reasons, which I shall get to shortly, they thought compassion was never appropriate, so they could not rely on it. What I now want to ask is whether this countertradition was correct. Respect for human dignity looks like the right thing to focus on, something that can plausibly be seen as of boundless worth, constraining all actions in pursuit of well-being, and also as equal, creating a kingdom of ends in which humans are ranked horizontally, so to speak, rather than vertically. Why should we not follow the countertradition, as in many respects we do already?

Now it must be admitted that the notion of human dignity is not an altogether clear notion. In what does it consist? Why should we think that all human life has it? The minute the Stoic tradition tries to answer such questions, problems arise. In particular, the answer almost always takes the form of saying, look at how far we are above the beasts. Reason, language, moral capacity—all these things are seen as worthy of respect and awe at least in part because the beasts, so called, don't have them, because they make us better than others. This view has its moral problems, clearly. It has long been used to deny that we have any obligations of justice toward nonhuman forms of life. Compassion, if slippery, is at least not dichotomous in this way: It allows of extension in multiple directions, including the direction of imagining the sufferings of animals in the squalid conditions we create for them.

There is another more subtle problem with the dignity idea. It was crucial, according to the Stoics, to make dignity something that is radically independent of fortune: All humans have it, no matter where they are born or how they are treated. It exerts its claim everywhere, and it can never be lost. If dignity went up or down with fortune, it would create ranks and orders of human beings: The well-born and healthy will be worth more than the ill-born and hungry. So the Stoics understood their project of making dignity self-sufficient as essential for the notion of equal respect and regard.

But this move leads to a problem: How can we give a sufficiently important place to the goods of fortune for political purposes, once we admit that the truly important thing, the thing that lies at the core of our humanity, doesn't need the goods of fortune at all? How can we provide sufficient incentive to political planners to arrange for an adequate distribution of food and shelter and even political rights and liberties, if we say that dignity is unaffected by the lack of such things? Stoic texts thus look oddly quietistic: Respect human dignity, they say. But it doesn't matter at all what conditions we give people to live in, since dignity is complete anyway. Seneca, for example, gives masters stern instructions not to beat slaves or use them as sexual tools. But as for the institution of slavery itself? Well, this does not really matter so much, for the only thing that matters is the free soul within, and that cannot be touched by any contingency.

Things are actually even worse than this. For the minute we start examining this reasoning closely, we see that it is not only quietistic, it is actually incoherent. Either people need external things or they do not. But if they do not, if dignity is utterly unaffected by rape and physical abuse, then it is not very easy, after all, to say what the harm of beating or raping a slave is. If these things are no harm to the victim, why is it wrong to do them? Seneca lacks not only a basis for criticizing the institution of slavery, but also a basis for the criticism he actually makes, of cruel and inhumane practices toward slaves.

Kant had a way of confronting this question, and it is a plausible one, within the confines of what I have called the countertradition. Kant grants that humanity itself, or human worth, is independent of fortune: Under the blows of "step-motherly nature" the good will still shines like a jewel for its own sake. But external goods such as money, health, and social position are still required for happiness, which we all reasonably pursue. So there are still very weighty moral reasons for promoting the happiness of others, reasons that can supply both individuals and states with a basis for good thoughts about the distribution of goods.

The Stoics notoriously deny this, holding that virtue is sufficient for *eudaimonia*. What I want to suggest now is that their position about human dignity pushes them strongly in this direction. Think of the person who suffers poverty or hardship. Now either this person has something that is beyond price, by comparison to which all the money and health and shelter in the world is as nothing—or she does not have something that is beyond price. Her dignity is just one contributor to her happiness, a piece of it that can itself be victimized and held hostage to fortune, in such a way that she may end up needy and miserable, even though she has dignity, and even virtue. This would mean that human dignity is being weighed in the balance with other goods; it no longer looks like the thing of surpassing, even infinite worth that we took it to be. There are, after all, ranks and orders of human beings: Slavery and abuse can actually change people's situation with regard to their most important and inclusive end, *eudaimonia* itself.

Because the Stoics do not want to be forced to that conclusion, they insist that external goods are not required for *eudaimonia*:

Virtue is sufficient. And basic human dignity, in turn, is sufficient for becoming virtuous, if one applies oneself in the right way. It is for this deep reason that the Stoics reject compassion as a basic social motive, not just because it is slippery and uneven. Compassion gets the world wrong, because it is always wrong to think that a person who has been hit by fortune is in a bad or even tragic predicament. "Behold how tragedy comes about," writes Epictetus, "when chance events befall fools." In other words, only a fool would mind the events depicted in Euripides' play, and only fools in the audience would view these events as tragic.

So there is a real problem about how, and how far, the appeal to equal human dignity motivates. Looked at superficially, the idea of respect for human dignity appears to provide a principled, even-handed motive for good treatment of all human beings, no matter where they are placed. Looked at more deeply, it seems to license quietism and indifference to things in the world, on the grounds that nothing that merely happens to people is really bad.

We have now seen two grave problems with the countertradition: what I shall call the *animal problem* and what I shall call the *external goods problem*. Neither of these problems is easy to solve within the countertradition. By contrast, the Euripidean tradition of focusing on compassion as a basic social motive has no such problems. Compassion can and does cross the species boundary, and whatever good there may be in our current treatment of animals is likely to be its work. As for the problem of external goods, compassion has no such problem, for it is focused in its very nature on the damages of fortune: Its most common objects, as Aristotle listed them in the *Rhetoric*, are the classic tragic predicaments—loss of country, loss of friends, old age, illness, and so on.

But let us suppose that the countertradition can solve these two problems, providing people with adequate motives to address the tragic predicaments. Kant makes a good start on the external goods problem, at least. So let us imagine that we have a reliable way of motivating conduct that addresses human predicaments, without the uneven partiality that so often characterizes compassion. A third problem now awaits us. I shall call it the *problem of watery motivation*, The name "watery" motivation comes from Aristotle's criticism of Plato's ideal city. Plato tried to remove partiality by removing family ties and asking all citizens to care equally for all other citizens. Aristotle says that the difficulty with this strategy is that "there are two things above all that make people love and care for something, the thought that it is all theirs, and the thought that it is the only one they have. Neither of these will be present in that city" (*Politics*, 1262b22–23). Because nobody will think of a child that it is all theirs, entirely their own responsibility, the city will, he says, resemble a household in which there are too many servants, so nobody takes responsibility for any task. Because nobody will think of any child or children that they are the only ones they have, the intensity of care that characterizes real families will simply not appear, and we will have, he says, a "watery" kind of care all round (1262b15).

If we now examine the nature of Stoic motivation, I think we will see that Aristotle is very likely to be correct. I shall focus here on Marcus Aurelius, in many ways the most psychologically profound of Stoic thinkers. Marcus tells us that the first lesson he learned from his tutor was "not to be a fan of the Greens or Blues at the races, or the light-armed or heavy-armed gladiators at the Circus" (I.5). His imagination had to unlearn its intense partiality and localism—and apparently the tutor assumes that already as young children we have learned narrow sectarian types of loyalty. It is significant, I think, that the negative image for the moral imagination is that of sports fandom: for in all ages, perhaps, that has been such a natural way for human beings to imagine yet other types of loyalty, to family, city, and nation. It was no accident that those White Sox fans selected a hockey chant as their way of expressing distress about the fate of the nation.

The question is whether this negative lesson leaves the personality enough resources to motivate intense concern with people anywhere. For Marcus, unlearning partiality requires an elaborate and systematic program of uprooting concern for all people and things in this world. He tells us of the meditative exercises that he regularly performs, in order to get himself to the point at which the things that divide people from one another do not matter to him. One side of this training looks benign and helpful: We tell ourselves that our enemies are really not enemies, but part of a common human project (*Meditations* II.1). Instead of seeing the enemy as an opponent, see him as a fellow human being, sharing a "portion of the divine," sharing similar concerns and goals, and engaged in the common project of making human life better. Passages such as these suggest that a strong kind of even-handed concern can be meted out to all human beings, without divisive jealousy and partiality. We see ourselves not as team players, not as family members, not as loyal citizens of a nation, but as members of the human kind, and our most important goal as that of enhancing the life of the human kind.

Now even in this good case problems are lurking, for we notice that this exercise relies on the thoughts that give rise to the animal problem and the external goods problem. We are asked to imagine human solidarity and community by thinking of a "portion of the divine" that resides in all and only humans: We look like we have a lot in common because we are so sharply divided from the rest of nature. And the idea that we have a common work relies, to at least some extent, on Marcus's prior denigration of external goods, for if we ascribed value to external goods we would be in principle competing with one another, and it would be difficult to conceive of the common enterprise without running into that competition.

But I have resolved to waive those two difficulties, so let me do so. Even then, the good example is actually very complex. For getting to the point where we can give such concern even-handedly to all human beings requires, as Marcus makes abundantly clear, the systematic extirpation of intense cares and attachments directed at the local: one's family, one's city, the objects of one's love and desire. Thus Marcus needs to learn not only not to be a sports fan, but also not to be a lover. Consider the following extraordinary passage:

> How important it is to represent to oneself, when it comes to fancy dishes and other such foods, "This is the corpse of a fish, this other thing the corpse of a bird or a pig." Similarly, "This Falernian wine is just some grape juice," and "This purple vestment is some sheep's hair moistened in the blood of some shellfish." When it comes to sexual intercourse, we must say, "This is the rubbing together of membranes, accompanied by the spasmodic ejaculation of a sticky liquid." How important are these representations, which reach the thing itself and penetrate right through it, so that one can see what it is in reality. (VI.13)[3]

Now of course these exercises are addressed to the problem of external goods. Here as elsewhere, Marcus is determined to unlearn the unwise attachments to externals that he has learned from his culture. This project is closely connected to the question of partiality, because learning not to be a sports fan is greatly aided by learning not to care about the things over which people typically fight. In the quoted passage, however, the link to partiality seems even more direct, for learning to think of sex as just the rubbing of membranes really is learning not to find special value or delight in a particular, and this extirpation of eroticism really does seem to be required by a regime of impartiality. Not being a fan of the Blues means, too, not being a fan of this body or that body, this soul or that soul, this city or that city.

But getting rid of our erotic investment in bodies, sports teams, family, nation—all this leads us into a strange world, a world that is gentle and unaggressive, but also strangely lonely and hollow. Marcus suggests that we have two choices only: the world of real-life Rome, which resembles a large gladiatorial contest (see Seneca, *De Ira* 2.8), each person striving to outdo others in a vain competition for externals, a world exploding with rage and poisoned by malice, or the world of Marcus's gentle sympathy, in which we respect all human beings and view all as our partners in a common project, but in which the terms of the project do not seem to matter very much, and the whole point of living in the world becomes increasingly unclear.

And this means something like a death within life. For only in a condition close to death, in effect, is moral rectitude possible. Marcus tries repeatedly to think of life as if it is a kind of death already, a procession of meaningless occurrences:

> The vain solemnity of a procession; dramas played out on the stage; troops of sheep or goats; fights with spears; a little bone thrown to dogs; a chunk of bread thrown into a fish-pond; the exhausting labor and heavy burdens under which ants must bear up; crazed mice running for shelter; puppets pulled by strings. (VII.3)

(This by an emperor who was at that very time on campaign in Parthia, leading the fight for his nation.) And the best consolation for that bleak conclusion comes also from the thought of death:

> Think all the time about how human beings of all sorts, and from all walks of life and all peoples, are dead. . . . We must arrive at the same condition where so many clever orators have ended up, so many grave philosophers, Heraclitus, Pythagoras, Socrates; so many heroes of the old days, so many recent generals and tyrants. And besides these, Eudoxus, Hipparchus, Archimedes, other highly intelligent minds, thinkers of large thoughts, hard workers, versatile in ability, daring people, even mockers of the perishable and transitory character of human life, like Menippus. Think about all of these that they are long since in the ground. . . . And what of those whose very names are forgotten? So: one thing is worth a lot, to live out one's life with truth and justice, and with kindliness toward liars and wrongdoers. (VI.47)[4]

Because we shall die, we must recognize that everything particular about us will eventually be wiped out. Family, city, sex, children, all will pass into oblivion. So really, giving up those attachments is not such a big deal. What remains, and the only thing that remains, is truth and justice, the moral order of the world. In the face of the looming inevitability of our end, we should not mind being dead already.

Marcus is alarming because he has gone deep into the foundations of cosmopolitan moral principle. What he has seen is that impartiality, fully and consistently cultivated, requires the extirpation of the eroticism that makes human life the life we know. The life we know is unfair, uneven, full of war, full of me-first nationalism and divided loyalty. But he sees that we can't so easily remove these attachments while retaining humanity. So, if that ordinary erotic humanity is unjust, get rid of it. But can we live like this, once we see the goal with Marcus's naked clarity? Isn't justice something that must be about and for the living?

IV

Let me proceed from now on on the hypothesis that Marcus is correct: Extirpating attachments to the local and the particular does deliver to us a death within life. Let me also proceed on the hypothesis that we will reject this course as an unacceptable route to the goal of justice, or even one that makes the very idea of justice a hollow fantasy. (This is Adam Smith's conclusion as well: Enamored as he is of Stoic doctrine, he thinks we must reject them when they tell us not to love our own families.) Where are we then placed?

It looks as if we are back where Aristotle, and Adam Smith, leave us: with the unreliability of compassion, and yet the need to rely on it, since we have no more perfect motive. This does not mean that we need give up on the idea of equal human dignity, or respect for it. But insofar as we retain, as well, our local erotic attachments, our relation to that motive must always remain complex and dialectical, a difficult conversation within ourselves as we ask how much humanity requires of us, and how much we are entitled to give to our own. But any such difficult conversation will require, for its success, the work of the imagination. If we do not have exceptionless principles, if, instead, we need to negotiate our lives with a complex combination of moral reverence and erotic attachment, we need to have a keen imaginative and emotional understanding of what our choices mean for people in conditions of many different kinds, and the ability to move resourcefully back and forth from the perspective of our personal loves and cares to the perspective of the distant. Not the extirpation of compassion, then, but its extension and education. How might such an extension be arranged?

The philosophical tradition helps us identify places where compassion goes wrong: by making errors about fault, about seriousness, about the circle of concern. But the ancient tradition, not being very interested in childhood, does not help us see clearly how and why it goes especially badly wrong. So to begin the task of educating compassion as best we can, we need to ask how and why local loyalties and attachments come to take in some instances an especially virulent and aggressive form, militating against a more general sympathy. To answer this question we need a level of psychological understanding that was not available in the ancient Greek and Roman world, or not completely. I would suggest (and have argued elsewhere) that one problem we particularly need to watch out for is a type of pathological narcissism in which the person demands complete control over all the sources of good, and a complete self-sufficiency in consequence. Nancy Chodorow long ago argued that this expectation colors the development of males in many cultures in the world. Recent studies of teenage boys in America, particularly the impressive work of Dan Kindlon and Michael Thompson in their book *Raising Cain*, has given strong local support to this idea. The boys that Kindlon and Thompson study have learned from their culture that men should be controlling, self-sufficient, dominant. They should never have, and certainly never admit to, fear and weakness. The consequence of this deformed expectation, Kindlon and Thompson show, is that these boys come to lack an understanding of their own vulnerabilities, needs and fears, weaknesses that all human beings share. They lack the language in which to characterize their own inner world, and they are by the same token clumsy interpreters of the emotions and inner lives of others. This emotional illiteracy is closely connected to aggression, as fear is turned outward, with little real understanding of the meaning of aggressive words and acts for the feelings of others. Kindlon and Thompson's boys, some ten years later, make the sports fans who chanted "U-S-A" at the ump, who think of all obstacles to American supremacy and self-sufficiency as opponents to be humiliated.

So the first recommendation I would make for a culture of respectful compassion is a Rousseauian one: that an education in common human weakness and vulnerability should be a very profound part of the education of all children. Children should learn to be tragic spectators and to understand with increasing subtlety and responsiveness the predicaments to which human life is prone. Through stories and dramas, they should get the habit of decoding the suffering of another, and this decoding should deliberately lead them into lives both near and far.

As children learn to imagine the emotions of another, they should at the same time learn the many obstacles to such understanding, the many pitfalls of the self-centered imagination as it attempts to be just. Thus, one should not suppose that one can understand a member of one's own family without confronting and continually criticizing the envy and jealousy in oneself that pose powerful obstacles to that understanding. One should not imagine that one can understand the life of a person in an ethnic or racial group different from one's own, or a sex different from one's own, or a nation, without confronting and continually criticizing the fear and greed and the demand for power that make such interactions so likely to produce misunderstanding and worse. What I am suggesting, then, is that the education of emotion, to succeed at all, needs to take place in a culture of ethical criticism and especially self-criticism, in which ideas of equal respect for humanity will be active players in the effort to curtail the excesses of the greedy self.

At the same time, since we have spoken of greed, we can also see that the chances of success in this enterprise will be greater if the society in question does not overvalue external goods of the sort that cause envy and competition. The Stoics are correct when they suggest that overvaluation of external goods is a major source of destructive aggression in society. If we criticize them to the extent of encouraging people to love their families, their friends, their work, their local context, even, to a certain extent, their nation, this does not entail the overvaluation of money, honor, status, and fame that Seneca saw at Rome and that we see in America now. Obviously enough, the urge for control over the sources of good is more pernicious when the good includes these highly competitive elements. If people care primarily for friendship, good work, and, let's even hope, social justice, they are less likely to see everything in terms of the hockey match and more likely to use Marcus's image of the common work or proj-

ect. Because this project is not a Stoic one, there will still be important sources of good to be protected from harm, and there will still
be justified anger at damage to those good things. But a lot of occasions for anger in real life are not good or just, and we can do a lot,
as a society, to prune away the greedy attachments that underpin
them. It is well known that privileged young people in America are
exceedingly focused on the attributes of wealth and status; psychological studies show that they are prone to humiliate others because
they don't have the same expensive ski vacations or expensive de-
signer clothes. We must consider how education can address these
problems, at all ages.

Next, we must speak about terrorism. This is a volume about terrorism, and I have taken the events of September 11 as my theme;
and yet I have suggested that the narrowness in our emotions is a
perfectly general problem, endemic to American life, not a problem
altogether new in the context of the "war on terrorism." We can now
go further: Crises are bad paradigms. An intense focus on our own
danger, such as terrorism evokes, may be a good incentive to turn
our imaginations outward. But Adam Smith is right: It is all too easy
to feel something in a crisis, and then to lapse, when daily life and
the fascination of one's own concerns reexert their hold. Human compassion always has this defect, as far as one can see. When there is
an earthquake or a flood, people pay attention to that part of the
world for a while, and even give money. Then they forget about that
part of the world, and stop giving money. The asymmetry is especially
obvious when our own interests hang in the balance. Terrorism makes
us pay attention—for a while. But how quickly, once things return to
normal, our imaginations stop conceiving of distant people. The eudaimonistic judgment no longer includes them.

Most of the preventable suffering and death in the world is not
caused by terrorism. It is caused by malnutrition, and lack of education, and all the ills connected to poverty. It is also caused by daily
small crimes, such as sex-selective infanticide and the systematically
unequal health care of women and girls. It is very easy to gain public
attention for dangers to the lives of girls and women when we can connect these dangers to evil terrorists; thus the women of Afghanistan
have won a sympathy that countless hungry suffering women all over
the world have not won. More generally, it is easy to gain attention for
a problem when it is dramatic and graphic. Thus, female genital mu-

tilation has energized Western women far more than the pedestrian topics of female hunger and lack of education, even though the latter affect vastly more women and cause more pervasive damage to human functioning.

There is, it seems to me, great danger in the idea that there is an ongoing "war on terrorism." There are many dangers actually, but the one on which I want to focus is the way such talk hooks our imaginations to a picture of violent struggle, inherently dramatic and self-involving, and fails to connect them to the daily sufferings of ordinary people. Drama can awaken the mind. But the analysis I have offered suggests that we will achieve no lasting moral progress unless and until the daily unremarkable lives of people distant from us become real in the fabric of our own daily lives, until our everyday eudaimonistic judgments about our important ends include them as ends, not just as temporary players in a drama in which we are the central actors.

How can this be done? Only by a vast reform of education. Children at all ages must learn to recognize people in other countries as their fellows and to sympathize with their plights. Not just their dramatic plights, in a cyclone or a war, but their daily plights. Children should learn how difficult it is for a child in rural Rajasthan to get adequate nutrition; how such a child has to work long hours herding sheep or goats; how, if that child is a girl child, she is likely to be married off before she is eight and to have no opportunity to make major life choices for herself. All this learning should be extended and deepened, as the child matures, through courses in world history, world politics, and the major world religions. We should learn how to visualize and recognize one another with some degree of human literacy. Thus, the Americans who in July 2002 mistook a family of actors from Kerala in South India, speaking and writing Malayalim, for Arab terrorists from some "terrorist group," and had them arrested when their flight landed, were displaying an appallingly high level of cultural and human illiteracy, no doubt reinforced by the divisive rhetoric of the "war on terrorism." A film actress from Kerala looks no more like an Arab terrorist than a farmer from Minnesota looks like a nightclub dancer from New York, and the script in which Malayalim is written looks no more like Arabic than our alphabet looks like the Hebrew alphabet. But Americans simply think of Asia as one vast place without internal differentiations. This is a failure of our educational systems, and we must do better.[5]

In concluding, I want to turn back to Euripides, reflecting, in concluding, about the role of tragic spectatorship, and tragic art generally, in promoting good citizenship of the sort I have been advocating here. Tragedies are not Stoic: They start with us "fools," and the chance events that befall us. At the same time, they tend to get their priorities straight. Thus, the overvaluations I have just been mentioning usually are not validated in tragic works of art. When people moan and groan about a social slight, or the loss of some money, that is, more often at least, an occasion for comedy. The great Athenian tragic dramas, to stick with those, revolve around attachments that seem central and reasonable: to one's children, one's city, one's loved ones, one's bodily integrity, one's health, one's freedom from pain, one's status as a free person rather than a slave, one's ability to speak and persuade others, the very friendship and company of others. The loss of these things is worthy of lamentation, and the tragic dramas encourage us to understand the depth of these losses and, with the protagonists, to fear them. In exercising compassion the audience is learning its own possibilities and vulnerabilities, as Aristotle said, "things such as might happen" in a human life. At the same time, often, the audience learns that people different in sex, race, age, and nation experience suffering in a way that is like our way and that suffering is as crippling for them as it would be for us.

Such recognitions have their pitfalls, and I have identified some of them in talking about *The Trojan Women*. We always risk error in bringing the distant person close to us: We ignore differences of language and of cultural context and the manifold ways in which these differences shape the inner world. These are the issues that our educational systems must address more effectively, as I have argued. But there are dangers in any act of imagining, and we should not let these particular dangers cause us to admit defeat prematurely, surrendering before an allegedly insuperable barrier of otherness. When I was out in the rural areas of Rajasthan, visiting an education project for girls, I asked the Indian woman who ran the project (herself, by the way, from Delhi) how she would answer the frequent complaint that a foreigner can never understand the situation of a person in another nation. She thought for a while and said, "I have the greatest difficulty understanding my own sister." In other words, there are barriers to understanding in any human relationship. As Proust said, any real person imposes on us a "dead weight" that our "sensitivity cannot remove." The obstacles to understanding a sister may in some instances be greater than those to understanding a stranger. At least they are different. And of course there are still other and equally great obstacles to understanding our own selves. All we can do is to trust our imaginations, and then criticize them (listening if possible to the critical voices of those we are trying to understand), and then trust our imaginations again. Perhaps out of this dialectic between criticism and trust something like understanding may eventually grow. At least the product will very likely be better than the obtuseness that so generally reigns in human relations.

As Euripides knew, terror has this good thing about it: It makes us sit up and take notice. It is not the endpoint of moral development, and it may be a trap, hooking our imaginations on drama rather than leading them toward a new attention to the daily. But terror can be at least the beginning of moral progress. Tragic dramas can't precisely teach anything new, since they will be moving only to people who at some level already understand how bad these predicaments are. But they can awaken the sleepers, reminding them of human realities they are neglecting in their daily political lives. The experience of terror and grief for our towers might be just that, an experience of terror and grief for our towers. One step worse, it could be a stimulus for blind rage and aggression against all the opposing hockey teams and bad umpires in the world. But if we cultivate a culture of critical compassion, such an event may, like Hecuba's Trojan cry, possibly awaken a larger sense of the humanity of suffering, a patriotism constrained by respect for human dignity and by a vivid sense of the real losses and needs of others. And in that case, it really will turn out that Euripides was right and Hecuba was wrong: The name of the Trojan land was not wiped out. It lives, in a work of the imagination to which we can challenge ourselves, again and again.

NOTES

An earlier version of this essay was published in the Winter 2003 issue of *Daedalus* (Volume 132, No. 1) on international justice. Reprinted by permission of Daedalus, the Journal of the American Academy of Arts and Sciences.

1. In this section I am drawing on the analysis of compassion for which I argue at greater length in Nussbaum, *Upheavals of Thought: The Intelligence of Emotions* (New York: Cambridge University Press, 2001).

2. See my "Duties of Justice, Duties of Material Aid: Cicero's Problematic Legacy," *Journal of Political Philosophy*, forthcoming.

3. Translation based on the French version of Pierre Hadot, translated into English by Chase, in *The Inner Citadel* (Cambridge, MA: Harvard University Press, 1998), with my modifications.

4. Translations from Hadot/Chase.

5. See my *Cultivating Humanity: A Classical Defense of Reform in Liberal Education* (Cambridge, MA: Harvard University Press, 1997).